# Working with Parents of a Newly Diagnosed Child with an Autism Spectrum Disorder

## A Guide for Professionals

Deb Keen and Sylvia Rodger

Foreword by Margot Prior

Jessica Kingsley *Publishers*
London and Philadelphia

Cover image and poem on p. 1 kindly provided with permission from Craig Roveta.
Raw material on p. 16 reproduced from Davey, 2002 with permission from Kathleen Davey.
Table 1.1 on p. 22 reproduced from Ingersoll, 2010 with permission from Sage Publications.
Box 2.1 on pp. 32–33 reproduced from American Psychiatric Association, 2000 with permission from the American Psychiatric Association.
Box 6.1 on pp. 106–107 reproduced from Prizant and Wetherby, 1985 with permission from Speech Pathology Australia.
Figure 7.3 on p. 127 reproduced from Mayer-Johnson, 1981 with permission from DynaVox Mayer-Johnson LLC.
Appendix to Chapter 7 on pp. 135–151 reproduced from Sigafoos, Arthur-Kelly, and Butterfield, 2006 with permission from Paul H. Brookes Publishing.


First published in 2012
by Jessica Kingsley Publishers
116 Pentonville Road
London N1 9JB, UK
and
400 Market Street, Suite 400
Philadelphia, PA 19106, USA

*www.jkp.com*

**Library of Congress Cataloging in Publication Data**
A CIP catalog record for this book is available from the Library of Congress

**British Library Cataloguing in Publication Data**
A CIP catalogue record for this book is available from the British Library

ISBN 978 1 84905 120 0
eISBN 978 0 85700 293 8

Printed and bound in Great Britain

# Contents

# Foreword

Since autism first came to our attention in the early 1940s with the insightful revelations of a 'new' disorder from Leo Kanner in the USA, there have been vast changes in our knowledge of almost all features of this disorder, or group of disorders as we now call it (Autism Spectrum Disorders, ASD). The early years of discussion about autism were characterised by puzzlement over diagnosis and classification, the origins of the disorder, whether biological or psychosocial/environmental, the nature of the cognitive and behavioural impairments, and the question of whether it could be treated in ways which would improve what appeared then to be very discouraging outcomes. Now, more than 60 years later, we have had major progress in our understanding of all of those domains, although many questions continue to challenge us, and autism remains a life-long burden.

We know much more now about the biological bases of ASD, but despite huge investment in research we do not yet have a clear picture of the origins of the complex set of developmental difficulties which characterise the spectrum. We understand pretty well the cognitive, social, communicative, and behavioural problems inherent in ASD, and this knowledge has underpinned the development of treatment, management strategies, and educational practice. Some of these advances are now indicating that we can change the developmental pathway of autism, especially if we begin intervention early in life. Nevertheless, there are still gaps in knowledge and expertise in most areas.

One of the most important and until now neglected areas has been 'what happens after diagnosis', that critical and heartrending time for families. Here there still is a gap in support and education at a time when parents are overwhelmed by what they are hearing, stunned with grief, and beset by the challenge of knowing what to do. Keen and Rodger's book attends to this gap. It is focused on the immediate aftermath of assessment and diagnosis, what parents need and want to know – explications of the nature of developmental problems in ASD, what is going to be needed for their child, and how to find information and to provide support. How I wish we had had such a book to hand decades ago, when we felt we were stumbling about in the dark!

*Working with Parents of a Newly Diagnosed Child with an Autism Spectrum Disorder* is focused on the early stages post diagnosis and is devoted to providing essential information and knowledge, as well as practical strategies for parents and professionals, to help to deal with the complex challenges these children present. It is based on experience coming from the authors' research expertise in designing and delivering parent education and support programmes. It covers theories of autism, past and present; it has a positive, strengths-based approach; it is based on excellent scholarship and expert knowledge of research in ASD; and it is notable for its authors' insights and expert clinical guidance throughout. This is a wonderful set of attributes on which to base such a comprehensive and well-directed book.

Keen and Rodger cover skill development, behavioural, developmental, social, communicative, and pragmatic approaches which are needed to bring about the best outcomes in the child with ASD, and notably the focus is family-centred, which is where most early development and learning takes place. A particular strength of the book is its emphasis on parent–professional partnerships in the task of developing a mix of strategies for adaptation and intervention which will most benefit the child in the context of the family. Such partnerships can work very well and are empowering and confidence-building for parents, as well as helping to reduce the inevitable stress of parenting children with ASD.

This book is practical, easily read and enlivened by good case examples and illustrations of ways to manage specific problems. While it is focused on autism, its principles are also relevant for families and practitioners caring for children with a range of disabilities. The authors provide a number of resources within the book, such as tools and measures to enhance understanding and management of particular difficulties (communication, sensory issues, play, to name just a few); along with reference to video material offering '*in vivo*' illustrations of teaching and learning. The material will be invaluable in meeting parents' needs as they begin their journey with their child with ASD.

Autism has been notable for the number and variety of treatments, even 'cures', which are constantly being promoted by their progenitors, often on the basis of pseudo- or false science and magical ideas, and which are too often misguided, costly, and not useful. Very few treatments have reliable scientific evidence and are genuinely able to change the course of autism. Some are a hoax, some can actually be unsafe for the child, and in many cases parents find themselves disappointed in the investment they have made when their faith and hopes in heavily promoted treatments are unrealised and their distress increased. It is difficult for parents to know how to cope with a barrage of offers and promises to cure autism, which come through the media as well as via misguided advice. Parents want the best for their child. But how can they discover what will really make a difference, and how can they accurately judge when a treatment that is glamorised with vivid stories of one or two children who apparently make amazing changes, is unlikely to truly affect their own child's autism.

In the concluding chapter the authors address these very important questions with a discussion about choosing appropriate treatments. They review treatment research, which is the essential foundation for identifying evidence-based intervention; that is, interventions which have really been shown to work in improving functioning in one or more domains of development in groups of children with ASD. They provide a set of principles of 'best practice' which parents can consider when they are looking at choices of potential interventions. They also offer a set of questions that parents can ask to acquire information which can help them make a good decision for their particular child, and note some reliable resources which parents can access as they build their knowledge of where to go and what to do.

Professionals from all disciplines concerned with autism will benefit greatly from this book, with its mine of information about the critical problems parents face when their child is first diagnosed with ASD, and will value the advice given on how to deal with these problems as partners in the endeavour. Practitioners will be able to further their own education to better guide good decisions and to achieve best practice in treatment and education. Working together with families, based on the research, knowledge, and clinical skills which Keen and Rodger bring to bear on the adjustment, adaptation, and learning processes that parents have to go through, can improve outcomes for all the family. This will reduce the anxiety and stress which so many parents have endured in the past as they take up the challenge of raising children with ASD.

*Margot Prior, AO*
*Professor of Psychology, University of Melbourne*

# Acknowledgments

This book represents the culmination of many years of research on the part of the authors, which would not have been possible without the participation of children with autism and their families. These families frequently had to find ways of arranging childcare, transport, and their time to attend workshops and be available for home visits. Many assessments and forms had to be completed by the families so that we could collect data to evaluate the effectiveness of our programme. We are indebted to them and their dedication to research that is so important to the development of improved practices for all families who may be faced with similar challenges.

We would also like to thank Craig Roveta for his wonderful artwork and poem, which enliven the cover and first page of our book. Craig's art is a demonstration to many families who may read this book of what is possible as they look to the future for their child with ASD. To Margot Prior, we are grateful for the time you've taken from your very busy schedule to read through our manuscript and to contribute such a thoughtful and supportive Foreword. Finally, we thank Alex Short and Vivienne Chavez for hours of editing and proofing.

# Preface

*Working with Parents of a Newly Diagnosed Child with an Autism Spectrum Disorder* was written for professionals involved in supporting families whose child has been diagnosed with ASD, including psychologists, occupational therapists, speech and language therapists, social workers, general medical practitioners, and educators. The approach is very much multidisciplinary, reflecting the training and experience of the authors in the fields of occupational therapy, psychology, and education. The impetus for the book came from the authors' research in early intervention for children with ASD at the time of diagnosis. They were struck by the lack of support and services for families at this time and what appeared to be a hiatus between diagnosis and commencement of an early intervention programme. Their research focused on the provision of a parenting education and support programme that would bridge this gap between diagnosis and early intervention for the child with ASD.

The organisation of the chapters in this book was influenced by the research conducted by the authors. The introductory chapter outlines the fundamental concepts that underpin this parenting programme and their approach to working with parents at the time of diagnosis. Chapter 2 gives an introduction to key information that parents usually seek about diagnostic criteria, characteristics, aetiology, prevalence, and prognosis of ASD.

Chapters 3 to 5 focus on working with families in a way that values the child with ASD, and the family, while maximising the effectiveness of the professional relationship. Chapter 3 on parent–professional partnerships explores the critical ingredients for a collaborative and respectful partnership. Chapter 4 on parental priorities guides professionals through the various ways they can help parents to determine appropriate and meaningful goals for their child with ASD. Chapter 5 on the provision of information examines principles underpinning adult education and the most effective ways in which professionals can provide information to families about constructive parenting strategies for a child with ASD.

Chapter 6 is critical to understanding the parenting strategies that can be used to facilitate a child's development, and the strategies described in this chapter are then incorporated in various ways into Chapters 7 to 9 about communication and behaviour, play, and sensory issues. These chapters provide practical ideas and techniques that parents can use in the home to support the development of their child with ASD.

Finally, Chapter 10 addresses some of the many questions professionals may have about early intervention programmes for children with ASD. Parents are often faced with a range of interventions and can find it difficult to determine the efficacy of these programmes. Throughout this chapter, professionals are given guidance about how to examine the evidence base of different intervention approaches, and a series of questions for parents to ask that will help in their decision-making.

We believe this book provides an important and comprehensive guide for professionals who are working with parents of children with ASD at one of the most difficult and confronting times – when their child is first diagnosed. We are confident that this book will help professionals adopt a family-centred approach toward assisting parents to understand their child with ASD and utilise effective parenting strategies in the home to support the transition of the child with ASD from diagnosis to early intervention.

Chapter 1

# Supporting Families Following Diagnosis

## An Introduction to Key Principles and Concepts

## INTRODUCTION

The term 'autism' was first used by Kanner in 1943 to describe a group of children who shared a number of characteristic features, with two of these perceived as having diagnostic significance: 'autistic aloneness' and 'obsessive insistence on sameness' (Kanner, 1943). Since these first descriptions of autism, criteria defining autism have been detailed in diagnostic manuals such as the World Health Organization's International Classification of Diseases 10th edition (ICD-10; World Health Organization, 1992) and the American Psychiatric Association's Diagnostic and Statistical Manual of Mental Disorders 4th edition (DSM-IV; American Psychiatric Association, 2000). Autism fits within a group of Pervasive Developmental Disorders (PDD) that include Autistic Disorder (AD), Asperger's syndrome (AS), and PDD Not Otherwise Specified (PDD-NOS). Together, this group of disorders has been referred to as Autism Spectrum Disorders (ASD) and is defined by impairments in socialisation, communication, and restricted and repetitive behaviours and interests. Throughout this book we will generally use the term ASD to refer to the population of children with whom we have worked and who may have a specific diagnosis of AD, AS, or PDD-NOS.

Parents can experience significant distress when their child is diagnosed with ASD (Keenan *et al.*, 2010). Research has found that around 37 per cent of parents feel dissatisfied with the way professionals disclose to them that their child has a disability (Sloper and Turner, 1993). In response to a questionnaire about diagnostic experiences of parents who have a child with ASD developed by Davey and Keen (in Davey, 2002), parents articulated many of the frustrations that can mark their diagnostic experiences, and examples of what some parents have said about these experiences follow (from Davey's questionnaires).

> Parent 1: Immediately after diagnosis I felt shocked, numb and confused. We were given little hope from the paediatrician. While I wanted the best for my child and wanted to help, I felt incapable, depressed, overwhelmed.

> Parent 2: The diagnosis process was excruciating. The professionals had no real understanding of autism. There was no advice on handling behaviours, encouraging language, diet, allergies, etc. I was referred to [disability service] who could spend one hour/fortnight and to [autism association] with a two-year waiting list... Parents are sent home with no useable information, no support and basically a terminal diagnosis.

> Parent 3: The entire diagnostic process took nearly two years. By this time I was fully aware, through research of my own, that my son would be diagnosed with autism. My son had already begun intervention by the time he was formally diagnosed.

The time of diagnosis and period of waiting for intervention is recognised as one of the most stressful periods for parents, particularly as there can be waiting lists for early intervention services. Diagnosis is the starting point for families to access intervention support services, but parents may experience delays of up to 24 months in accessing services once their child receives a diagnosis (MacDermott *et al.*, 2006).

The needs of children with ASD are extensive and this places great demands on the skills and knowledge of parents to deal with the child's impaired communication and social interactions (Aarons and Gittens, 1992). Parents need a new set of knowledge and skills to optimise their child's social interactions from an early age in order to prevent later behaviour issues. This is critical, as parents of children with ASD are known to experience significant stress and lower levels of parenting competence than parents of children without disabilities (Hassall, Rose, and McDonald, 2005; Hastings and Johnson, 2001). Stress and low self-esteem in mothers has been linked to adverse outcomes for children, including less than optimal parenting, failure to engage with services, decisions to seek out-of-home care for their child, impeded child development, and higher rates of child psychopathology and antisocial behaviour (Llewellyn *et al.*, 2005; O'Connor, 2002).

The aim of this book is to assist professionals to provide appropriate and timely support to parents, leading to parenting practices that facilitate the child's development and help parents seek early intervention services that will best meet the needs of their child and family. We draw on our experiences of developing and evaluating an intervention programme for parents that involved a workshop followed by ten home visits made by trained facilitators over a five-week period. Through this programme, parents were provided with relevant ASD-specific information, assisted to identify and prioritise goals for their child and family, and received support to individualise strategies presented at the workshop to facilitate their child's social communication at home (Keen *et al.*, 2007; Rodger, Braithwaite, and Keen, 2004; Rodger *et al.*, 2008).

The facilitators who have worked in the programme with us have come from a variety of professional backgrounds including psychology, special education, speech pathology, and occupational therapy. The approach we have taken to working with families and strategies that have been employed with parents are not discipline-specific, and any professional who is supporting children with ASD and their families can benefit from the material presented in this book. There are times, of course, when specialist expertise is invaluable, and this can readily be incorporated into the programme. The parent programme which we developed and which informs the content in this book was underpinned by a number of key concepts drawn from the research literature, our own research and clinical experience. In the remainder of this chapter we outline these important concepts.

## SKILL DEVELOPMENT

Parents of children with ASD can be faced with what on the surface can appear to be quite conflicting information about the most effective treatments for enhancing their child's development. In particular, there are two well-recognised approaches to skill development, which differ from each other in their theoretical underpinnings, but actually share many similarities when it comes to implementation. These two approaches are known as the *behavioural* approach and the *developmental/relationship-based* or *social-pragmatic* approach. In this book we recommend strategies that draw from both approaches.

### Behavioural Approaches

Behavioural approaches are based on learning theory. A cornerstone of this approach is the three-term contingency model that describes the functional relationships between antecedents, behaviour, and consequences (see Figure 1.1; Alberto and Troutman, 2006).

According to this model, the occurrence of any voluntary (or operant) behaviour is shaped by what happens before (antecedents) and after (consequences) the behaviour. Put another way, in any situation (antecedent), the probability of a behaviour occurring is a function of the consequences. Behavioural interventions involve the control or manipulation of antecedents (such as establishing operations and discriminative stimuli) and consequences (reinforcement and punishment) to increase or decrease the occurrence of target behaviours.

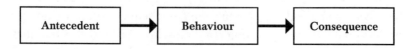

*Figure 1.1 Three-term contingency model*

*For example, imagine a typical playground scenario where Tom is playing in the sandpit with a toy truck and Bill is sitting beside him with a bucket. Bill wants to play with the truck so he takes it from Tom. Tom then hits Bill and takes back the truck while Bill is crying. Figure 1.2 illustrates this sequence of events using the model. Tom's hitting (behaviour) is more likely to occur again in the future because it has been reinforced in that he got his truck back (consequence) after Bill had taken it from him (antecedent).*

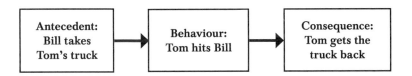

*Figure 1.2 Example of the three-term contingency model*

Applied Behaviour Analysis (ABA) is '…the process of applying sometimes tentative principles of behaviour to the improvement of specific behaviours and simultaneously evaluating whether or not any changes noted are indeed attributable to the process of application' (Baer, Wolf, and Risley, 1968, p. 91). In simple terms, ABA is about the use of systematic instruction based on empirically validated learning principles to teach functional skills. Instructional technologies based on behavioural principles have been developed and refined over the past 50 years or so, and we now have available to us many techniques to address the learning needs of children with ASD. It is beyond the scope of this book to detail these instructional technologies but there are some excellent resources available for those interested in further reading (e.g., Alberto and Troutman, 2006; Duker, Didden, and Sigafoos, 2004).

One of the best-known applications of ABA to individuals with ASD is a programme that was developed by Ivar Lovaas in the 1970s and later published (Lovaas, 1987, 1993). Essentially this approach involves the intensive teaching of targeted skills within a highly structured teaching environment using a discrete trial teaching format (Frea, 2000). There are five key components to conducting Discrete

Trial Training (DTT), whereby each trial has a clear sequence with a defined beginning and end. The components are:

1. gaining the child's attention

2. presentation of a discriminative stimulus (e.g., an instruction/ direction)

3. learner response (correct, incorrect, or no response)

4. feedback (reinforcement for correct response or prompting when incorrect or no response)

5. an inter-trial interval, after which another discrete trial begins.

These discrete trials are presented repeatedly in a one-on-one situation for each target behaviour until the correct behaviour is acquired.

The Lovaas programme has been one of the most researched approaches to the treatment of ASD, and there is a body of evidence to support the efficacy of this approach in delivering positive learning outcomes for children with ASD (Sallows and Graupner, 2005).

While research has shown the effectiveness of discrete trial training, a number of issues have been identified. Given the highly structured and artificial context within which learning takes place, skills learned may not generalise well. Generalisation refers to the transfer of learning to other settings/people outside the training situation. If a child is taught, for example, how to greet his mother when she gets home from work, he may not be able to demonstrate this greeting skill with other people in his family or in other locations, such as at school. Failure to generalise decreases the functionality of what is learned, and while generalisation strategies can be incorporated into an intervention, many children may require specific teaching in a variety of different contexts.

Another issue with the discrete trial format is that independence may be inhibited due to creation of stimulus dependency. For example, a child who has been taught to play with a toy following the direction to do so may wait for the parent to tell her to play with a toy rather than initiating the play herself. This lack of generalisation and spontaneity has been particularly evident in the area of communication. As pointed out by Prizant and colleagues, even Lovaas himself stated that the DTT format may have been responsible for producing very situation-specific and restricted verbal output (Prizant, Wetherby, and Rydell, 2000). There has also been research to suggest that, for some children, the discrete trial format may lead to more occurrences of challenging behaviour than other, more naturalistic approaches (Sigafoos *et al.*, 2006).

In an attempt to improve the generalisation and maintenance of learned behaviours, while still drawing on ABA, contemporary behavioural approaches have developed strategies that are more child-centred and naturalistic. Interventions for children with ASD such as incidental teaching (McGee, Morrier, and Daly, 1999), milieu teaching (Kaiser, Ostrosky, and Alpert, 1993), and Pivotal Response Training (Koegel *et al.*, 1999a; Koegel *et al.*, 1999b) are examples of these contemporary behavioural approaches. As these approaches emphasise the importance of learning within natural contexts and environments, they provide strategies that can be used by parents in the home and within the context of family routines. Adult responsiveness to the child's spontaneous communication, use of child-preferred activities/items, and following the child's lead are encouraged as ways to promote child-initiated communication, spontaneity, and generalisation.

## Developmental Social-Pragmatic Approaches

These aspects of contemporary behavioural approaches are shared with developmental social-pragmatic approaches, but a number of differences remain (Prizant *et al.*, 2000), as illustrated in Table 1.1.

From a theoretical perspective, developmental social-pragmatic approaches are underpinned by psychological theories of child development and the social-pragmatic model of language development. Skill acquisition and behavioural changes are conceptualised in relation to developmental stages which inform goal-setting. Although development may be delayed in children with ASD, there is an assumption that the sequence of development is the same as their typically developing peers (Ingersoll, 2010). From a developmental perspective, different aspects of a child's development, including communication, socialisation, and play, are seen as interconnected, so that multiple goals may be identified and targeted for a child within a single activity (Prizant *et al.*, 2000).

**Table 1.1 A comparison of intervention techniques for Naturalistic Behavioural and Developmental, Social-Pragmatic (DSP) Approaches**

| | Naturalistic Behavioural Approach | Developmental Social-Pragmatic (DSP) Approach |
|---|---|---|
| Setting | Natural | Natural |
| Teaching episodes | Child initiated | Child initiated |
| Materials and activities | Child selected | Child selected |
| Target skills | Specific social-communication skills (e.g., two-word phrases, pointing, pretend play schemes) | General social-communication skills (e.g., social engagement, nonverbal communication) |
| Facilitative strategies[a] | Not a defined component | Adult responsiveness (i.e., contingent imitation, indirect language stimulation, affective attunement) |
| Elicitation strategies | Environmental arrangement (i.e., in sight-out-of-reach, controlling access, gaining attention) | Environmental arrangement (i.e., communicative temptations, playful obstruction, wait time) |
| Prompt strategies[a] | Varied according to child's initiation (i.e., physical guidance, modeling, explicit instruction) | Not a defined component |
| Reinforcement properties | Natural | Natural |
| Reinforcement contingencies | Loose shaping, reinforce attempts toward target | Reinforce all communicative behaviours |

a. Techniques that are not a defined component of one of the approaches.

*Reproduced from Ingersoll, 2010 with permission from Sage publications.*

Examples of interventions for children with ASD that fall within this approach include the Developmental, Individual Difference, Relationship-based model (DIR or Floortime; Greenspan and Wieder, 1999), the Denver (and more recently the Early Start Denver) model (Rogers *et al.*, 2000), the Hanen programme (Manolson, 1985), Social Communication, Emotional Regulation and Transactional Support model (SCERTS; Prizant *et al.*, 2004), and relationship-focused responsive teaching (Mahoney and Perales, 2003). We shall describe some of these in Chapter 10 when considering the selection of evidence-based interventions. Of particular importance to the developmental social-pragmatic approaches as they are adopted for use with children who have ASD are a developmental milestone known as 'joint attention' and the notion of adult responsiveness.

### Joint Attention

Delays in communication skills are one of the early signs of ASD, and often manifest in the child's lack of response to his or her own name and the absence of joint attention behaviours. Joint attention typically emerges in infants between three and nine months of age and refers to the co-ordination of attention in a triadic relationship involving the child, an object, and another person (Mundy, Gwaltney, and Henderson, 2010). Behaviours such as pointing, showing, and shifts in eye gaze are employed to achieve this shared attention. It is possible to initiate and respond to joint attention bids. Directing a parent's attention to a favourite food is an example of a child initiating joint attention. Following a parent's pointing gesture as the parent asks the child to 'look' at a toy is a form of responding to the joint attention bid of the parent. Children with ASD both initiate and respond to joint attention bids less often than other children, although problems with initiating joint attention bids tend to be more persistent over time than responding (Mundy *et al.*, 2010). These differences in the joint attention behaviour of children with ASD are evident as early as 15–18 months and have been identified as one of the early red flags for ASD diagnosis (Wetherby *et al.*, 2007). Joint attention appears to be critical to later language development (Luyster, Kadlec, Carter, and Tager-Flusberg, 2008), and researchers have been very interested in finding effective ways to increase joint attention skills, which may then have a cascading effect on subsequent social learning (Mundy *et al.*, 2010).

## *Responsivity*

Adult responsiveness has been defined as responses to an infant's or child's behaviours that occur immediately after and are semantically related to, or are imitations of, the behaviour (Yoder *et al.*, 1998). The rate of a child's communicative development appears to be related to his or her mother's level of responsiveness (Yoder and Warren, 1999), in that communicative competence varies in relation to the level of adult responsiveness experienced by the child (Hart and Risley, 1995). Hart and Risley (1995) assert that small differences between caregivers in their level of responsiveness have a cumulative effect over the course of the child's development. This has been supported by the work of Siller and Sigman (2002), who looked at synchrony between mothers and children. Synchrony refers to how the mother is responsive to the child's focus of attention. Synchronous behaviours includes showing, pointing, or offering toys that are the child's focus of attention, or verbalising in a way that maintains the child's ongoing activity by offering reinforcement or a comment. Siller and Sigman (2002) found that caregivers of children with ASD who demonstrated higher levels of synchrony had children who developed superior joint attention and language over periods of 1, 10, and 16 years when compared to children of caregivers with lower levels of synchrony.

There are only a small but now growing number of studies that have examined adult responsiveness to early communicative behaviours in children with ASD (Watson, 1998). Some studies have reported that caregivers of children with ASD tend to redirect and regulate their child's behaviour more than caregivers of typically developing children and children with an intellectual disability. In contrast, however, Siller and Sigman (2002) found no differences between caregivers of children with ASD and caregivers of typically developing or developmentally delayed children in levels of responsiveness during play sessions. It is likely that levels of responsivity vary considerably among parents of children with ASD, but the research is now fairly convincing that responsivity plays an important role in children's language development.

Evidence of the efficacy of interventions that target joint attention behaviours and specifically focus on increasing parental responsiveness through caregiver training have emerged over the past decade (Aldred, Green, and Adams, 2004; Kasari *et al.*, 2010). Outcomes from these studies are encouraging and are consistent with the approach taken in this book to encourage responsivity and synchrony in parents when interacting with their child with ASD at home.

## FAMILY-CENTRED APPROACH AND PRACTICES

Our intervention programme with families is underpinned not only by a particular approach to skill development, as outlined above, but also by an approach to working with families based on family systems theory (Begun, 1996). Many support services for families who have a child with a disability are committed to working within a family systems framework. Family systems theory acknowledges that the child with a disability is first and foremost a valued family member (Dunst, Trivette, and Deal, 1994). While the needs of the child with ASD, particularly at the time of diagnosis, are pressing on the minds of parents, family systems theory recognises the interrelatedness of family members and the needs of all family members, not just the member with ASD. This interrelatedness means that something which affects one member will inevitably impact all other members. The family 'system' is continually changing and adapting to meet the needs of individuals within it, and also responding to the demands that are placed on the family by the external environment in which it is embedded.

Based on family systems theory, a family-centred approach to service provision has evolved which draws from both the help-giving and empowerment literatures (Dempsey and Keen, 2008). This approach is driven by an understanding of the critical role played by the family in the child's life (Turnbull and Turnbull, 2001). The central role of the family to children with disabilities has been recognised, incorporated, and at times mandated in government policy on service provision in a number of countries (e.g., Individuals with Disabilities Education Act [IDEA] in the USA and the Commonwealth and State Disability Services Acts in Australia; Keen and Knox, 2004).

Recognition and acknowledgement of the contribution parents could make to their child's development was not always enlisted in the case of parents who had a child diagnosed with ASD. In the 1960s, the prevailing theory about ASD was that a 'cold' maternal parenting style caused the disorder (Bettelheim, 1967). Upon diagnosis of the child, parents were usually encouraged to institutionalise their child, primarily so that the child could grow up in what was thought to be a more nurturing environment (Turnbull and Turnbull, 1986). The clear message to parents was that the child would be better off in the care of others who were more qualified to meet the child's needs. 'Relationships between parents and professionals within this context were marked by professionals making judgments about the suitability of parents to raise their own children and be responsible for making decisions about how best to meet their child's needs. Control over the child's life was in many cases arrested from parents and assumed by professionals' (Keen, 2007, p. 340).

It is now understood that ASD is a neurobiological disorder. Further, working within a family-centred framework has real relevance to young children with ASD, who spend most waking hours in their early years interacting with their parents. This provides abundant learning and teaching opportunities throughout the day to encourage and enhance skills. Parents also have a detailed knowledge and understanding of their own child, a unique and caring relationship, and can be the child's greatest resource. Professionals know more generally about child development, behaviour, and ASD, and bring specific expertise which a parent may not have. Parents are a constant in the child's life, while professionals tend to come and go over time. These differences in knowledge and expertise between parents and professionals are complementary and work to the advantage of the child with ASD.

## Parent–Professional Partnerships

Central to family-centred practice, therefore, is the relationship that is established and maintained between professionals and parents. Effective parent–professional relationships are collaborative in nature and characterised by mutual respect, trust, honesty, mutually agreed goals, and shared planning and decision-making (Keen, 2007). One of the main reasons why partnerships fail is lack of sensitivity to the feelings of the family (Knox *et al.*, 2000). The judgmental approach of professionals in the 1960s toward mothers of children with ASD exemplified this lack of sensitivity, and resulted in non-collaborative relationships where parents were often excluded from decision-making.

Lucyshyn, Dunlap, and Albin (2002) defined true collaboration as 'the establishment of a respectful, trusting, caring, and reciprocal relationship in which interventionists and family members believe in each other's ability to make important contributions to the support process; share their knowledge and expertise; and mutually influence the selection of goals, the design of behaviour support plans, and the quality of family–practitioner interactions' (p. 12). We shall examine the parent–professional relationship in more detail in Chapter 3.

## CONCLUSION

In this chapter we have outlined a number of key concepts that underpin the work we've undertaken with families who have a child with ASD, and that have guided the writing of this book. Two approaches to skill development – behavioural and developmental social-pragmatic – inform the range of strategies and techniques we recommend that professionals use when helping parents engage with their children in those early weeks and months following diagnosis. The value of targeting joint attention behaviours and adopting a responsive parenting style are highlighted.

Help is provided to families during these first few months within a family-centred framework. A family-centred approach is based on family systems theory that recognises the interconnectedness of family members and the importance of collaborative relationships between parents and professionals. Helping parents to identify goals and learning priorities for their child at home, gain accurate and useful information about ASD, use parenting strategies that enhance their child's development, and select appropriate interventions are approached from a family-centred perspective. An outline of the steps we advocate in this book for supporting families in the initial months following diagnosis is shown in Figure 1.3. Working collaboratively with families on their priorities using practices informed by scientific evidence can make an important contribution to the quality of life of children with ASD and their families.

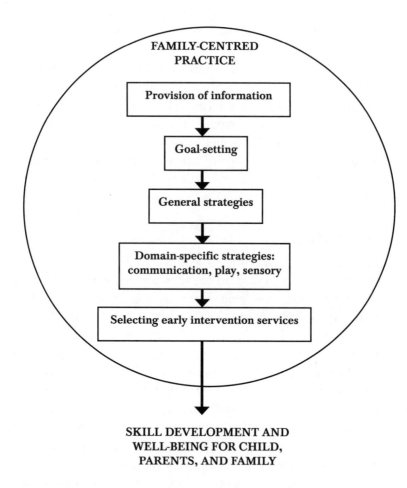

*Figure 1.3 Steps in supporting families following diagnosis*

Chapter 2

# About ASD

## INTRODUCTION

Twenty years ago the awareness of something called 'autism' in the general population was low but with an increase in prevalence of the disorder, which we will discuss in this chapter, awareness has increased. Even so, information about ASD is often accessed through the internet and the quality and accuracy of this information can vary significantly. When parents are first told that their child has ASD, it is essential that they receive accurate information about the disorder.

In this chapter we will examine the diagnosis of ASD in some detail. To do this, we will first look at the diagnostic criteria for ASD and how a diagnosis is made, what is known about the underlying causes of the disorder, and how prevalent it is today. We will also provide an overview of the core impairments of ASD and explore three cognitive theories that have been proposed to explain some of the common characteristics seen in children on the autism spectrum.

## GENERAL DESCRIPTION

The term PDD refers to a group of five disorders described within the Diagnostic and Statistical Manual IV-TR[1] (DSM-IV-TR; American Psychiatric Association, 2000) that includes:

- Autistic Disorder (AD)

---

1   The DSM-V is due to be released in May 2013 and may contain significant changes to the diagnostic criteria for ASD.

- Asperger's Syndrome (AS)

- Pervasive Developmental Disorder Not Otherwise Specified (PDD-NOS) or Atypical Autism

- Rett's Disorder

- Childhood Disintegrative Disorder.

Some of these PDDs form a group of disorders that have been referred to as ASD with core impairments in socialisation, verbal and nonverbal communication, and restricted and repetitive behaviour patterns (American Psychiatric Association, 2000). Researchers and clinicians now generally agree that there is an autism spectrum (Lord and Risi, 2000), with wide variability and complexity of expression of symptoms (Filipek *et al.*, 1999). ASD refers to a subgroup of PDDs that manifest in early childhood (Wing, 1996) and include AD, AS, and PDD-NOS.

The term 'autism' was first used by Leo Kanner to refer specifically to children with classic, or Kanner's, autism, which is recognised in infancy and characterised by the full expression of what is now known as AD (Kanner, 1943). While Hans Asperger's description of AS was contemporary with Kanner's work, this diagnostic category has only been widely used since its inclusion in the DSM-IV in 1994.

## Autistic Disorder

The criteria for a diagnosis of AD under the DSM-IV-TR are provided in Box 2.1. A child must present with unusual behaviours in the areas of communication, socialisation, and interests and activities prior to the age of three years to be classified as having AD. Within this category, individuals may sometimes be described as having high-functioning autism (HFA), in that they meet the behavioural criteria for the disorder but have average or above average intelligence.

## Asperger's Syndrome

The diagnostic criteria for AS are similar to AD, with two major points of difference being the absence of early language delays or communication impairments and relatively normal cognitive skills. However, the differences are reduced to the presence or absence of language delay if individuals with HFA are considered and compared with those with AS. There has been significant debate in the research and professional literature about whether AS and AD are separate and distinct disorders (Howlin, 2004).

Howlin (2003) conducted a review of studies that had compared individuals with AS and HFA and concluded that lack of agreement on diagnostic criteria and other factors across these studies made comparison almost impossible. In general, when differences between AS and HFA were detected, they were often small and inconsistent. Differences that were identified might also be found to disappear when IQ and/or chronological age were controlled, in many cases. As pointed out by Howlin (2004), it is important to remember that the basis for the distinction between AS and AD in the DSM-IV is not empirical but clinical in nature.

The lack of empirical support for separate and distinct categories as described in the DSM-IV-TR has led many to favour a dimensional approach to diagnosis, as represented by the notion of an autism spectrum. This approach is reflected in the proposed changes to the diagnostic categories that will be contained in the next edition of the DSM, due for release in 2013.

## Pervasive Developmental Disorder Not Otherwise Specified (PDD-NOS)

Some children meet some, but not all, of the criteria for AS or AD and when this occurs, they are likely to be diagnosed with PDD-NOS. The criteria for this diagnosis are less clear, so that in these children the core symptoms may present in a mild form or in uncharacteristic ways (Heflin and Alaimo, 2007).

Although ASD is neurobiological in origin, as yet there is no biological marker. Symptoms can be subtle and may go unrecognised even though they are always present in the first three years of life (Filipek et al., 1999). Some children may not be identified and diagnosed until middle childhood or even into adolescence or adulthood.

## Box 2.1 DSM-IV-TR criteria for a diagnosis of Autistic Disorder

**Diagnostic criteria for 299.00 Autistic Disorder**

A. A total of six (or more) items from (1), (2) and (3), with at least two from (1), and one each from (2) and (3)

(1) qualitative impairment in social interaction, as manifested by at least two of the following:

    a. marked impairment in the use of multiple nonverbal behaviours such as eye-to-eye gaze, facial expression, body postures, and gestures to regulate social interaction

    b. failure to develop peer relationships appropriate to developmental level

    c. a lack of spontaneous seeking to share enjoyment, interests, or achievements with other people (e.g., by a lack of showing, bringing, or pointing out objects of interest)

    d. (d) lack of social or emotional reciprocity

(2) qualitative impairments in communication as manifested by at least one of the following:

    a. delay in, or total lack of, the development of spoken language (not accompanied by an attempt to compensate through alternative modes of communication such as gesture or mime)

    b. in individuals with adequate speech, marked impairment in the ability to initiate or sustain a conversation with others

    c. stereotyped and repetitive use of language or idiosyncratic language

    d. lack of varied, spontaneous make-believe play or social imitative play appropriate to developmental level

(3) restricted repetitive and stereotyped patterns of behaviour, interests and activities, as manifested by at least two of the following:

a. encompassing preoccupation with one or more stereotyped and restricted patterns of interest that is abnormal either in intensity or focus

b. apparently inflexible adherence to specific, non-functional routines or rituals

c. stereotyped and repetitive motor mannerisms (e.g., hand or finger flapping or twisting, or complex whole-body movements)

d. persistent preoccupation with parts of objects

B. Delays or abnormal functioning in at least one of the following areas, with onset prior to age 3 years:

(1) social interaction

(2) language as used in social communication, or

(3) symbolic or imaginative play

C. The disturbance is not better accounted for by Rett's Disorder or Childhood Disintegrative Disorder.

*Reprinted with permission from the Diagnostic and Statistical Manual of Mental Disorders, Fourth Edition, Text Revision (Copyright © 2000). American Psychiatric Association.*

## CAUSATION

The cause of ASD is still unknown but it is generally understood that there are likely to be multiple causes, with both genetic and environmental factors (including *in utero*) implicated. Research involving twins has provided sound evidence of a genetic influence in ASD. The likelihood of both twins having ASD when they are monozygotic (identical) is much greater than when the twins are dizygotic (fraternal; Rutter, 2005). In addition to twin studies, research has found that siblings of a child with ASD are much more likely to be affected by ASD than would occur in the general population (Hall, 2009).

To date, no single gene has been identified and it is thought unlikely that this will occur. Instead, it is thought that multiple genes on several chromosomes are involved, and this makes the identification of these genes particularly challenging. This is compounded by the interaction of these genes with as yet unidentified environmental factors which lead to the presentation of autistic symptoms (Rutter, 2000, 2005). In a small number of cases ASD is linked to specific genetic disorders, including Fragile X, tuberous sclerosis, and Angelman's syndrome.

In addition to genetic studies, researchers have investigated the structure and function of the brain in individuals with ASD to identify those areas most affected by the disorder. One of these researchers, Eric Courchesne, has worked with colleagues using structural and functional magnetic resonance imaging (MRI and fMRI) to better understand the underlying impairments in brain functioning that are associated with the cognitive and behavioural impairments that are characteristic of ASD. They have found that there is premature overgrowth in some brain structures and that there is a lack of 'neural pruning' in the early years (Courchesne *et al.*, 2001).

Apart from MRI research, autopsy studies have provided another source of information about brain structure and have identified differences in the cerebellum, brain stem, frontal lobes, and amygdala of the brain. There has been particular interest in examining the links between abnormalities in the frontal lobe region and autistic symptoms, as the frontal lobes play a role in emotional expression and executive functioning – which will be discussed later in this chapter (Hall, 2009).

## PREVALENCE

Evidence has emerged in the international literature that ASD prevalence rates are rising and that the demographics of this population are changing. Clinical opinion and the empirical literature indicate an apparent increased prevalence of ASD. It is, however, difficult to answer the question as to whether prevalence has increased or whether the increase is due to other factors (Liu, King, and Bearman, 2010). No study is likely to answer this question because over the last 20 years there have been significant changes in diagnostic criteria, an increased public awareness of ASD, and changes in the types and availability of therapeutic and educational services (Jordan and Jones, 1999). Determining the prevalence of behaviourally defined disorders is more difficult than determining prevalence of conditions for which biological markers exist. In reviewing prevalence studies, it is important to understand the diagnostic criteria used, the period in which these studies were conducted, and the developmental context. Undoubtedly, prevalence rates and diagnostic criteria are linked. Furthermore, with the widespread adoption of the term Autism Spectrum Disorder, children may be diagnosed as having ASD without differentiation of subtype.

Early studies reported prevalence of infantile autism of 4–5 per 10,000 (Lotter, 1966). Over recent years, prevalence figures appear to have increased, due to improved clinical recognition and acknowledgement of a broader clinical phenotype (Filipek *et al.*, 1999). Prevalence figures cited also vary, depending on the diagnostic definition used (e.g., AD, AS, ASD). Arvidsson and colleagues' (1997) longitudinal study of three- and six-year-old children revealed the age-specific prevalence for childhood AD as 31 in 10,000 children. They caution that the rates reported must be regarded as a minimum, as it is likely that high-functioning children with autism have been missed at this young age. Chakrabarti and Fombonne (2005) reported prevalence rates of 16.8 per 10,000 for AD and 45.8 per 10,000 for other PDDs. The prevalence of ASD in Australia is now reported to be 1 in 160 children aged 6 to 12 years. This makes ASD more prevalent than blindness, deafness, cerebral palsy (CP), leukaemia, and diabetes combined (MacDermott *et al.* 2006).

Prevalence studies have consistently reported that ASD is more common in males than females, at a ratio of about 4:1. The rates of intellectual impairment within the ASD population are less clear. An interesting investigation was conducted by Edelson (2006) in relation to this issue. She examined the evidence behind claims in the research literature that the majority of children (up to 75%) with ASD have an intellectual disability. A total of 215 articles published between 1937 and 2003 were reviewed to identify the source and type of evidence behind statements made in relation to the rates of intellectual disability. Edelson found that 74 per cent of the claims came from non-empirical sources, 53 per cent of which did not trace back to empirical data. Furthermore, when empirical evidence was used, it was published between 25 and 45 years prior to the study and often relied on results from measures of development or adaptive behaviour rather than intelligence. There have been some studies that have found rates much lower than those commonly cited. For example, Chakrabarti and Fombonne (2005) found rates of intellectual impairment as low as 25 per cent within a population of children with PDD.

## DIAGNOSIS AND ASSESSMENT

Diagnosis is important, even in very young children. Early diagnosis leads to inclusion in early intervention programmes, resulting in significant improvements in cognitive, communication, and behavioural functioning. Appropriate early intervention can help families to formulate appropriate expectations for their children's progress and behaviour, enables educational planning and treatment, provision of family support and education, and can reduce parental stress. With improved awareness and understanding of ASD, early identification is more possible now than in previous years. Much work has been undertaken to determine the most efficient, effective, and reliable means of identifying children as early as possible so that they may benefit from early intervention. Researchers have been able to determine early signs that can act as 'red flags' to alert parents and professionals of children who may be at risk of an ASD diagnosis, to closely monitor the child's development over time (Wetherby *et al.*, 2007; Wetherby *et al.*, 2004).

Diagnostic evaluations for ASD usually consist of some combination of developmental history, direct observation of behaviour, and testing, which includes standardised assessments of adaptive functioning, communication skills, and cognitive ability. Diagnostic evaluation requires a comprehensive multidisciplinary approach, including measures of parental report, child observation and interactions, and clinical judgement. The development of a profile of strengths and weaknesses to support intervention efforts is also recommended (Filipek *et al.*, 1999).

A range of standardised measures have been developed to assist clinicians in making a diagnosis, and examples of these are shown in Table 2.1. Some of these tools are designed to be used for screening purposes, while others are diagnostic. A screening tool can be used with young children in high-risk categories, such as those with a sibling already diagnosed with ASD. They may also be included in a range of development screening tests for children undergoing routine health checks. Children identified positively on these screening tests can then be referred for more comprehensive diagnostic assessment. Screening tests vary in their specificity (the number of children correctly identified as *not* having ASD) and sensitivity (the number of children correctly identified as *having* ASD). As screening tests are usually quick and easy to administer, they can be very useful, but it is important to remember that they will sometimes fail to identify a child with ASD or may identify a child as having ASD when the child does not have the disorder. Standardised diagnostic assessment tools take longer to administer than screening instruments and are more comprehensive in their examination of the child's behaviour.

**Table 2.1 Diagnostic tools**

| Measure | Authors |
|---|---|
| Autism Diagnostic Interview (ADI–R) | Rutter, Le Couteur, and Lord (2003) |
| Autism Diagnostic Observation Scale (ADOS) | Lord, Rutter, DiLavore, and Risi (2001) |
| Parent Interview for Autism (PIA) | Stone and Hogan (1993) |
| Asperger Syndrome Diagnostic Interview (ASDI) | Gillberg, Gillberg, Rastam, and Wentz (2001) |
| Australian Scale for Asperger Syndrome | Garnett and Attwood (1998) |
| Children's Autism Rating Scale (CARS) | Schopler, Reichler, DeVellis, and Daly (1980) |
| Autism Behaviour Checklist (ABC) | Krug, Arick, and Almond (1980) |
| Autism Screening Instrument for Educational Planning (ASIEP) | Krug, Arick, and Almond (1979) |
| Gilliam Autism Rating Scale (GARS) | Gilliam (1995) |
| Modified Checklist for Autism in Toddlers (M-CHAT) | Robins, Fein, Barton, and Green (2001) |
| Communication and Symbolic Behaviour Scales (CSBS) | Wetherby and Prizant (1993) |
| Social Communication Questionnaire (SCQ) | Rutter, Bailey, and Lord (2007) |
| Diagnostic Interview for Social and Communication Disorders (DISCO) | Leekam, Libby, Wing, Gould, and Taylor (2002) |

Ideally, the child will be seen by a psychologist, speech pathologist, and occupational therapist, who each provide important information about the child's adaptive behaviour, developmental level, communication, socialisation, and sensory functioning, which can inform diagnosis and assist with intervention planning. In addition, reports from early childhood or kindergarten teachers provide useful information about how the child functions in naturalistic contexts with other children.

## IMPAIRMENTS IN ASD

ASD is characterised by core impairments in communication, socialisation, and restricted and repetitive behaviours and interests (American Psychiatric Association, 2000). There are additional areas that, while not core to the diagnosis of ASD, are consistently associated with the disorder. A description of these core and associated impairments follows.

### Socialisation

It has been noted that at least 50 per cent of parents who have a child with ASD suspect a problem before their child reaches their first birthday (Ornitz, Guthrie, and Farley, 1977). Parents typically report that their child was not cuddly and was resistant to contact, or that he or she was passive and floppy (Prior and Ozonoff, 1998). While children with ASD appear to form social attachments to their caregivers, they tend to seek help and comfort less often, and show less attention to people, objects, and events than do their typically developing peers (Prior and Ozonoff, 1998). Osterling and Dawson (1994) conducted a fascinating retrospective study of home videotapes involving infants who would later be diagnosed with ASD. In their study they examined the type and frequency of social behaviours that are usually evident in typically developing infants of the same age, such as joint attention, which involves the child's ability to co-ordinate attention between themselves, another person, and an object or event (see page 23). By 12 months of age, the children in the videotapes displayed fewer social and joint attention behaviours (such as responding to their name, showing objects to others, and looking at the face of another and pointing) than typically developing infants. One of the most challenging things for parents of a child with ASD can be the apparent lack of engagement or connectedness of the child, which may be evident through the child's resistance to physical contact and preference for being alone.

## Communication

The communicative abilities of children with ASD vary widely, from children who fail to develop any speech and remain mute throughout their lives, to those more mildly affected who have well-developed speech. Even for these individuals, however, difficulties persist in the pragmatics or meaningful use of language, and in the social aspects of engaging in a conversation. They may, for example, talk at length about a prescribed interest and not enter into the turn-taking usually associated with a conversation.

For some, speech may be limited to a few words, which are not used in a functional way to communicate. Some children engage in echolalic speech, where words or phrases that they hear are repeated immediately or after a period of delay. A parent might ask their child 'Do you want a drink?' and the child repeats 'Want a drink', which makes it difficult for the parent to understand whether the child's repetition of the phrase is an answer, or merely a repetition of what was just heard without communicative intent. Children who experience these limitations benefit from the introduction of an augmentative or alternative communication system, and this will be discussed in more detail in Chapter 7.

Other aspects of communication are also affected in individuals with ASD, including the use of gesture, whereby the type and range of gestures may be limited and the use of gesture may be asynchronous with speech (de Marchena and Eigsti, 2010). Fewer children with ASD use pointing gestures compared to typically developing peers, although they are more likely to point as a way of requesting something than they are to point for the purpose of commenting (Mundy and Sigman, 1989; Stone et al., 1997).

## Restricted and Repetitive Behaviours and Interests

A feature of the early descriptions of children with ASD, dating back to those by Leo Kanner in 1943, was the presence of ritualistic behaviour, reliance on non-functional routines, and restricted and prescribed interests and obsessions. The play of these children was often observed to be ritualistic and associated with unusual toy use

(Wulff, 1985). These behaviours continue to feature in the DSM-IV-TR as a core symptom of ASD (American Psychiatric Association, 2000). Table 2.2 shows examples of restricted and repetitive behaviour typically seen in children with ASD. It is important to remember that these behaviours can vary enormously within an individual over time, and between individuals.

**Table 2.2 Examples of restricted and repetitive behaviours**

| Pattern of Behaviour | Examples |
| --- | --- |
| Adherence to rituals and routines that must be performed precisely the same way each time and which, if interrupted, can lead to anxiety and challenging behaviour. | Having a particular route that must be followed between home and school; constantly knocking on the wall while walking to the bathroom; only eating from a red coloured plate. |
| Sterotyped behaviours involving parts of or the whole body. | Rocking; hand flapping; some forms of self-injury. |
| Stereotyped behaviours involving objects. | Carrying and twirling a piece of string. |
| Sensory sensitivities. | Distress at the sound of an air-conditioner or hand dryer; licking the carpet. |
| Highly prescribed interests in certain topics, objects or events. | Insistence on wearing a piece of clothing at all times; fascination with numbers and/or letters; intense interest in and extensive knowledge about dinosaurs. |

According to Wing (1988, 1996), rigidity of thought and behaviour represents a core deficit in imagination, but others have argued that individuals with ASD may be able to imagine but have difficulty distinguishing their imaginings from their real experiences (Jordan and Jones, 1999).

## Sensory Issues

It is well documented that children with ASD frequently experience idiosyncratic responses to sensory stimuli, though the reason for this is unknown (Baranek, 2002; Bogdashina, 2003; Gal, Cermak, and Ben-Sasson, 2007). Since not all people with ASD experience sensory perception and processing problems, these have not been considered core criteria for a diagnosis of ASD (American Psychiatric Association, 2000). Studies suggest that unusual sensory responses (e.g., hypo- and hyper-responses), preoccupations with sensory features of objects, perceptual distortions, and paradoxical responses to sensory stimuli exist in between 42 per cent and 88 per cent of children with ASD (Kientz and Dunn, 1997). More recently Tomcheck and Dunn (2007) reported that up to 95 per cent of children with ASD experience sensory processing impairments. Where they do occur, unusual sensory and perceptual features tend to present early in development (i.e., before 12 months of age). The occurrence of sensory symptoms does not seem to be related either to ASD symptom severity or to children's IQ (Rogers, Hepburn, and Wehner, 2003).

## What is Sensory Processing?

Sensory processing involves making sense of information from the various human senses. Information is received by multiple senses simultaneously, requiring an interplay and comparison of information with past experience. The resulting behavioural, emotional or motor responses reflect multiple contributing factors (Smith-Myles *et al.*, 2000). These responses demonstrate the level of integration of different types of sensation that is known as 'sensory processing' (Miller and Lane, 2000; Miller *et al.*, 2005).

*Sensory modulation* is the critical balance or regulation of facilitating and inhibiting sensory inputs (Dunn, 1999; Miller, Coll, and Schoen, 2007). This enables response to some inputs and disregard of others (e.g., ignore the wall clock ticking and focus on what the kindergarten teacher is saying). Modulation enables balancing of responses so that they match the task. Sometimes this requires habituation to certain familiar inputs so that they are not attended to (e.g., a radio playing while we are reading). Children with ASD often have difficulty disregarding specific inputs, as they seem to experience them more acutely than other people (e.g., the noise of the wall clock ticking is perceived so intensely that the child cannot ignore it).

There is a neurological threshold continuum from low to high that is experienced across all sensory systems (i.e., vision, hearing, touch, taste, smell, movement). Children with low thresholds tend to be *oversensitive* or *over-responsive*. In other words, it only takes a low-level stimulus before the child registers it. As a result he or she often experiences distress from noises, light sensitivity, discomfort with certain textures, aversions to smell and taste, and insecurity with height and movement. These children tend to react in an avoidant manner to these stimuli.

On the other hand, children who have high sensory thresholds are *undersensitive* or *under-responsive* to sensory input. For these children it takes a high-level stimulus to be registered and attended to before they respond. These children often show lack of attention to sounds, and decreased awareness to pain, temperature, and injury. They may demonstrate disregard for persons and objects in the environment and may have delayed reactions as a result of poor sensory registration. Children with over- or under-responsiveness to sensation react to stimuli in certain characteristic ways (Bogdashina, 2003; Smith-Myles *et al.*, 2000). For example, a child with over-responsiveness may rock when overwhelmed, in an apparent attempt to calm himself; a child with under-responsiveness may make humming noises to stay focused.

In children with ASD, both over- and under-responsivity can occur in the same child and there may be fluctuations within and between systems and over time (Bogdashina, 2003). Further, many children engage in odd, stereotypical behaviours for reasons other than sensory seeking. For example, they may want to avoid something or someone in the environment, or to obtain a desired object, or their odd stereotypical behaviours may be part of a rigid pattern or routine.

## COGNITIVE THEORIES

As we have described above, ASD is characterised by impairments in communication, socialisation, restricted and repetitive behaviours and interests, and sensory issues. Attempts to understand the nature of these impairments has given rise to a range of cognitive theories, with the three most influential being theory of mind, executive function, and central coherence.

### Theory of Mind

A delay in formation of a theory of mind as an explanation for ASD gained traction in the 1980s (Baron-Cohen, Leslie, and Frith, 1985). Theory of mind, sometimes referred to as mindreading, relates to a person's ability to understand and reason about the mental states of others (Holroyd and Baron-Cohen, 1993; Leslie and Frith, 1988). There has been much interest in measuring theory of mind to determine when this emerges in typical development, and how children with ASD may differ from this typical trajectory. One way typically used to measure theory of mind is to assess a child's understanding of 'false belief' tasks (Holroyd and Baron-Cohen, 1993). To pass a false belief task, a child must distinguish between his or her own true belief and someone else's false belief (Wimmer and Perner, 1983). The Sally-Anne task is a commonly used false belief task (Baron-Cohen *et al.*, 1985). In this task the child is introduced to two characters, Sally and Anne, and is told a scenario (usually acted out with dolls or drawings). In the scenario, Sally hides an object in location A and leaves the room. While out of the room, Anne moves the object to another location, B. On returning, Sally will have a false belief that the object is still in location A. The child is then asked where he or she thinks Sally will look for the object. To pass this task a child has to understand that Sally has a false belief about where the object is located and that this is different from the child's own understanding about where the object really is, in location B in this instance (Swettenham, 1996).

Typically developing children generally pass these false belief tasks at around four years of age (Baron-Cohen *et al.*, 1985; Muris, Steerneman, and Merckelbach, 1998). In contrast, children with ASD frequently fail false belief tasks (Baron-Cohen, 1991; Baron-Cohen *et al.*, 1985; Frith and Happé, 1999; Swettenham, 1996). Attempts to explain these performance differences has led researchers to measure the relative influences of chronological age, mental age, and verbal mental age on theory of mind performance (Baron-Cohen, 1991; Happé, 1995; Leslie and Frith, 1988). Children with Down syndrome, intellectual impairment, and learning disabilities with a lower mental age than children with ASD have been shown to perform better on a range of theory of mind tasks (Baron-Cohen *et al.*, 1985; Frith, Happé, and Siddons, 1994; Yirmiya and Shulman, 1996). These results indicate that mental age alone fails to account for the theory of mind difficulties encountered by children with ASD.

There does, however, appear to be an important relationship between theory of mind performance and verbal ability, and research has shown that verbal ability influences theory of mind performance

(Charman and Baron-Cohen, 1992; Happé, 1994; Leekam and Perner, 1991; Ozonoff, Rogers, and Pennington, 1991). Happé (1995) compared children with ASD (n = 70), intellectual impairment (n = 34), and typically developing children (n = 70) on two theory of mind tasks. She found that children with ASD required a far higher verbal mental age to pass false belief tasks than did children from the comparison groups. A correlation between higher verbal mental age and enhanced theory of mind performance in children with ASD has been supported by a number of research studies (Charman and Baron-Cohen, 1992; Charman and Campbell, 1997; Leekam and Perner, 1991; Muris et al., 1998). In an attempt to explain the relationship between verbal ability and theory of mind, Happé (1995) has suggested that children with ASD who pass these tasks may be using a verbally mediated, cognitive problem-solving approach that differs qualitatively from the way typically developing and intellectually impaired children understand false belief. They therefore need much greater verbal competence if they are to have a chance of passing theory of mind tasks. Some have also argued that children with ASD have deficits in verbal memory (Ozonoff et al., 1991) and processing narrative (Tager-Flusberg and Sullivan, 1994), which may impact their theory of mind performance.

## Executive Function

Executive function has been described as the 'faculties that are needed for the individual to work in a motivated fashion toward a goal that may not be reached instantly' (Gillberg and Coleman, 2000, p. 108). Executive functioning refers to the organisational and planning aspects of cognition and is therefore critical to cognitive functioning. The following skills are central to executive function:

- focusing skills
- time concepts
- sequential thinking
- motivation.

It is thought that the areas of the brain associated with executive function, including the frontal lobes, may be affected in individuals with ASD, leading to deficits in these skills (Ozonoff, South, and

Provencal, 2005). Difficulties in forward planning and cognitive flexibility can result in problems with changes in routine, transitions from one activity to another, abstract reasoning, information processing and sequencing issues. This may help to explain some characteristics of the disorder such as restricted and repetitive behaviours, rigid routines and prescribed interests.

## Central Coherence

The saying 'He can't see the wood for the trees' illustrates the concept of central coherence well because it refers to the ability to move between the detail (wood) and the big picture (the tree). Typically developing children have a tendency to process information for meaning by looking at the big picture. They are able to extract the most relevant information from a story or conversation and understand the overall meaning.

**Table 2.3 Strengths and weaknesses of weak central coherence**

| Strength | Weakness |
|----------|----------|
| Completing a jigsaw using the unique shape of each piece without reference to the picture of the completed puzzle. | Completing a jigsaw using the picture of the completed puzzle for reference. |
| Being able to identify faces by accessories (e.g., a pair of reading glasses). | Being able to identify faces by the person, rather than their accessories. |
| Remembering strings of unrelated words. | Remembering sentences. |
| Remembering an array of completely unrelated items. | Remembering an array of items that belong to a particular category, such as things that are found in a kitchen. |

It has been argued that children with ASD have weak central coherence in that they tend to have a cognitive style that is very detail-focused and they have difficulty processing information at the global level or switching from detail to concept and back again (Frith, 1989). At times this can be a strength in that individuals with this processing style can have excellent attention to detail and pick up things that others may miss. They may also be able to remember and retain random information that is difficult for others who use meaningful associations between pieces of information to aid memory. These strengths and weaknesses are illustrated in Table 2.3, and are drawn from the work of Francesca Happé, who has undertaken extensive research in this area (Happé, 2000; Happé, Briskman, and Frith, 2001). The tasks listed in the 'strengths' column are those in which children with ASD may outperform their peers of a similar mental age. The tasks listed in the 'weaknesses' column are representative of those in which children with ASD perform less well, compared with peers of a similar mental age.

## CONCLUSION

Over the past decade the number of identified cases of ASD has risen significantly internationally, and while much of this increase can be accounted for by changes in diagnostic criteria and increased awareness, it is likely that there has been some increase in prevalence. ASD is comprised of Autistic Disorder, Asperger's syndrome and Pervasive Developmental Disorder Not Otherwise Specified. These diagnostic categories are currently under review and there are likely to be significant changes to the diagnostic criteria when the DSM-V is released in 2013.

Ideally, diagnosis should involve a multidisciplinary assessment of the child, and early identification of children at risk of the disorder is beneficial to ensure that early intervention can be implemented. As yet, the cause of ASD is unknown. What is known is that ASD is a neurobiological disorder involving both genetic and environmental factors. Structural and functional analyses of the brain have revealed abnormalities in specific areas, including the frontal lobes, which are responsible for executive functions and emotional expression.

Three prominent cognitive theories of ASD have helped to explain some of the characteristics evident in children with the disorder, but none of these theories provides a comprehensive explanation of all characteristics. The core impairments of ASD involve social, communication, and behavioural aspects. Sensory issues are common, although not core to the disorder. There is significant variability in the way in which these impairments are expressed in individual children who share the ASD diagnosis. These aspects may also change in presentation over time.

Chapter 3

# Parent–Professional Partnerships

## INTRODUCTION

Effective parent–professional partnerships are a cornerstone of family-centred services, which are considered best practice in early intervention. These partnerships are collaborative in nature and are characterised by mutual respect, trust and honesty, mutually agreed upon goals, and shared planning and decision-making (Keen, 2007). This chapter will outline what is meant by family-centred practice when working with families, and identify the key principles underpinning the development of effective partnerships with families who have a member with ASD. It focuses on working with immediate and extended families, as well as developing partnership-based home programmes and effectively using space within the home environment to meet individual family members' needs. Mutually agreed goals and shared planning and decision-making will be the focus of Chapter 4.

As mentioned above, central to family-centred practice is the relationship that is established and maintained between professionals and parents. Professionals can evoke strong feelings that are both positive and negative in their interactions with parents (Seligman and Darling, 2007). Developing effective relationships can be challenging, and may be further impacted by the additional stress often experienced by parents of children with ASD. It is well known that parents of children with emotional, behavioural, and communication problems such as those characteristic of ASD experience greater levels of stress (e.g., Baker *et al.*, 2003), with mothers of children with ASD typically experiencing higher levels of stress than fathers (Dabriwsja and Pisula, 2010). Mothers were found to use emotion-oriented coping and social diversion strategies more frequently than fathers. This and previous studies highlight the need to take into account the nature of gender differences in parental stress associated with particular childhood disabilities, and to help parents develop effective coping strategies related to their individual coping styles and gender differences (Dabriwsja and Pisula, 2010). Of particular importance is the finding that parenting stress may inhibit the positive effects of supporting the child's development (Osborne *et al.*, 2008), and potentially contribute to difficulties establishing collaborative relationships with professionals.

Some recent research by Kayfitz, Gragg, and Orr (2010) which explored the *positive* experiences of Canadian mothers and fathers of children with ASD (n = 23) found that parents of children with ASD have co-occurring positive experiences, and that these are related to lower levels of parenting stress. In addition, mothers reported more positive experiences than fathers. This study highlights the importance of recognising and reinforcing these positive experiences and helping parents to recognise and acknowledge them, as this may help them gain a more balanced perspective about parenting children with ASD. Professionals who develop collaborative relationships with parents are more likely to be able to explore both the positive and negative aspects of parenting, and be able to support parents to find meaning and cope better with the challenging aspects of family life.

## WORKING WITH FAMILIES AND FAMILY-CENTRED PRACTICE

### Families and Extended Families

When working with children, it goes without saying that the family unit is pivotal. Family members will provide the child with life-long support; they have expert knowledge about the child through their daily lived experiences with him or her; and have an understanding of his or her likes and dislikes, and the environmental context of family life. In most cases family members will continue to be the child's best advocates in the health, education and welfare systems that they will engage with throughout their lives (Rodger and Keen, 2010).

In contemporary society there are many different family configurations, sharing a variety of different living arrangements (Darlington and Rodger, 2006). Relatives may be either close or more distant, and may differ in the way they participate in the life of the child. The family network generally extends beyond relatives to include friends, neighbours, paid carers, and other members of the community, with whom the family has regular contact (e.g., a swimming teacher). The family's network of relatives, friends, and community members has the potential to be an important source of support to the child and family, but their capacity to be supportive is related to their acceptance of the child with a disability, and their ability to acknowledge the many challenges faced by parents in raising a child with a disability (Cuskelly and Hayes, 2004). This acceptance and acknowledgement may not happen easily or automatically. For example, grandparents have been found to fall into one of two categories: those who do and those who do not provide support to parents (Mirfin-Veitch and Bray, 1997). In most cases, grandparents who are less supportive and involved seem to have difficulties accepting their grandchild's disability.

## Family-centred Practice

Family-centred practice has evolved in acknowledgement of the pivotal role of families when a child has specific developmental challenges. Family-centred practice is a broad practice philosophy now widely recognised as best practice in child and family health care (Carpenter, 2007; Hannah and Rodger, 2002; MacKean, Thurston, and Scott, 2005). It refers to a transdisciplinary philosophy of care and service delivery that views the family unit as the client, incorporating parents/carers, the child with a disability, and his or her siblings, and attends to the skills and resources needed by all family members to manage the ongoing care of the child with a disability (Rosenbaum et al., 1998).

Family-centred practice was originally an extension of 'client-centred practice' (King et al., 2004), an orientation to intervention in which the client's participation is focal. Family-centred practice draws from family systems theory, eco-cultural theory and transactional models of child development which assume that children develop best when the requirements of the whole family are addressed. A substantial body of evidence is developing which supports the use of interventions which fit within the description of family-centred practice for improving outcomes for children with disabilities, as well as all family members (Dunst *et al.*, 1991; King *et al.*, 1999; Law *et al.*, 2003). The links between outcomes for children with disabilities and parents' (particularly mothers') well-being and help-giving practices are well documented (Dempsey *et al.*, 2009; Dunst, Trivette, and Hamby, 1996; Hassall, Rose, and McDonald, 2005; Hastings and Brown, 2002; Raina *et al.*, 2005).

Within family-centred practice family members' involvement in decision-making is strongly encouraged (Rosenbaum *et al.*, 1998). Irrespective of the level of involvement in intervention that parents choose, they are viewed as equal members of the team of professionals surrounding their child, and are respected for their valued knowledge and expertise (Brown, 2003). Hence, the adoption of family-centred practice in the delivery of services to children and their families involves professionals acting in ways that promote parents' involvement in their child's intervention, and address the contextual influences on the developing child.

A consensus definition (Allen and Petr, 1996) of family-centred services is that:

> Family-centred service delivery, across disciplines and settings, views the family as the unit of attention. This model organises assistance in a collaborative fashion in accordance with each individual family's wishes, strengths, and needs. (p. 64)

Family-centred services recognise the central role of the family as promoting the development of a child, and that *both* the family and the professionals bring different knowledge and skills to their working relationships in order to provide effective intervention to the family (Hannah and Rodger, 2002). The needs and priorities of the family determine how and when services are provided, with the emphasis on the strengths and resources of the whole family and not only on individual family members. Goals and desired outcomes are mutually defined by the family and the professionals involved.

Rosenbaum and colleagues (1998) identified some guiding principles of family-centred practice including that:

1.  parents have ultimate responsibility for the care of their children

2.  family members are treated with respect as individuals

3.  the needs of all family members are considered

4.  parents' expertise about the child's and family's status and needs is recognised

5.  families decide the level of involvement they wish in decision-making for their child

6.  all family members are involved to the extent they wish to be.

Family-centred practice and services are both underpinned by the premise that collaboration and partnership are central means that professionals and families use to work towards common goals and combine their efforts to achieve outcomes which the child and the family have agreed upon (Case-Smith, 1999).

## DEVELOPING EFFECTIVE RELATIONSHIPS WITH PARENTS

When children are the recipients of intervention, relationships have been reported to be intensified as both child and parents/guardians are incorporated (Hjorngaard and Taylor, 2010). The relationship with parents is even more crucial with children who do not necessarily understand the nature and reason for the intervention. Some authors, such as Hjorngaard and Taylor (2010), who are both parents of children with neurodevelopmental disorders, suggest that, rather than assume a shared understanding of the terms 'partnership' or 'collaboration', it is important for parents and professionals to explore their views and meanings about these terms, as well as their expectations of the relationship. This lays the foundation for developing a shared understanding of how the 'partnership' will work for each individual parent–professional encounter. The basis for this is for professionals to find out about each family's unique culture and parenting approaches. Hjorgaard and Taylor consider that the more time spent undertaking the groundwork for a mutually respectful partnership, the greater the trust likely to be developed in the intervention process and in an understanding of the roles of both partners. They reflected that '…the most respectful and meaningfully collaborative partnerships for [my] family were with therapists who spoke to us as parents and to [my] child in particular in a manner that indicated we were equals' (p. 81).

Identifying practitioner skills and behaviours that facilitate the development of such effective partnerships is important, because the development of a trusting and respectful relationship is unlikely to occur automatically (Dunlap *et al.*, 1997; Dunst *et al.*, 1994; Summers *et al.*, 2005). Dunst, Trivette, and Johanson (1994) found the highest ranked characteristic of good partnerships was 'trust', followed by mutual respect, open communication, and honesty. As practitioners are often required to work with a diverse range of families with complex and differing needs, it can be challenging to succeed in building strong and respectful relationships with every family (Rodger *et al.*, 2008).

To some degree, compatibility between practitioner and family appears to reflect a 'goodness of fit' (Rodger *et al.*, 2008). Understanding the ecology of a family and ensuring a 'good fit' has been found to influence intervention outcomes (Fox *et al.*, 1997; Moes and Frea, 2000; Vaughn *et al.*, 1997). Practitioners can gain an understanding of family ecology and use this information to establish rapport and guide goal-setting and intervention such that they are compatible with family goals and priorities. One technique is to gather information about family rituals and routines (see Table 6.1 in Chapter 6) that help to define the family, and about how time is spent by family members individually and as a family unit. A range of methods of goal-setting are discussed in detail in Chapter 4.

There is also a growing body of research evidence demonstrating that parents engaged in collaborative relationships with professionals experience less stress and higher levels of parenting competence, and report that these early intervention programmes are more family-centred (Broggi and Sabatelli, 2010). Broggi and Sabatelli measured two relationship characteristics, namely satisfaction and control. They suggested that these dimensions may be useful in further conceptualising and evaluating parent–professional relationships in early intervention. They did caution, however, that individual parents' preferences need to be considered carefully, as not all parents want to exercise high levels of control over their child's intervention.

Parents experiencing high satisfaction and high control tend to experience generally positive and supportive relationships and to be more active decision-makers. They concluded that relationship type might influence early intervention outcomes and that evaluating these relationship characteristics at various points in the early intervention process provides professionals and families with opportunities for discussion, and can help to clearly identify ways in which collaborative relationships can be developed with individual families (Broggi and Sabatelli, 2010).

Individual professionals' attitudes are important if effective relationships are to be established with parents and families. Rodger and Keen (2010) identified a number of considerations such as:

1.  professionals' values/beliefs (e.g., respect, dignity), attitudes towards team work, cooperation and willingness to work with team and family members to reach satisfactory solutions for individual families

2.  professionals' knowledge and skills in communication and collaboration, leading to development of effective partnerships.

Professionals also need to develop a high degree of personal and professional adaptability to respond to the multiple issues influencing how families with children manage on a daily basis. Development of high-level communication skills (e.g., negotiation, consultation, conflict resolution) that aid in the development of collaborative partnerships with parents is also critical.

Provision of information, taking into consideration educational levels, literacy, cultural and language issues, adult learning principles and learning style preferences, also needs to be well developed in family-centred practitioners (Rodger, 2006). This will be addressed in Chapter 5.

## RECOGNISING AND ACKNOWLEDGING DIFFERENCES

Just as all families are individual, so are their choices in terms of how they engage with professionals and services regarding their level of involvement in their child's intervention and related decision-making.

Corlett and Twycross (2006) found that, while professionals need to have effective negotiation and communication skills in working with families and children, parents also need to be able to negotiate the nature of their roles. Therefore, professionals need to create positive relationships with parents, in which the latter feel empowered to undertake such negotiation.

Seligman and Darling (2007) highlighted that parents come to interactions with professionals with a range of predispositions and expectations, some of which may be based on the image of professional dominance resulting from professionals' education and status in the community. This is important for professionals to be aware of, as it may impact on parents' comfort with engaging as 'equal' partners in relationships. Some parents may view professionals with respect and even awe, submitting to their recommendations unquestioningly, while others may resent professionals apparently controlling their lives (Seligman and Darling, 2007). Professionals are typically expected to be affectively neutral and not become emotionally over-involved with their clients. In this regard the professional role is the antithesis of the parental role. Parents may also have preconceived notions of the nature of the professional role and hold expectations that may be either realistic or unrealistic. Similarly, Seligman and Darling (2007) cautioned professionals to be aware of their own predispositions towards children with disabilities and their families, some of which may be stigmatising and negative. A study by Dillenburger et al. (2010), described later in this section, highlights some of the differences in views that might exist between parents and professionals.

While professionals have a 'clinical' perspective of the child, based on their particular professional background and skill set, their professional socialisation, and perceptions of their professional dominance, this perspective has its limitations, and these can include viewing the child's condition out of his or her family context, and over-focusing on the diagnostic condition, and profession-specific treatment priorities. It is important for professionals to be able to:

- be empathic
- listen carefully to parents
- try to understand the role of parents to appreciate their perspectives

- be aware of their own feelings and attitudes

- be respectful

- focus on the child's strengths and positive attributes as well as areas of need

- communicate using clear straightforward language

- spend time with parents when needed. This is especially important when parents are coming to terms with new information, such as around the time of diagnosis.

(Seligman and Darling, 2007)

While professionals are increasingly taking on new roles, such as from 'therapist expert' to 'equal partner' when working with parents, parents are also required to undertake new roles when developing partnerships with professionals. Some of these include roles as entrepreneurs, activists, and child advocates, who need to seek information, maintain control, become aware of their rights and responsibilities, and at times challenge authority (Esdaile and Olson, 2003; Seligman and Darling, 2007).

Recent research has documented that parents and professionals have different perspectives on the needs of children with ASD and their families, and stresses experienced by parents. Dillenburger and colleagues (2010) explored these similarities and differences in a comprehensive study of 95 Irish parents and caregivers of children with ASD, and 67 professionals who were working with these families, including therapists, social workers, psychologists, teachers, nurses, etc. They collected data using two questionnaires: the Family Autism Needs Questionnaire, which addresses child-and-parent-related information, current provision and future needs, and experiences and perspectives; and the Professional Autism Needs Questionnaire, which addresses views of professionals working with families with ASD and professional-related information. They found that families' and professionals' views do not always concur, although both groups agreed that families make extraordinary sacrifices, siblings are affected and parents experience significant stress. Parents reported that educational and social service supports were inadequate and that they needed to rely on family and friends for support. Parents and professionals differed in their views about interventions and family stress. Professionals tended to overestimate some issues experienced by parents, such as stress and the impact of the child with ASD on family life (such as recreation and leisure, holidays and excursions, social and community engagement). Eighty-eight per cent of parents perceived that their own stress levels were high, and had been so for an average of five years. Parents and professionals generally agreed that increased support, information and training were needed for parents of children diagnosed with ASD. Parents were worried about present unmet needs of their child and planning for the child's future. Professionals were more concerned about externalising behaviours such as poor sleep patterns, challenging behaviours and routines, and hyperactivity, while parents were more concerned about behaviours associated with ASD, such as deficits in interaction, play, social skills, and communication. Finally, parents were more aligned with Applied Behaviour Analysis (ABA) interventions than professionals (Dillenburger *et al.*, 2010).

Dillenburger *et al.* (2010) further highlighted the impact of discrepancies between the views of parents and professionals on collaborative working relationships, and posited that this may increase stress for parents. Given these different perspectives, professionals need to listen carefully to parental concerns (which may well be different to those of professionals) before decisions are made about intervention priorities and associated educational strategies. They also suggested that the diversity of multidisciplinary support had the potential to cause more stress to parents, particularly if this was not well co-ordinated, and argued that multidisciplinary teams need to work together to provide consistent and coherent management of children and their families. In summary, Dillenburger and colleagues proposed that the differences between the views of parents and professionals need to be recognised and acknowledged by professionals and policy-makers if they are to meet families' needs and provide services that are truly family-centred.

Implementing family-centred practice is not without its challenges. A re-evaluation of traditional practice domains, intervention models, and ways of working with parents has been required in many clinical situations (Humphry, 1995; Lawlor and Mattingly, 1997; Litchfield and MacDougall, 2002; Rosenbaum *et al.*, 1998). Lawlor and Mattingly (1997) argued that a shift towards intervention which addresses the concerns and values of the caregiver cannot easily be 'tacked on' to existing practices because of differences in core practice assumptions. Their argument is supported by comments from professionals when asked about their experiences in implementing family-centred practice. Litchfield and MacDougall (2002) found that professionals commented upon role confusion, a sense of losing control and credibility, a fear of de-skilling, and stress at the expectation of multi-skilling, as they addressed wider issues affecting parents' concerns.

What is recommended by both parents and advocates of family-centred practice is that professionals:

1. interact as friends, guides, or informants

2. convey a belief in parents' abilities

3. provide timely, practical information.

(Hannah and Rodger, 2002; Harrison *et al.*,
2007; Washington and Schwartz, 1996)

## WORKING WITH INFORMAL NETWORKS AND MEMBERS OF THE EXTENDED FAMILY

A practice that is congruent with family-centred practice is the facilitation of family-to-family support and informal and formal networking. This recognises the expert knowledge families have to share with one another, their capacity to empathise through shared but individual lived experiences, and the importance of facilitating both formal and informal community networks (Rodger and Keen, 2010). It is recognised that families with fewer informal supports (e.g., friends, relatives, neighbours) require more assistance to engage with other families who might be able to provide mutual support through more formal means (e.g., support group meetings, coffee mornings organised by parents or professionals; Darlington and Rodger, 2006). Hannah and Rodger (2002) also highlighted the need to incorporate practices that strengthen family systems and encourage the wider use of community resources through provision of general, locally relevant information pertaining to children's development, education, health, and family well-being.

## DEVELOPING PARTNERSHIP-BASED
## HOME PROGRAMMES

Many intervention approaches for children with ASD require some form of home programme activities, practice of skills/tasks at home, and incorporation of strategies for generalisation and transfer across environments (e.g., kindergarten, childcare, home, community). Many parents of children with neurodevelopmental disabilities consider home programmes to be 'part of life' and necessary for maximising progress and using time efficiently (Novak, 2011). While Novak's research has been primarily with children with CP, it is very possible that, given the pervasive impact of conditions such as ASD and CP on children's development and families' lives, many of the principles emanating from her research may be relevant to home programmes for children with ASD. This still requires empirical investigation, but at face value there appears to be much that can be applied from this research. Novak (2011) introduced the term 'partnership-based' for home programmes that were perceived by parents to provide benefits including support, realism, flexibility, motivation, generalisable activities, practice reminders, progress updates, and role clarification. A randomised controlled trial demonstrated that these programmes provided parents and children with many advantages over rigidly prescribed, professional-directed home programmes (Novak, Cusick, and Lannin, 2009). Partnership-based home programmes are characterised by:

1. establishing effective collaborative relationships

2. setting parent and child goals

3. selecting therapeutic activities that focus on family goals underpinned by best available evidence

4. supporting parents to implement the programme via education, home visiting, progress updates to sustain motivation

5. evaluating outcomes for child and family.

Parents in Novak's (2011) study advised other parents to accept their child's disability, avail themselves of help, be honest, develop routines that work for their families, and view home programmes as essential components of their child's intervention. Rather than casting parents into the role of pseudo-therapists, parents felt that engaging in these programmes enhanced their relationships with their children, and helped them to feel more confident in managing their children's needs. Parents advised professionals to provide support, ensure that they co-ordinated their multidisciplinary services across the team, provided prognostic information, and were open to parents' ability to comply with suggestions (Novak, 2011). Parents recommended that compliance pressure was counterproductive, and that, instead, focusing on parents' goals and providing support was more likely to lead to strategies that were motivating for parents to use at home. Chapters 6 to 9 will highlight how professionals can help parents to utilise strategies at home that will become part of their daily family lives, providing multiple opportunities to support their children's development and learning, rather than focusing on specific therapy activities that need to be performed strictly each day.

## CONSIDERING THE HOME ENVIRONMENT

In relation to working with parents of children with ASD at home, Pengelly, Rogers and Evans (2009) found that, due to the complexity of problems experienced by children with ASD and their families, having dedicated physical space for the child with ASD to relax and be alone, as well as separate space for other family members at home, was important and provided personal, emotional, and occupational benefits for family members. Pengelly and colleagues (2009) determined that establishing a 'good fit' between individuals with ASD and their home environments was important, as space at home influences children's behaviour, parents' stress levels, and the occupational engagement of family members. For example, modifying the environment to allow the child with ASD greater control can avoid sensory overload and resultant behaviour problems, and the use of quiet space allows self-calming. They found children with ASD needed personal space that allowed them to de-stress and calm down safely, either alone or with their parents. Children responded better to having some choice of space, and specific spaces associated with specific activities or occupations, such as the bedroom for sleeping and other spaces for playing. (Siblings also need safe spaces away from the child with ASD to engage in play, homework, and other activities.) Separate space for the child with ASD to settle and calm was also helpful for parents, allowing them to de-stress away from the child. This research highlights the importance of professionals discussing the home environment with parents, so that they are aware of strategies that allow them to utilise space at home for the benefit of the child with ASD as well as other family members.

## CONCLUSION

This chapter has described the importance of establishing effective partnerships with parents and other family members, including the child with ASD. These partnerships are the cornerstone for the provision of effective family-centred services to children with ASD and their families. The complexities of the multiple relationships involved in this endeavour were stressed. Professionals are cautioned not to make assumptions about parents' and families' needs, and not to overestimate the degree of stress potentially being experienced by parents. They need to consider family strengths, and not assume a deficit-oriented approach in working with children with ASD and their families. This chapter has highlighted principles of family-centred service delivery, relationship building, and working with extended family members. Some characteristics of partnership-based home programmes were described, based on work with families of children with CP (Novak et al., 2009), which may have application to children with ASD and their families. Finally, the importance of considering the home environment, and ensuring a match between the personal and physical space needs of various family members, was discussed.

Chapter 4

# Establishing Parental Priorities

## INTRODUCTION

This chapter describes how professionals can assist parents to develop priorities for their young child with ASD at or around the time of diagnosis, and before they are formally linked with an early intervention service. First, the importance of relationships and using a strengths focus in goal-setting will be addressed. Second, goal-setting will be described, as this is the process by which priorities (represented as child and family goals) are established. This will be followed by a discussion about several goal-setting approaches that can be used with parents at this early stage following diagnosis, such as open-ended or informal interviews, structured interview formats such as using daily logs, and the Canadian Occupational Performance Measure (COPM) (Law *et al.*, 2005). A newly developed approach to goal-setting using the Family Goal-setting Tool (Rodger *et al.*, in press) will be described. Finally, documenting and regular review of goals and priorities will be discussed.

## RELATIONSHIPS AND GOAL-SETTING

As discussed in Chapter 3, forming effective relationships with children and their families is the key to family-centred early intervention practice (Law and Mills, 1998; Rosenbaum *et al.*, 1998). If professionals and clients have a shared view of the issues facing the child and family, and the parents' desired outcomes, they can work in partnership to achieve those outcomes. Central to this partnership is developing an understanding of the clients' (parents' and families') priorities or goals, as these inform professionals' interventions. Parents need to be able to make their wishes known to early intervention health or educational professionals and/or teams if they are truly to collaborate in the provision of early intervention and therapy services (Clark and Bell, 2000). Eliciting these priorities may not always be easy (Wilkins *et al.*, 2001), as parents can become overwhelmed by all the things that their child is not yet able to do. This can especially be the case soon after an ASD diagnosis, as the diagnostic process focuses on the child's problems or deficits in communication, social interaction, play, and symbolic behaviour. Prioritising where to start is important, as it is rarely possible or appropriate to address everything at once.

King (2009) proposed a relational goal-oriented model (RGM) to support the optimal delivery of services to children and families. This model is based on relationships and is goal-oriented in nature. It focuses on family needs and strengths, as well as individualisation and enablement. In the RGM, services should:

1. address overarching goals, desired outcomes and the fundamental needs of clients

2. consider relational processes that allow development and change

3. attend to the worldviews and priorities of clients

4. be informed by the approaches, knowledge, skills, and strategies of expert practitioners.

The RGM addresses the overarching goals of clients, practitioners, and managers. It acknowledges parents' desires for a creative and supportive environment that provides opportunities for their child's growth and belonging. In addition to the importance of goal-setting with parents, King (2009) described the need for short-term intervention session goals and medium-term goals that meet parents' needs through individualised therapy goals and treatment plans.

## USING A STRENGTHS FOCUS

Before setting any goals for their child and family, it is important to help parents to reflect on their child's strengths and interests, as well as the family's strengths and resources, rather than focusing on a list of problems or deficit areas that are typically identified leading up to an ASD diagnosis. This is described as using a strengths-based approach (McCashen, 2005).

The strengths approach originated in the field of mental health (e.g., Rapp, 1998), and has recently been adopted within the context of early childhood and family support settings (Green, McAllister, and Tarte, 2004). The strengths approach emphasises a partnership between parents and service providers (Raghavendra *et al.*, 2007). It focuses on the family's role in decision-making about the child's intervention and priorities/goals, and recognises parents as the experts on their child's status and needs (McWilliam, Tocci, and Harbin, 1998). The aim is to empower families to recognise their inherent strengths and problem-solving capacity, reinforce the family's existing capacities, build on their strengths, and facilitate client-directed changes that are meaningful and significant. Young children, particularly those with ASD, also pose a significant challenge in collaborative goal-setting, due to their limited cognitive and communicative skills development. Hence therapy goals are most often collaboratively set by the adults who know them best, namely parents, kindergarten or childcare teachers, and/or professionals.

## WHAT IS GOAL-SETTING?

Goal-setting is the process whereby health and/or educational professionals individually or collectively engage in a discussion with clients (e.g., child, parents, family members) to determine what they wish to focus on. In the case of a newly diagnosed young child with ASD, parents will be prominent in this discussion. Professionals working from a child- and family-centred perspective aim to collaborate with parents in determining the direction of therapy/intervention (Rodger and Keen, 2010). Commonly, health and/or educational services engage in annual planning or goal-setting processes with families. This typically occurs in order to develop an annual family team plan. These are variously called Early Intervention Plans (EIPs),

Individual Family Service Plans (IFSPs), Individual Educational Plans (IEPs), or family plans, depending on the type of service context. The development of these plans is contingent on an effective goal-setting process from which a prioritised list of agreed goals emerges. Frequently, different professionals oversee the intervention strategies related to specific goals. For example, communication goals such as developing choice-making skills may become the focus of the speech pathologist, and specific self-care or fine motor goals may be focused on by occupational therapists. Alternatively, goals such as sitting at a small table and staying 'on task' or encouraging choices (once the system for communication is decided upon) are likely to be addressed by all professionals working with the child/family. The latter is essential if the child with ASD is to generalise skills learned across settings, people, and situations.

## WHY IS GOAL-SETTING IMPORTANT?

Goal-setting can have a powerful impact on parents' and families' engagement in interventions and outcomes. As early as the 1970s, Mosey (1973) reported that '… goals set by the learner are more likely to be attained than goals set by someone else' (p. 37). Engagement in goal-setting provides an additional sense of responsibility and participation in the intervention process (Mosey, 1973). Research evidence has also demonstrated that goals that are explicit and challenging can enhance and sustain a client's motivation and lead to improved performance (Bandura, 1997). Oien, Fallang, and Ostensjo (2009) found that the active involvement of parents of children with CP in the process of goal-setting and implementation, increased their feelings of competency and partnership with professionals. The setting of small, clear, and achievable goals was found to direct parents' and professionals' attention towards the child's learning potential and mastery, facilitating a shared focus on success. In Oien and colleagues' (2009) study, service providers found parents to be very competent in selecting important and functional goals that were meaningful within the context of their families' everyday lives.

Poulsen, Rodger, and Ziviani (2006) proposed that understanding self-determination theory (SDT; Deci and Ryan, 2000) could help further professionals' understanding of the psychological processes involved in goal-setting. The facilitation of empowering interactions in which clients actively participate in decision-making and attain self-managed goals also underpins optimal motivation and healthy psychological functioning (Law and Mills, 1998; Poulsen *et al.*, 2006). Personal choice and self-determination are powerful motivators in shaping an individual's behaviour, such that motivation is likely to increase due to an individual's intrinsic desire for competence in meaningful activities (Majnemer, 2011). Identifying goals and establishing the parents' or family's motivation to address chosen goals is critical to successful intervention, especially with young children where parents are the key adults engaged with their child and family on a daily basis. Engagement of children and parents in goal-setting is the first step to understanding their needs, interests, and motivations.

Based on information obtained from interview, or using specific goal-setting tools, professionals can find out about the parents' and family's preferences, engagement patterns (when, where, how, and with whom particular activities occur), and perceptions of their own and their child's competence with these activities. This leads to collaborative identification of personally meaningful goals, the establishment of baseline data on perceived competence with current goal performance, and the development of strategies for goal achievement. In summary, involvement of parents in goal-setting is more likely to lead to ownership of intervention goals, enhance motivation to engage with intervention strategies, and lead to better outcomes for their child and family.

## APPROACHES TO GOAL-SETTING

There are a number of ways in which professionals can engage in goal-setting discussions with parents. There are two approaches regarding the sequence of assessment and goal-setting. The first is that the professionals undertake a comprehensive assessment of the young child's functioning/developmental status and then, on the basis of these assessments, team members identify areas of concern, which are discussed with parents. As a result of these assessment findings and parents' concerns, a set of goals is determined. Typically, such comprehensive assessment is undertaken in the lead-up to making an ASD diagnosis and does not need to be repeated.

The second approach, espoused by Rodger (2010) holds that the first step of information gathering requires professionals to undertake goal-setting discussions with the parents and the child (where appropriate or possible). It is only once these goals are established that professionals undertake the specific assessments required to determine what intervention strategies may be useful (e.g., determining the possible reasons for the problems identified). This latter approach reduces the amount of unnecessary and time-consuming assessment undertaken with a young child, and helps the professionals involved focus specifically on identified goals/areas of parental concern. Hence, goal-setting processes are pivotal to both the specific assessment and the intervention processes that follow.

## Types of Goal-setting Conversations

### Interviewing

When using interviewing as the prime method for obtaining the parents' views about goals for their child, it is important from the outset to inform them about the purpose of the meeting and the outcome that is desired. For example, we might tell parents that 'this discussion session aims to provide an opportunity for you to discuss (1) your key concerns at the moment, (2) what you would like your child to achieve next in terms of development or skills, and (3) what you would like us to focus on during intervention sessions.'

In establishing the purpose of the meeting, it is important to ensure that parents' perspectives are valued and seen as important to the professional (or team), that the professional (or team) is keen to hear their views, and that they wish to work together with the parents in achieving desired outcomes for their whole family. It is important that parents know who is available to assist (which professionals are employed by the service; who is on that team), and what types of services are available (e.g., respite as well as individual therapy). It is often useful to provide some prompts for parents so that they can prepare for such discussions, and for them to be able to discuss these with other family members prior to the goal-setting meeting.

Frequently mothers attend these appointments, as fathers' work commitments often make involvement difficult. Scheduling meeting times that suit fathers' work commitments, or asking mothers to discuss goals and priorities with their partner prior to the meeting, can be helpful. Other family members, such as grandparents or others who have significant involvement with the child, (e.g., through babysitting activities), can also offer suggestions about what are priorities for them. Some useful prompt questions for parents to consider prior to the meeting are listed in Box 4.1.

---

**Box 4.1 Prompts for goal-setting
conversations with parents**

- What would you like your child to be able to do/achieve in the next 6–12 months?

- What can't your child do right now that you would like him or her to be able to do?

- Are there any everyday activities (e.g., getting in the car to go out, going shopping) that are difficult for your family to do because of your child's ASD?

- Are there any daily routines or rituals that are difficult (e.g., mealtimes) for you and your family as a result of your child's ASD?

- Are there any things that you would like to be able to do to help your child, or that would provide you with more time for other family members?

- Is there something your child is good at that you would like to encourage, or would like to happen more frequently?

- Does your child have a particular interest that you would like to develop further?

---

Professionals can ask parents to bring some notes/thoughts with them to these meetings based on the prompt questions provided. This might aid their memory or capture discussions they have had with partners/other family members. If parents are feeling overwhelmed, as is often the case soon after an ASD diagnosis for their child, and just don't know where to start (because there are so many things they want the child to do), professionals can help them focus on the things that are most challenging for them to manage (such as tantrums or sleeping) at that point in time. Sometimes questions such as 'If there was one thing you could change right now about your child's behaviour/abilities that would make your life easier, what would that be?' can be helpful.

At the goal-setting meeting it is often useful to start with parents' reflections on what is going well for their child and family at that point in time, what has the child achieved recently (since the last meeting), or if this is the first goal-setting meeting, whether they have noticed particular things that the child has begun to do or learn in recent times. These can provide an indication of developing skills that might be capitalised upon. If it is an initial goal-setting meeting, finding out about the child's special interests (e.g., toys, games, objects, fascinations, obsessions), and his or her likes and dislikes can be a useful window into the child's world and preferences.

The questions listed in Box 4.1 can also be asked during the goal-setting session itself. It is important to focus not just on the child with ASD, but also on other family members, such as parents and siblings, to see if there are specific needs in the broader family unit that can be met by the professionals or team. For example, the parent may wish the child with ASD to be able to play with a sibling for a short time and take turns (see Chapter 8); or may wish for greater assistance to manage sleep-time routines when the child is at his or her grandparents' house (where the child is regularly cared for).

Once the goals are identified, the parents can be asked to prioritise these so that they can determine which ones to start working towards first. Sometimes there is a natural order in this, such as the need to establish some means of communication (e.g., a Picture Exchange Communication System [PECS]; Bondy and Frost, 1994; see Chapter 7, page 128 and Chapter 10, page 213) prior to working on requesting. At other times, it may be that the focus becomes working on a goal where achieving some quick success is important for both the child and the parents, who can easily become frustrated with limited progress. On other occasions, tackling behaviours that are disruptive, such as tantrums or concerns about nutritional intake, may be important priorities. There are rarely any hard-and-fast rules with prioritisation, hence gaining input from the parents is critical regarding what might alleviate any current stress and help them to remain positive about their child's progress.

### Daily Logs and Routines

Sometimes when parents are overwhelmed by the extent of their child's deficits and do not know where to start with establishing goals, it can be useful to talk through a typical weekday and weekend day in their family's life. Twenty-four hour logs originated in occupational therapy as a means of understanding an individual's time use and the activities they engage in (Mosey, 1973). They enable professionals to talk with parents about a typical day in the life of their child with ASD and their family. Questions such as 'What does a typical day look like for your child and family?' can provide an informative picture of the child's and family's daily life patterns. Parents sometimes find it difficult to describe a 'typical' day, as life with a child with ASD can be very unpredictable. In these situations it can be helpful to choose a day in the previous week and focus on that particular day. (See Table 4.1 for an example of a log that professionals can complete as they talk parents through the day.) Probes related to key times during the day can assist professionals to know:

- Where activities happen?

- Who is present?

- What actually happens?

- Whether there are any concerns regarding these regular daily events/activities?

- Whether these activities run smoothly?

- What makes this so, or not so?

- Whether time of day or other situational circumstances impact on the child's functioning?

Additional prompts are provided in Box 4.2.

**Box 4.2 Prompts for parents when discussing a typical day**

- What time does your child with ASD get up in the morning? What happens then? Talk through morning routines, breakfast, childcare. Where do these occur? Who is present? How do these routines happen? What self-care skills does the child have/need to acquire? Are there any flash points during the morning?

- What happens during the morning? What type of play does he or she engage with? Are there any scheduled activities on particular weekdays, such as play group, kindy gym, childcare, visit to friends, shopping, etc.?

- What does lunchtime look like? What does your child eat? Where? With whom? What self-care skills does the child have/need to acquire?

- How does your child/family spend the afternoons? What play activities/lessons (e.g., swimming) does he or she engage with?

- What is early evening like? What routines occur (bath, dinner, bed)? Are there concerns with any of these? How does your child go off to sleep? What time? Who is involved? What works? What does not work? What self-care skills does the child have/need to acquire?

- Are there any routines/rituals that are important to your family (such as Friday night or Sunday dinner with grandparents, eating out, stories before bed)? Are there any problematic routines associated with the child's autistic obsessions? Are there things your family would like to be able to do but cannot or do not do because of the child with ASD?

- How does your child with ASD manage transitions between activities/situations/routines or environments?

- How does your child with ASD manage car trips/transport between home/childcare/kindy/family/friend's homes?

**Table 4.1 Daily log for typical weekday and weekend day**

Directions: List in detail all activities which are part of your child's and family's day.

| Time | Typical Weekday | Typical Weekend Day |
|------|-----------------|---------------------|
| 6.00 – 7.30am | | |
| 7.30 – 9.00am | | |
| 9.00 – 10.00am | | |
| 10.00 – 12.00 noon | | |
| 12.00 – 2.00pm | | |
| 2.00 – 3.00pm | | |
| 3.00 – 5.00pm | | |
| 5.00 – 7.00pm | | |
| 7.00 – 9.00pm | | |

For each activity, is this something the child/family need to do, want to do, have to do? Consider how well the child/family does the activity and whether this is satisfying for them, or whether improvement or change is required.

*Adapted from Activity Configuration Part A (Mosey, 1973).*

The information gained from such discussions can lead parents and professionals to identify difficult times during the day (e.g., challenges to family routines), as well as antecedents and consequences of particular behaviours. This may well provide the basis for identifying particular priorities. For example, it may become clear that all mealtimes are troublesome for parents, given the child's restricted food preferences and insistence on sameness, as well as rigidity about use of particular cutlery or crockery. Many parents of children with ASD report that these eating and mealtime difficulties are both pervasive and stressful for them (Marquenie *et al.*, 2011; Provost *et al.*, 2010), in contrast to parents of typically developing young children who generally experience pleasant family connections during mealtimes (Evans and Rodger, 2008). A number of inventories that address family routines and rituals are summarised in Table 6.1 in Chapter 6.

Other tools such as the Child's Challenging Behaviour Scale (CCBS; Bourke-Taylor *et al.*, 2009) might be useful for parents who are experiencing challenging behaviours and caregiving difficulties and wish to identify goals related to these. The CCBS is a brief, psychometrically sound instrument to measure parents' ratings of their child's behaviours that are challenging and associated with reduced maternal well-being. This tool also taps into the child's responses to family routines and disruptions.

## GOAL-SETTING TOOLS

A number of goal-setting tools have been developed for working with individuals and families. Some of these originated within the occupational therapy profession. These tools can be used in combination or separately.

### The Canadian Occupational Performance Measure

One of these tools is the COPM (Law *et al.*, 2005) which has been in use within occupational therapy clinical and research practice since the early 1990s. The COPM is a criterion-based measure of occupational performance (that is, how well a person can perform a particular activity or occupation). Based on the Canadian Model of Occupational Performance (Canadian Association of Occupational Therapists, 2002), it identifies occupational performance problems (self-care or activities of daily living, productivity such as school, work, chores, and play/leisure) through a client-centred interview. The interview format includes questions regarding discrepancies between what clients want, need or are expected to do, and what they are currently able to do.

A client-centred approach is essential to the COPM interview (Law *et al.*, 1990). Parents are able to complete the COPM interview and ratings on their children's occupational performance, and can identify goals related either to themselves as parents or to their family as a whole (such as being able to sit down for a family meal together or go on a family outing). Parents rate the importance, performance, and satisfaction with performance for each problem area on a ten-point scale. A high score indicates greater importance, performance level, and satisfaction. Importance scores are used to prioritise goals. The difference between mean performance and satisfaction scores pre- and post-intervention indicates the extent of change in performance, with a change of two or more points reported to be clinically significant (Cardillo and Smith, 1994).

The psychometric properties of the COPM have been reported in numerous studies, indicating excellent reliability, validity, and sensitivity (Carswell *et al.*, 2004; Parker and Sykes, 2006). A sensitising effect has been noted following repeated use with clients (VanLeit and Crowe, 2002), which leads to a small positive shift in perceived performance and satisfaction with performance. Despite this, the test–retest reliability of the COPM is high (Carswell *et al.*, 2004). In terms of construct validity, the COPM has low correlations with other health instruments because occupational performance is a distinct construct (Dedding *et al.*, 2004) and only a moderate number of items match those on other standardised assessments (Chan and Lee, 1997). The use of the COPM in paediatric settings has increased over recent years, and it is the most commonly used tool when goal-setting with children (Tam, Teachman, and Wright, 2008). Using the COPM, Rodger, Braithwaite, and Keen (2004) found that parents of children recently diagnosed with ASD identified between three and six goals ($M = 4$) in the areas of communication, behaviour, social interaction, play, and self-care (ranked in order from the most commonly to the least commonly identified).

## The Family Goal-setting Tool (FGST)

The FGST was developed by a clinical and research team (Rodger *et al.*, in press) to aid in the process of developing annual goal-setting with families of children with developmental disabilities, including ASD.

An audit of family plans in one Australian early intervention service over four years led to a list of 40–45 potential goals that could be depicted as goal cards. Boardmaker™ symbols were then used to represent a skill, task, or issue on each of 77 individual cards. These cards were then supplemented by other goals, and appropriate activities, based upon the clinical knowledge and experience in early childhood development and intervention of the tool's authors, and based also upon the need to address information provision, which research using the Measures of the Processes of Care (MPOC; King,

Rosenbaum, and King, 1995) had consistently found to be lacking. The cards were then critiqued by team members to identify gaps and determine potential areas of confusion or need for clarity.

The 77 cards were classified into seven domains, which were corroborated by ten independent, multidisciplinary early intervention professionals. The domains are:

1. information, resources and parent/carer support

2. inclusion of child/family in community/participation

3. social relational support

4. daily living skills

5. communication

6. gross motor/mobility

7. play and early academic skills.

Families are presented with the set of 77 cards and asked to consider and place each card in one of three piles: 'yes' – indicating that they are interested in pursuing that skill, issue, or topic; 'maybe' – indicating that the subject depicted on the card is a potential area of concern, or interest; or 'no' – indicating that they are not interested in pursuing that particular goal. The process of sorting the cards frequently leads to discussion about the cards and the needs of the family. The 'yes' pile cards are discussed further and families are assisted to prioritise their top three to six cards representing activities/issues that they wish to work on. It is often possible to combine individual cards into an overall priority area (e.g., combine 'family community outings' and 'using community facilities' into 'increased community participation'). The selected cards become the focal point for establishing early intervention goals.

A key finding from the pilot study undertaken to evaluate the FGST was that it allowed parents a greater sense of ownership in the goal-setting process. The literature suggests that active parent involvement in goal-setting increases perceptions of competency, ownership, and satisfaction with services (Broggi and Sabatelli, 2010; Oien et al., 2009). The project findings suggested that this increased sense of parental control reduced the anxiety felt by parents who were uncertain of the appropriateness and suitability of their chosen goals. Using the tool was perceived by both parents and team members to increase parents' confidence in choosing goals for their families, and communicating their needs to professionals. Parents also consistently reported that using the tool led to a greater knowledge of services available to them at the early intervention service.

Researchers have found that limitations in information exchange and provision are consistently considered weak points in family-centred practice (Dyke *et al.*, 2006; Nijhuis *et al.*, 2007; Raghavendra *et al.*, 2007; Wilkins *et al.*, 2010). The FGST appears to address this need through prompting both parents and service providers to consider previously unrecognised areas of intervention or support.

Another finding (Rodger *et al.*, in press) was that the FGST helped team members to engage and involve families from different cultural and language backgrounds. The tool demonstrated potential to overcome communication barriers, thanks to the accessibility of the picture card format. This was similarly relevant for use with families with low literacy levels. However, this particular implication requires further exploration.

It also emerged that in comparison to previous goal-setting methods (i.e., mainly interviews), the FGST required a similar amount of time to complete but resulted in clearer, more focused goals. Team members felt it was important to spend the time goal-setting with parents through a structured process, rather than launching into therapy sessions without strong direction as to what parents wanted.

## DOCUMENTATION AND EVALUATION OF GOALS

Once goal-setting is completed it is useful for parents to be provided with a copy of the goals that have been agreed upon, so that they can refer back to them. Depending on the agency there will be specific mechanisms or processes for doing this. Frequently parents are asked to sign a copy of the Individual Education Plan (IEP) or Individual Family Service Plan (IFSP) goals agreed to. In providing parents with copies of goals or individualised plans it is important to ensure the readability of these documents for parents, and to ensure that they are parent-friendly. A recent study of IFSPs provided to parents found that the readability level of these documents was way above the Grade 5 reading level that is generally recommended for ease of reading for lay persons (Pizur-Barnekow *et al.*, 2010). It is well known that inaccessible and unusable documents decrease family involvement and can lead to decreased achievement by children. Both the use of medical terminology, and lack of incorporation of family routines, are known to make IFSPs confusing and inaccessible to parents (Pizur-Barnekow *et al.*, 2010). Therefore, it is important to write these documents in a manner that is easy for parents to read and understand. This requires attention to readability level, page formatting, diagrams and illustrations, and examples, as well as provision of opportunities to ask questions in relation to the content.

Goals should be reviewed regularly, informally at least six-monthly and formally at least annually. With young children who have recently been diagnosed with ASD, it is important to monitor the relevance of the goals regularly, discuss progress in relation to goals and outcomes expected, and make modifications as required. Sometimes a goal may be achieved more quickly than anticipated, and in this case either another goal can be set, or the first goal can be modified to support generalisation. For example, if the goal was to establish a particular sleep routine at home before bed, this could well be generalised to a grandparent's house, or aspects of the routine could be used for daytime naps at childcare. As with the goal-setting process, both parents and professionals should be involved with evaluation of progress towards goal achievement, and decision-making about 'where to next'.

## CONCLUSION

This chapter has described reasons for engaging parents in goal-setting for their children and families, and why goal-setting is important in assisting parents to identify priorities for their child and family. Various methods of goal-setting with parents, including informal discussions, interview checklists, and specific goal-setting tools, have been described. The importance of documenting goals for both parents' and professionals' record-keeping, and the importance of regular review of goals set, have also been highlighted.

Chapter 5

# Providing Information
# to Parents

## INTRODUCTION

We know that families of children with ASD are at an increased risk of stress and other negative outcomes, including psychological distress, decreased coping, and social isolation (e.g., Sanders and Morgan, 1997; Tonge *et al.*, 2006). Hence, there is a need to provide information to parents in a manner that empowers and helps them to draw on family resources to cope with what lies ahead following an ASD diagnosis. Support and counselling at the time of diagnosis is important. However, as Bromley *et al.* (2004) emphasise, information and training are also vital to enhance parental capacity to manage long-term. The aims of this chapter are to:

1. provide an overview of parent education/information provision within the context of an ASD diagnosis and the child's early years

2. clarify definitions of terms such as parent education and support

3. propose a framework to guide the provision of education and information to parents.

In so doing, the framework considers information content, learning processes, and outcomes from the perspectives of the child, parents, and family members. It also provides a perspective on evaluation within the context of family-centred practice.

## INFORMATION PROVISION

The unique needs of children with ASD challenge parenting confidence and competence, and may require parents to assume atypical, unexpected, and probably unfamiliar parental roles, including child advocate, care co-ordinator, and co-therapist. Therefore, parents need assistance in developing the requisite knowledge, skills, and attributes to understand, adapt to, and contend with their child's needs (Bell, 2007). Within the context of family-centred practice, parents are encouraged to be collaborative and active partners in treatment planning and implementation (Becker-Cottrill, McFarland, and Anderson, 2003; Crockett et al., 2005). Equally, professionals working in early intervention are called to shift from an expert intervention model to one in which parents are taught to maximise their children's development and learning within daily routines/ activities (Mahoney and Wiggers, 2007). It is critical for parents to be informed partners in decision-making about their children, and hence information is frequently cited as the most commonly expressed need of parents of young children with disabilities (Bailey et al., 2006).

### Lifespan Information Needs

At the time of diagnosis, parents of children with ASD have reported having specific informational needs including:

1.  appropriate information about the nature of ASD

2.  sources of emotional and practical support

3.  risk factors for the child

4.  information about early intervention services and parent group.

(Mansell and Morris, 2004)

Furthermore, post-diagnosis, parents continue to need balanced information and support, particularly at critical transition periods such as school entry, primary to high school, and transition to adulthood (Hare et al., 2004). In the absence of consistent service provision across the child's lifespan, these information and support needs are often filled by parent organisations, which are generally regarded positively by parents (Mansell and Morris, 2004). Beyond the time of initial diagnosis, parents will find that their family roles and information needs will evolve according to the development of the child and the evolution of the family unit.

Parents do not just rely, however, on professionals or other parents for support and information. They frequently access a range of other sources of information such as the internet, books, mass media, and parent and professional conferences. The advent of the internet has increased access to a wide range of information for parents and professionals, which is of variable quality and authenticity. Information overload is common, and parents may require assistance to make sense of the information they have gathered and apply it to their particular family situation. Furthermore, professionals need to be skilled in assisting parents to access, process, and apply this information.

## PARENT EDUCATION

At one level, almost any activity parents become involved in within their young child's early intervention could be regarded as educational. Bell (2007) noted that 'parenting education' may refer to training parents to provide intervention, skills development, and increasing self-awareness, as well as information sharing. Parent education has been referred to as 'parent training', 'parent psycho-education' (Bristol, Gallagher, and Holt, 1993), 'educative counselling' (in which parents are provided with information about their child's disability across the lifespan as the child's condition changes; Seligman and Darling, 1989), and 'parent-mediated intervention' (in which children's development is facilitated by enhancing parents' strategies for interacting with their children; Mahoney *et al.*, 1999; Mahoney and Wiggers, 2007). Within this chapter, we refer to 'parent education' with regards to information provision and sharing between parents and health professionals.

The goal of parent education is therefore to promote the development and competence of the child by enhancing parents' knowledge about childrearing, parenting, and relationship skills. The specific knowledge required will vary, depending on parents' desired learning outcomes and ultimately their prioritised goals for their child with ASD. For example, information provided to parents at the time of diagnosis may relate to a myriad of topics such as: how ASD is diagnosed, how ASD presents, underlying causes, types of interventions, local support groups, and how to support children's development at home. The skill development component of parent education may involve concepts such as learning about strategies and techniques for playing (see Chapter 8) and communicating with their young child at home (see Chapter 7), or learning techniques such as shaping, chaining, and discrete trial training to teach specific tasks or skills (Smith, Donahoe, and Davis, 2000; see Chapter 8).

## Parent Education and Early Intervention

Parent education is now regarded as a critical feature of early intervention programmes for children with ASD (e.g., Tonge *et al.*, 2006). One of the most salient reasons for including parent education/information provision within early intervention services is the recognition that, to be effective, early intervention needs to be embedded into families' daily routines so that it is contextually relevant (Schuck and Bucy, 1997; Segal, 2004) and supports generalisation of skills (Brookman-Frazee *et al.*, 2006; Stewart, 2009). Utilising families' daily routines offers many opportunities to develop and practise new skills and behaviours throughout the day. This is consistent with social-pragmatic interventions for children with ASD that emphasise teaching language skills in everyday interactions in naturalistic contexts, using contextual supports such as visual and gestural supports, emotional expression, and enhancing social communication (Ingersoll and Dvortcsak, 2006; Wetherby and Prizant, 2000).

Mahoney and colleagues (1999) reported on two studies which involved 250 mothers whose children received early intervention services. They found that mothers' highest preferences were for parent education activities (child information and family instruction activities), which were 25 per cent higher than their preferences for family support activities. Subsequent literature has provided further evidence establishing that parents want information and instruction about helping their children at home (Bailey and Powell, 2005). An evaluation of family-centred rehabilitation services in Canada for children with physical and developmental disabilities (Law *et al.*, 2001) found that while parents rated most services highly in terms of respectful supportive care, co-ordinated and comprehensive care, and enabling and partnership, they were often found to be lacking in terms of information provision. So how do we provide parent education in a manner that is best suited to parents' informational needs?

## Underlying Assumptions for Information Provision

Mahoney and colleagues (1999) proposed four assumptions to guide parent education in early intervention settings. First, parent-mediated interventions are philosophically compatible with family-centred practice. This occurs when parents are provided with opportunities to set and prioritise goals for their child and family (Rodger, Braithwaite, and Keen, 2004; Rodger and Keen, 2010), and when they can choose the extent of their involvement in family-centred intervention (Brown, 2004; see Chapter 3). Brown proposed that within family-centred services there is a continuum of participation that involves the family as informant, assistant, coworker, partner, collaborator, and service director. In order to provide family-centred parent education, the format and style of parent education, and the relationships between parents and professionals as collaborators, must be considered. This requires instruction to be delivered sensitively, in such a way that parents are respected and their roles dignified.

Second, parent-mediated intervention is a multi-faceted construct embedding a continuum of approaches and content. Content refers to what is taught during formal sessions – such as general parenting strategies, information about a child's development and learning needs, or the direct teaching of specific skills, such as management of problem behaviour or use of an augmentative communication system. Outcomes may include increased parent knowledge, enhanced parent–child relationships, and/or the child's acquisition of specific skills. The relationship between parent education content and outcomes was advocated initially by Mahoney and colleagues (1999).

Third, engaging in parent-mediated intervention should be a parent's choice, not a requirement (Brown, 2004). Some reports indicate that parent education is easier with parents who are relatively well educated and less stressed by their socio-economic contexts (Kaiser and Fox, 1986). Choice also refers to the type, format, timing, content, goals, and intensity of involvement in parent education and training and parent-mediated intervention.

Finally, parent education requires professionals to have specific expertise in relation to adult learning constructs (Knowles, Holton, and Swanson, 1998; Rankin and Stallings, 2001), as well as techniques for coaching and teaching skills to parents (Graham, Rodger, and Ziviani, 2009; Greber, Ziviani, and Rodger, 2007a, 2007b). Parents come to education sessions with previous life experiences, particular expectations, and expertise about their own child and family, necessitating that professionals engage with them as adult learners. Professionals conducting such programmes need to be grounded in family-centred practice, be skilled at managing interpersonal interactions with parents, have condition-specific information, have skills in the processes and principles of adult education, and have skills for teaching parents (e.g., coaching, demonstrating, providing constructive feedback; Graham *et al.*, 2009; Turnbull *et al.*, 2007).

## A FRAMEWORK FOR PARENT EDUCATION

A framework to guide the provision of parent education is illustrated in Figure 5.1. This framework extends the initial work of Mahoney and colleagues (1999). Specifically, this framework anchors parent education within the family-centred service philosophy, as discussed in Chapter 3 and elsewhere (e.g., Rodger and Keen, 2010; Rosenbaum *et al.*, 1998). This places greater emphasis on the process of facilitating parent learning by considering adult learning principles, acknowledging the influences of contextual variations, and incorporating multiple stakeholders' perspectives in the evaluation of outcomes. The core components of this framework are the educational content, the process of facilitating adult learning, and the outcomes for child, parent/s and the family unit. Principles regarding information provision are discussed in the following sections.

### Family-centred Service Provision

In order for information provision to be family-centred, information needs to be provided in a flexible manner that is tailored to the particular family, with the timing and content of the information adapted to meet the individual family's requirements (Drennan, Wagner, and Rosenbaum, 2005). A family's informational needs are likely to change across the lifespan. Within this context, the impact of disability across the child's and family's lifespan must be acknowledged (Lesar, Trivette, and Dunst, 1995).

## Principles Regarding the Content of Education

The content of parent education provision is dependent on many factors. Child factors may include the child's age and stage of development, strengths, and needs. Family and setting factors could involve the family context, presence of siblings, mental health of the parents, parents' knowledge of ASD, and the setting in which information is sought. Due to these many factors, there can be no definitive list of content topics for parent education for children with ASD. An analysis of the informational needs of parents seeking information can inform the provision of appropriate information at any particular stage. Topics might include:

- information about the child's stage of development and needs
- background about the aetiology of ASD
- the key impairments which comprise the spectrum
- locally available services
- parent support groups
- strategies that support parent-child interaction.

Over time, once initial information has been provided, and questions about causation and characteristics of ASD answered, parents are likely to want to learn how to develop specific discrete skills in their child, how to manage behaviour, and how to facilitate the child's functioning in everyday home and community contexts.

## FAMILY-CENTRED SERVICE PHILOSOPHY

| Content of Education | Process of Facilitating Learning | Evaluate Outcomes |
|---|---|---|
| Content of information provision depends on:<br>• family context<br>• stage of the lifespan of child and other family members<br>• presence of other siblings<br>• family members' informational needs.<br><br>Content is multi-faceted and dependent on:<br>• child's age/stage<br>• strengths and deficits<br>• parents' knowledge of condition<br>• the setting<br>• professionals' skills<br>• parents' access to support groups<br>• parents' stress levels. | Consider adult learning principles.<br>Conduct needs assessment and undertake learning goal-setting.<br>Ensure appropriate literacy levels of written materials.<br>Help parents individualise information for own family needs.<br><br>Consider socio-cultural context:<br>• language used<br>• strengths focus<br>• power status<br>• learning environment<br>• expertise of group members<br>• sharing and discussion<br>• opportunities for practice<br>• feedback on progress. | **Parent**<br>• increased knowledge<br>• enhanced parent–child relationship<br>• enhanced parent–child interaction<br>• increased effective communication<br>• less stress, depression<br>• better coping skills<br>• enhanced parenting competence/self-efficacy<br>• empowerment<br>• satisfaction.<br>**Child**<br>• acquisition of specific skills<br>• enhanced relationship with parent<br>• enhanced social interaction patterns with siblings<br>• improved communication.<br>**Family**<br>• less stressed family routines<br>• more positive family interactions<br>• engages in family activities<br>• improved family quality of life. |

## EARLY INTERVENTION CONTEXT

*Figure 5.1 Model of parent education focusing on principles regarding content, learning process, and outcomes in early intervention context*

*Adapted from Mahoney et al., 1999.*

## Principles Regarding the Process of Facilitating Learning

The process or way in which information is shared with parents is one of the most critical aspects of parent education. To date the 'how' of parent education has received little attention in the literature. A process of facilitating learning based on adult learning principles addresses this gap and is presented in Figure 5.1.

Knowles and colleagues (1998) identified the six key principles of adult learning that are outlined in Table 5.1. A number of parent education strategies can be used that are based on these adult learning principles. Some examples specific to parents of children with ASD are provided in Table 5.1. Information provision must be tailored for parents' individual needs because adults are not homogeneous learners. Parents need opportunities to think about their own child and family in the context of the information provided, and to work out what is a balanced approach to early intervention for their family. This is particularly important, given the myriad of websites and intervention approaches available for individuals with ASD, many of which have limited empirical support (Francis, 2005; Simpson, 2005).

Another important consideration is that learning occurs in a socio-cultural context, that is, learning is an activity situated in a social, cultural, historical, and institutional milieu (Wenger, 1998; Wenger, McDermott, and Snyder, 2002). Learning is regarded as a social process where the focus is on empowering the learner to develop his or her own self-efficacy, which enhances the learning of new skills. This requires awareness of the language used by professionals, a focus on strengths rather than deficits, and awareness of differentials in power and status between those facilitating the learning and the adult learners. Professionals play a key role in establishing the learning environment (community of practice) that occurs in dyadic (parent–professional) encounters, as well as groups. This learning milieu is based on mutual respect, understanding of joint learning enterprises, and the role of parents in knowledge production, not just the consumption of knowledge derived from experts (Neufeld, 2006; Neufeld and Kneipmann, 2001; Wenger *et al.*, 2002).

**Table 5.1 Six key principles of adult learning illustrated using parent education strategies**

| Adult learning principles | Implementation strategies for parents of children with ASD |
|---|---|
| 1. Learners have specific needs to know. | Conduct needs assessment (e.g., existing knowledge, skills, and beliefs). Engage in mutual planning processes re parent and child goals. Identify expectations and learning preferences (e.g., styles and content preferences). |
| 2. Adult learners are self-directed. | Professional acts as coach, facilitator, or consultant rather than teacher. Assist parents with personal and goal-setting regarding their child. Provide some control over the learning process (e.g., give parents choice and their own say regarding content and activities). |
| 3. Adult learners have prior experiences which influence learning. | Recognise prior knowledge, needs and interests. Take into account experiences with other children, knowledge of other children with ASD, media exposure to ASD, contact with other parents. Establish whether these experiences with ASD have been positive or negative. Determine discrepancies between what is already known and what needs to be known to achieve goals. Share and discuss experiences in group context or individual sessions. |
| 4. Readiness to learn indicates potential for engagement in activities and achievement of learning outcomes. | Help parents identify their own need to know. Mothers and fathers may have different background experiences and hence different needs to know. |

| | | |
|---|---|---|
| 5. | Adult learners have a problem- or life-centred orientation to learning. | Respond by using real-life situations, as they are motivated by learning that is meaningful, relevant, and helpful. |
| | | Link theory to practice. |
| | | Provide practical, how-to information, and opportunities for practice and application. |
| | | Provide a supportive, non-threatening environment in individual or group workshop sessions. |
| | | Give feedback on progress interacting with child with ASD, implementing strategies. |
| | | Vary media for delivery of information. |
| 6. | Motivation to learn is enabling when it involves solving real-life problems. | Help parents engage with their own problem-solving (e.g., how to play or communicate better with their unresponsive child with ASD). |
| | | Show how learning will achieve desired goals for the child. |
| | | Discuss and plan for direct application of learning. |

*Based on Knowles et al., 1998; Neufeld, 2006.*

There is much that can be learned by parents within a group context that offers opportunities to share collective experiences about everyday life with a child with ASD. The acknowledgement of group members' expertise is testimony to the diverse life experiences adults bring to learning situations and the importance of the 'situatedness' of learning, and the recognition of a community of learners (Wenger *et al.*, 2002). Adults' life experiences can provide a rich source of information and support in group situations. Group discussions, parent-to-parent mentoring, and informal question-and-answer sessions during workshops are effective learning strategies that emphasise the sharing of experiences with other parents. The importance of social interaction with other parents and social network building with other families in similar situations cannot be underestimated (Rodger, 2006).

## Best Practice in Evaluation of Outcomes

The final component of the framework for parent education illustrated in Figure 5.1 is the evaluation of outcomes. From a family-centred perspective, it is not only child outcomes but also parent and family outcomes that are of interest.

- *Child outcomes* might relate to the acquisition of specific skills, enhanced interaction with parents or siblings, and improved play or communication skills.

- *Parent outcomes* might include enhanced parent–child relationships, increased effective communication skills, better coping skills, improved parental mental health, or enhanced parenting competence and self-efficacy.

- *Family outcomes* may involve more positive family interactions, less stressed and more flexible family routines, and positive engagement in extended family activities.

It is imperative that parent education interventions are evaluated in terms of these multiple perspectives and that the outcomes for child, parent, and family are made explicit. Tools such as the Measures of Processes of Care (King, Rosenbaum, and King, 1995) are useful in evaluating parent satisfaction with information provision, as well as other aspects of family-centred practice in clinical and research settings. Effective measurement of outcomes also requires the assessment of family routines and engagement of families in community activities. Measures such as the Beach Center Family Quality of Life Scale (Beach Center on Disability, 2005), the European Parent Satisfaction Scale About Early Intervention (EPASSEI; Lanners and Mombaerts, 2000), the Family-Centeredness Scale (Thompson *et al.*, 1997), and the Life Participation for Parents tool (Fingerhut, 2009) that evaluates the impact of family-centred practice on parents, may also be useful.

Empowering interventions enable families to acquire competencies to solve problems, meet their needs, and attain family goals. Brookman-Frazee (2004) compared a partnership-based intervention for parents of children with ASD with a clinician directed intervention. They found that mothers in the partnership condition demonstrated less stress and higher confidence than mothers in the clinician directed condition, while children in the partnership condition demonstrated more positive affect, higher levels of responding, and more appropriate engagement with their parents. Tonge and colleagues (2006) determined that a parent education and behaviour management intervention, and a parent education and counselling intervention, led to improved parental mental health, with the former programme being more effective in reducing parental insomnia, anxiety, somatic symptoms, and family dysfunction at six-month follow-up. These studies provide evidence for parent education interventions based on partnerships that are empowering for parents.

## CONCLUSION

It is sometimes argued that information leads to knowledge, and this in turn leads to consumer empowerment. Appropriate information provision may well be instrumental in empowering parents. Well-delivered parent education that duly considers relevant content in relation to families' needs and lifecycle stages, the learning process, and adult learners' particular needs, has an important part to play in early intervention for parents of children with ASD. Professionals need to consider the best means of evaluating such interventions in terms of child skill acquisition, parent satisfaction, knowledge, learning outcomes, and parenting competence, as well as broader family quality of life outcomes. Well-designed research which compares various types of parent education (e.g., formats – one-off sessions versus a series of sessions; delivery methods – online versus face-to-face; and the specific content) in terms of the benefits for children, parents, and families will add to our knowledge base. Given the limited empirical evidence for parent information provision, it is incumbent upon professionals to design educational interventions based on philosophically and theoretically sound principles such as those described in this chapter.

Chapter 6

# Home-based Parenting Strategies

## The Building Blocks

**INTRODUCTION**

Parents may be a child's greatest resource in the early years. The home can provide an environment rich in opportunities for responsive interactions between a parent and child. During these interactions, social and language behaviours can be modelled by parents and imitated by the child, leading to frequent opportunities for learning and practising newly acquired skills. Following a diagnosis of ASD, parents are often keen to know what they can do at home to develop their child's skills, particularly in the areas most affected by ASD. Effective parenting strategies that fit the family ecology and which can be embedded within daily routines can offer many opportunities throughout the course of the day for the child to learn and practise new skills.

This chapter is designed to provide the building blocks that underpin a range of home-based strategies that parents can employ to support the development of their child with ASD. In a sense, this chapter provides a framework for parents to guide the implementation of specific strategies that will support their child's development in areas of communication, play, self-help, and other activities of daily living that are detailed in later chapters. A range of parenting strategies will be detailed in this chapter, including:

- environmental arrangement
- turn-taking
- offering choice
- visual supports.

These parenting strategies are underpinned by a strong theoretical framework and supported by a significant body of evidence related to the way in which parent–child interactions can support a child's social and communication development. Throughout this chapter we illustrate the parenting strategies discussed, using examples given by parents of children with ASD who participated in the parenting programme we developed to support parents at the time of diagnosis (Keen *et al.*, 2010). Pseudonyms are used in these examples but the words are direct quotes from the parents.

## RESPONSIVITY

We know from previous research that the social communication skills of children with ASD can be enhanced when parents adopt a responsive parenting style (Landa *et al.*, 2011). Chapter 1 introduced the concept of 'adult responsivity'. Fundamental to the social-pragmatic approach to intervention for children with ASD adopted in this book, 'responsivity' refers to the way in which an adult responds to a child's behaviour by imitating, or in other ways being sensitive to the child's focus of attention.

It has been understood for some time that children benefit from interacting with parents who are sensitive to their child's focus of attention and to activities in which the child shows interest (Siller and Sigman, 2002; Yoder *et al.*, 1998). Various terms have been used to describe this style of parenting, including 'synchrony' (Siller and Sigman, 2002) and 'responsivity' (Yoder *et al.*, 1998). A number of elements combine to produce a responsive parenting style, including reciprocity, contingency, and, as mentioned above, reflecting the interests of the child (Ingersoll, 2010b). 'Reciprocity' refers to how participants in a socio-communicative exchange share control, rather than one participant dominating or controlling the interaction. If an interaction is unbalanced, communicative breakdowns can result or, in the case of a child with ASD, the child may lose interest in participating. Reciprocity can help to maintain and prolong communicative interactions, particularly when the parent's responses are contingent on the child's communicative initiations. A 'contingent' response demonstrates an understanding of the child's intended message, and acknowledges and builds on this message.

As we will discuss further in Chapter 7, it can be difficult to understand what a child with ASD may be trying to communicate when the communicative forms used are subtle or idiosyncratic (Keen, 2005). Frequent breakdowns in the communicative exchange can generate a great deal of frustration for both the child and the parent, and can reduce the frequency and duration of communicative interactions. A responsive parenting style should therefore be combined with other strategies, which we will detail in this and later chapters. A responsive style contrasts with a directive style of interaction, whereby a parent might choose an activity or toy for the child rather than the child choosing, or may redirect a child away from something in which he or she is showing interest. An example may help to illustrate these different interaction styles.

*Imagine a young child with ASD playing on the floor with a music box. As he looks at and touches the toy, his mother, who is seated beside him on the floor, looks at the toy and names it, saying, 'It's a music box.' Contrast this with the same situation except that the child's mother, instead of naming the music box, picks up a toy drum, and tries to draw the child's attention to it by hitting the drum and saying, 'Hear the noise this drum makes'. In the first example, the mother is following the child's focus of attention and joining with the child in the activity by commenting on the toy in which the child is showing interest. In the second example, the mother is being playful with the drum but is directing the child's attention away from the music box toward an object that may or may not be of interest to the child.*

The essential elements of a more responsive parenting style include allowing the child to make choices about what he or she will do, following the child's lead, and sharing in the child's focus of attention. There are times when a directive approach is necessary to ensure that basic chores are done or to ensure the safety of the child and others. There are times during each day, however, when a responsive or synchronous approach is advantageous and desirable. Times when the child is engaging in free play are particularly suitable for responsive interactions that enable the child to select a toy or activity, and the parent to follow the child's interest in that selection.

---

**A FATHER TALKS ABOUT BEING RESPONSIVE**

You feel the frustration because you're not interacting because the communication isn't happening, and that's the fundamental issue with autism, is that you're not communicating. And so by following [what he's interested in], you've got some commonality, you've communicated something, you're doing something together. And then if you move from that to something else together, then you've overcome that anxiety and that frustration on both sides, and that's really important.

I think I found that my natural tendency was always to want to help him or to show him what to do, and some of the earliest frustrations, some of the earliest sad times I can remember were when Peter just didn't respond when I tried to show him things, and it was only when I started to tune into what he was doing and just went along with what he was doing, so that we were then doing it together, and suddenly he started to interact because he felt that we had something to talk about, or something to communicate about.

So I remember, he still does it, plays around with the CD player. Your natural tendency is to try to explain to him, we should put a CD on and we should listen to the music, 'cos that's what we do... But he of course is interested in the buttons and looking at the numbers and the lights. So once I let go of the need to have him listen to it the way I do, and actually got in and enjoyed watching the numbers go up and down, and pressing the buttons, it was great, because we learnt about numbers, he's really good at counting now. Nowadays of course he is often quite happy to put a CD on and just sit and listen to it. So that was a very useful transition...from what was a block, from where we weren't able to communicate, and there was frustration on both sides, to being able to interact, and it's sort of led on to other things. (Quote from Paul, father of Peter)

---

Some important research was conducted by Siller and Sigman (2002) into the links between parent synchrony and language development in children with ASD. In this study, the researchers measured how often parents attempted to adopt their child's focus of attention during a play session involving mother and child. They also examined the child's level of engagement with toys. Parents were divided into one of three groups, depending on whether they had a child with typical development, ASD, or developmental delay. All the children in the three groups were similar in mental age (around two years of age) and language development. Parents were then videotaped interacting with their child for four minutes in a room set up with a range of toys laid out on the floor. The videotapes were coded with respect to both child and parent behaviours that represented synchronous or asynchronous behaviour. These included whether the parent tried to shift the child's attention away from a toy or activity in which he or she was engaged, or maintained the child's focus on the activity by offering reinforcement or a comment.

The results of this study revealed that, on average, parents of children with ASD showed just as much synchronous behaviour as did the parents of the children with typical development or developmental delay. Given that children with ASD tend to be less engaged in the world around them (Warren and Kaiser, 1986; Wimpory et al., 2000), it was encouraging to discover that this didn't decrease the responsiveness of parents. As would be expected, there was variability in the levels of synchrony shown by parents from all groups in the Siller and Sigman study, and the researchers found that, for the ASD group, parents who showed higher levels of synchrony during play had children with superior joint attention and language skills at the ages of 1, 10, and 16 years when compared with children whose parents showed lower levels of synchrony.

Significantly, some studies have been able to show that parents of children with ASD can learn to decrease their asynchronous behaviour and increase their synchronous interactions with their child. In a study conducted by Aldred and colleagues, when parents learned to be more responsive using a range of specific parenting strategies, their children also demonstrated a significant increase in expressive vocabulary (Aldred, Green, and Adams, 2004). In another study, Mahoney and Perales (2005) were able to implement an intervention that increased maternal responsivity, and when this occurred, the children of these mothers also showed increases in specific developmental behaviours.

These studies of parent responsivity highlight the important role professionals can play in teaching parents to use a responsive parenting style. The strategies outlined later in this chapter support responsivity by helping parents to embed specific parenting techniques in daily routines.

## EMBEDDING STRATEGIES IN FAMILY ROUTINES

Routines and rituals are considered important events in the lives of families, and contribute to a common identity among family members (Werner DeGrace, 2003). Rituals may include mealtime routines, weekend leisure activities, bedtime stories, and birthday celebrations. The precise nature of these routines and rituals will vary across families, and these routines are influenced by a family's customs and beliefs. In order to learn or practise a new skill or behaviour, children with ASD benefit from a structured environment that affords opportunities for consistency and repetition. Routines involve predictable sequences of events that can help a child anticipate and make sense of situations. Many family routines provide these important factors because they occur frequently over the course of a day or week and involve a structured sequence of events that are usually repeated in a similar way each time.

Parents who have a child newly diagnosed with ASD often report high levels of parenting stress, and there are considerable demands on their time as they come to understand their child's unique needs (Aarons and Gittens, 1992). For these reasons, parents may find it difficult to set aside special time to work with their child on specific therapeutic or educational goals. Making use of existing routines can make it easier for parents to support their child's development during the course of their day. At the end of the week, a parent may end up spending more time implementing the strategies described in this chapter by incorporating them into daily routines than if they were to set aside a structured 30-minute intervention session each day. A routine can act as a reminder to parents to implement a strategy that will enhance social and communicative interactions with their child – using parenting strategies within routines just becomes part of the day.

**Table 6.1 Routines and rituals inventories and interview guides**

| Name of instrument (authors) | Purpose | Format | Scoring/psychometric properties | Domains |
|---|---|---|---|---|
| **Routines Based Interview (RBI)** (McWilliam, Casey, and Sims, 2009; Scott and McWilliam, 2000; McWilliam, 2003a, b) | To facilitate information gathering and intervention planning in early intervention services, principally: 1. to develop a list of functional outcomes 2. to assess child and family functioning 3. to establish a positive relationship with the family. | Semi-structured interview, which follows six steps: 1. beginning statements 2. routines as the agenda 3. information from routines 4. satisfaction with routines 5. concerns and priorities 6. outcome writing. Interview commences with asking family to identify main concerns for their child and family. Then discuss daily routines, from beginning to end of a typical day. At the beginning of the interview, families are asked what their main concerns for their child and family are. The basic structure is questions about daily routines, from the beginning to the end of a typical day. | For each routine, rate goodness of fit (1 = poor to 5 = excellent) for satisfaction with routine. If possible, teacher provides input on goodness of fit between child and routines in classroom. Additional information is recorded about child's engagement, independence, communication, and social competence within each routine. Note which domains are addressed by the routine (physical, cognitive, communication, social/emotional adaptation). Once all major routines have been discussed, identify desired outcomes and rank according to priority. The RBI has been widely used for over 20 years. Preliminary studies have demonstrated that the RBI produces better outcomes, more functional outcomes, and enhanced family satisfaction compared to standard interviewing techniques (McWilliam et al., 2009). | *Prompt/key routines* 1. waking up 2. diapering/dressing 3. feeding/meals 4. getting ready to go/ travelling 5. hanging out/watching TV 6. bathtime 7. nap/bedtime 8. grocery store 9. outdoors. RBI Report Form (McWilliam, 2003a, b). The Scale for Assessment of Family Enjoyment within Routines (Scott and McWilliam, 2000). |

| The Family Routines Inventory (FRI) (Boyce et al., 1983) | | | | Ten subscales (number of items): |
|---|---|---|---|---|
| | Each family is different with regard to the types of routines and traditions they follow. Routines provide a structural integrity to family life; they are symbolic of family cohesion and affirm family identity. The FRI is a direct measure of the extent of strength-promoting routinisation within families.<br><br>Inventory provides parents' views about occurrence and frequency of a series of family routines.<br><br>Inventory contains 28 items spread across 10 subscales. For each statement, both frequency and importance scores are collected. | A parent report questionnaire, in which parents indicate whether the routine exists in the family, and if so, the frequency with which it is performed, and the level of importance of the routine from four categories:<br><br>1. always everyday = 3<br>2. 3–5 times a week = 2<br>3. 1–2 times a week = 1<br>4. almost never = 0<br><br>allowing a maximum frequency score of 84. | Three levels of scoring:<br><br>*Frequency of Routines (0–28)*<br>The absolute number of routines endorsed by each family.<br><br>*Frequency Score (0–84)*<br>The frequency with which the routine occurs:<br><br>3 = daily performance<br>2 = 3–5 times per week<br>1 = 1–2 times per week<br>0 = almost never.<br><br>*Importance (0–84)*<br>How important routine is to family:<br><br>3 = very important<br>2 = somewhat important<br>1 = not at all important.<br><br>There are three scoring options: *raw* score (of all routines endorsed), *weighted* score, and *frequency* score (raw score weighted by frequency of participation). The frequency scoring is the optimal method, with test–retest reliability = 0.79 and established content validity. | 1. workday routines (8)<br>2. weekend or leisure time (2)<br>3. children's routines (5)<br>4. parents' routines (1)<br>5. bedtime (2)<br>6. meals (3)<br>7. extended families (2)<br>8. leaving and homecoming (3)<br>9. disciplinary routines (1)<br>10. chores (1). |

| Name of instrument (authors) | Purpose | Format | Scoring/psychometric properties | Domains |
|---|---|---|---|---|
| **Family Rituals Questionnaire (FRQ)** (Fiese and Kline, 1993) | The FRQ is a 56-item, forced choice questionnaire which asks participants to respond by considering how their family typically interacts in 7 different settings, across 8 different dimensions of family rituals. | Parent report questionnaire.<br><br>There are 7 different sections, which each relate to a specific family setting. Then, participants are asked to respond to 8 pairs of statements, which each measure the 8 dimensions of family rituals.<br><br>When presented with each pair of statements, the respondent picks the one which best describes the typical behaviour of their family in that setting, and then indicates the extent to which the description is true for their family (really true, or sort of true). | *Family Ritual Routine Score* = sum of responses to roles and routines dimensions.<br><br>*Family Ritual Meaning Score* = sum of responses to occurrence, attendance, affect, and symbolic significance.<br><br>Internal consistency co-efficients have been scored at 0.52–0.90 and test-retest reliability of 0.88 has been established. | *Seven family settings:*<br>1. dinner time<br>2. annual celebrations<br>3. special celebrations<br>4. weekends<br>5. vacations<br>6. religious holidays<br>7. cultural/ethnic traditions.<br><br>*Eight dimensions of rituals:*<br>1. occurrence<br>2. roles<br>3. routines<br>4. attendance<br>5. affect<br>6. symbolic significance<br>7. continuation<br>8. planning (deliberateness) in family activities.<br><br>As reported by the authors of FRI (Fiese and Kline, 1993), the 'Continuation' dimension has not proven to be very predictive in comparison to the dimension 'Planning', which has been found to be strongly related to health and well-being outcomes (Fiese, personal communication, 27 May 2008). |

| Child Routines Inventory (Sytsma, Kelley, and Wymer, 2001) | Routines are events that occur at about the same time, in the same order, or in the same way every time. Significant findings link *lack* of routines to child behaviour problems, poor parenting practices, and parental psychopathology. This empirically driven, content-valid parent report tool measures their child's routines.<br><br>Parents rate how often their child engages in each routine by circling a rating, ranging from 0 (= never) to 4 (= nearly always) of *how often* your child has engaged in this routine *in the last month.* | Parent report questionnaire.<br><br>36 items are scored using a 5-point rating scale (0–4), rating the frequency and consistency in how the child engages in a routine over the past month: 0 = never; 4 = nearly always.<br><br>Three additional items are scored for children who have not attended school in the past month.<br><br>Sum all 36 (39) items to get total score. | Initial validation and development found excellent internal consistency ($\alpha = 0.90$) and good test–retest reliability ($r = 0.86$) (Sytsma et al., 2001).<br><br>No significant differences between gender after controlling for treatment history.<br><br>Age norms for 5–12-year-olds have been calculated for each clinical subscale and total score. Five- and 12-year-olds tend to score differently on homework routines, so specific instructions for scoring these domains are provided.<br><br>Missing values: Can estimate up to one missing value per subscale.<br><br>Sum value of items completed in subscale, and divide by number of items completed. This obtained value can be used to estimate missing value. | *Four clinical subscales (number of items):*<br>1. daily living routines (11)<br>2. household responsibilities (9)<br>3. discipline routines (11)<br>4. homework routines (5).<br><br>*Two validity checks:*<br><br>*Defensive responding.* To detect respondents with tendency to present their child as having unrealistic frequency of routines, or respondent prone to higher ratings. Sum scores for three questions (10, 20, 30). Sums of 10 or greater are suspect.<br><br>*Inconsistency index.* Seven pairs of questions are correlated since testing similar constructs; therefore, would expect similar scores.<br><br>Collect the absolute differences between scores in the seven pairs and sum. Sums greater than 9 are suspect. |

| Name of instrument (authors) | Purpose | Format | Scoring/psychometric properties | Domains |
|---|---|---|---|---|
| **Family Life Interview** (Llewellyn *et al.*, 2010) | Interview format for families to rate the sustainability of their everyday family routines. | Comprises a self-report instrument completed by parent during a semi-structured interview with practitioner. Contains 48 items, each scored on a 9-point rating scale. | Rasch analysis demonstrated construct validity via hierarchical ordering of items, demonstrating sustainability of routines with 118 families. Meaning and fit were easier for parents to endorse than balance and predictability of routines.<br><br>Uni-dimensionality needs further development work. Excellent internal consistency demonstrated by 0.87 person reliability index. ICC for test retest was 0.72 for 39 pairs of data indicating moderate to good test–retest reliability. | Covers dimensions of sharing workload and responsibility, balancing needs and demands, integrating the child, accessing special services, financial resources, and home and neighbourhood. |

Another advantage of embedding strategies in family routines and rituals is that these activities occur naturally. When a skill or behaviour is taught in a more artificial and highly structured context, children with ASD have to learn to generalise this to more naturally occurring contexts, and this is often problematic (Lovaas *et al.*, 1973). When behaviours are taught in naturalistic environments, the child learns to use these behaviours at the time and place they are required, and the behaviours are subject to naturally occurring reinforcers that will help maintain them over time (Schlosser and Lee, 2003).

There are a number of ways in which professionals can learn about family routines and rituals that may provide opportunities for implementing parenting strategies to enhance the child's development. Routines and rituals can be used as a means to investigate the organisation, structure, health, well-being, and connectedness of families. One approach is to ask parents to keep a diary of their family activities for one week, noting the type of activity and when, with whom, and how it occurs. The diary can provide a stimulus for discussion, with the professional to identify routines and rituals that may provide an ideal platform for embedding one or more of the parenting strategies to enhance social communicative interactions between parent and child. There are also a number of structured assessments or inventories that parents can be asked to complete about their family – such as the Child Routines Inventory (Sytsma, Kelley, and Wymer, 2001) and the Family Routines Inventory (Jensen *et al.*, 1983). See Table 6.1 for a more comprehensive list of inventories and interview guides.

## STRATEGIES

We have commented in this chapter that evidence is mounting to support an intervention approach for children with ASD that emphasises child initiation, motivation, and spontaneity within natural contexts. This approach focuses on encouraging daily interactions between the parent and child that enhance social communication skills. Specific, evidence-based strategies that can be used to help achieve these outcomes have been identified in the research literature and are discussed below. These strategies, which recognise parents as the primary facilitators of their child's communication and language development in the early years, should be used in conjunction with individualised treatment goals based on each child's strengths and needs, and developed in partnership with parents and their intervention priorities for their child (see Chapters 3 and 4).

## Visual Supports

In Chapter 1 we described how children with ASD initiate joint attention (e.g., direct the parent's attention to a favourite toy) and respond to others' bids for joint attention (e.g., follow a parent's pointing gesture) less than other children. The development of language and gesture is often delayed in children with ASD and it is common for expressive language to be superior to receptive language. These delays and differences in development can have a significant impact on the child's later social and communicative development. Helping parents to understand these differences and ways to communicate effectively with their child is a high priority, in order not only to assist their child's development, but also to reduce the frustration (so clearly described by Peter's father) that they may feel in trying to comprehend and address the needs of their child.

Obtaining a comprehensive communication assessment and beginning a communication intervention programme are high priorities for parents following diagnosis. These may occur through visits to a speech pathologist or as part of an early intervention programme. Many families find that there is a period of time following diagnosis before they can access these services. This may arise due to factors such as waiting lists, lack of services in their geographic location, or financial constraints. In these situations, there are many ways in which professionals can support parents to implement strategies immediately in the home to facilitate social communication with their child. Some of the most effective ways parents can facilitate communication in the home is by modifying their own language and using simple visual augmentative communication strategies.

When a child's expressive skills are superior to their receptive communication skills, which is typical of children with ASD (Hudry, 2009), a child's ability to understand what is being said to him or her can be overestimated. It can also lead to apparent inconsistencies in a child's responses to parents' communication. Consider the following example.

*Joan and her son Thomas are in the kitchen together and Joan is getting ready to go shopping. She takes her shopping bags out of a drawer, picks up her car keys, and tells Thomas they are going shopping and to get in the car. Thomas walks out to the garage and gets into the car as requested. The following day, Joan is in Thomas' bedroom, where he is playing with some toy cars. She tells Thomas they are going over to visit a friend and asks him to get in the car. Thomas continues to play with his toy cars. Joan wonders why Thomas doesn't do as she has asked. She knows that he has followed this instruction in the past. At first she thinks that he is just being non-compliant, and is too interested in playing with his cars to leave. She thinks about this and then has an idea. Joan goes into the kitchen where she keeps her car keys and takes the keys into Thomas' bedroom. She holds up the car keys, and repeats her earlier instruction to get in the car, at which point Thomas gets up from his play and goes to the car.*

This example illustrates a number of important aspects of communicative interactions between children with ASD and their parents. Children can become highly reliant on the context in which an instruction is given. They may be quite adept at tuning in to nonverbal cues and may respond to these without actually understanding what has been said. Joan was able to discover that the car keys were an important visual cue for Thomas and aided his understanding of her request. This example also demonstrates how understanding of verbal instructions can be assumed, and failure to comply with an instruction incorrectly interpreted as deliberate non-compliance. This interpretation can lead to unfortunate consequences for both the child and the parent.

Professionals can play an important role in raising parental awareness of the expressive/receptive divide and in encouraging parents' use of visual augmentation by employing objects and/or photographs of objects, and activities when communicating with their child. Visual supports can be applied in a range of contexts, including visual schedules to help with learning and following routines, through to providing a mode of communication. A related strategy that parents can use immediately in the home is to reduce the language processing burden on their child by slowing down their speech and decreasing the number of words they use when giving directions or asking questions.

---

**MOTHERS TALK ABOUT USING FEWER WORDS**

So if he's to follow instructions, before he was more verbal, we might have just used one word. We would say, 'Peter, shoes,' or 'Peter, put shoes on.' Just so that he knew what the key instructions were, and he wasn't getting confused by lots of language. (Quote from Margaret, mother of Peter)

What we've found works really well with Karen is keeping sentences as short as possible, and even narrowing them down to two words or one word to get the message across. We also go very slowly, so we'll take time, perhaps count to ten, and give Karen time to respond. (Quote from Nancy, mother of Karen)

---

In Chapter 7, we will explore communication in more detail, and consider further some of the ways in which parents may use augmentative and alternative communication strategies in the home.

## Environmental Arrangement

Environmental arrangement is a technique used in behavioural interventions to increase engagement and motivation, so that the child is more likely to initiate a response which may be prompted and shaped into a target behaviour that has been previously identified as part of a learning goal. Environmental arrangement has been central to a number of intervention programmes for children with disabilities, including those with ASD. Kaiser, Ostrosky, and Alpert (1993) combined environmental arrangement and milieu teaching approaches (which also promote arrangement of the environment) in a staff training intervention for preschool teachers of children with severe disabilities. The strategies used in the study included:

- making materials available that were of interest to the child
- placing materials within the child's view but out of reach
- providing materials that the child needed assistance to operate

- providing small portions so that the child needed to request more

- not providing all materials a child needed to complete an activity (sabotage)

- doing something the child didn't want you to do (protest)

- violating a child's expectations (silly situations).

Kaiser and colleagues found that teachers were able to learn to use these strategies, and that the children's communication skills improved as a result.

In developmental social-pragmatic interventions, environmental arrangement has also been used and referred to as 'communicative temptations' (Wetherby and Prutting, 1984). As with environmental arrangement, communicative temptations are used to facilitate or entice children to participate in communicative interactions. Each communicative temptation sets the occasion for at least one communicative function, such as requesting, rejecting, or commenting, although many temptations may stimulate a number of functions (Prizant and Wetherby, 1985). A list of communicative temptations is provided in Box 6.1.

While environmental arrangement and communicative temptations are similar techniques used to elicit communications from children, they are implemented quite differently. Prompts and shaping, which are central to the way in which environmental arrangement is used in behavioural approaches, are not emphasised in the use of communicative temptations, where the main focus is on establishing a social communicative exchange. Underpinning this exchange is a responsive parenting style, whereby any response from the child is interpreted as meaningful and valid. (Prompting for a 'correct' response produces a much more adult-directed context by casting the parent in a teaching role rather than an equal partner in the exchange.)

## Box 6.1 Communicative temptations

1. Eat a desired food item in front of the child without offering any to the child.

2. Activate a wind-up toy, let it deactivate, and hand it to the child.

3. Give the child four (4) blocks to drop in a box, one at a time (or use some other action that the child will repeat, such as stacking the blocks or dropping the blocks on the floor), then immediately give the child a small animal figure to drop in the box.

4. Look through a few books with the child.

5. Initiate a familiar and an unfamiliar social game with the child until the child expresses pleasure, then stop the game and wait.

6. Open a jar of bubbles, blow bubbles, then close the jar tightly. Hand the closed jar to the child.

7. Blow up a balloon and slowly deflate it. Hand the deflated balloon to the child or hold the deflated balloon up to your mouth and wait.

8. Hold a food item or toy that the child dislikes out near the child to offer it.

9. Place a desired food item or toy in a clear container that the child cannot open while the child is watching. Put the container in front of the child and wait.

10. Place the child's hands in a cold, wet, or sticky substance, such as jello, pudding, or paste.

11. Roll a ball to the child. After the child returns the ball three (3) times, immediately roll a round rattle or a toy on wheels to the child.

12. Wave and say 'bye bye' to a toy upon removing it from the play area. Repeat this for a second and third toy, and do

nothing when removing a fourth toy. These four trials should be interspersed throughout the other temptations, rather than be presented in a series.

13. Hide a stuffed animal under the table. Knock, and then bring out the animal. Have the animals greet the child the first time. Repeat this for a second and third time, and do nothing when bringing out the animal for the fourth time. These four trials should also be interspersed when presented.

14. Put an object that makes noise in an opaque bag and shake it. Hold up the bag and wait.

15. Engage the child in an activity of interest that necessitates the use of an instrument for completion (e.g., crayon for drawing, spoon for eating, or wand for blowing bubbles). Have a third person come over and take the instrument, go sit on the distant side of the room, while holding the instrument within the child's sight, and wait.

*Reprinted from Prizant and Wetherby, 1985 with kind permission from Speech Pathology Australia.*

When a child has just been diagnosed with ASD, parents often benefit from an initial focus on establishing a relationship with their child. Using communicative temptations, parents can move out of a teaching or directing role and are able to interact in a responsive way with their child, without concern for eliciting a particular behaviour or 'correct' response. This can create a more relaxed context that helps to establish and build the parent–child relationship. A balanced approach is ideal, enabling parents to appreciate that moving in and out of different roles (teaching, being directive, and being responsive) is natural, but that children with ASD do benefit from a responsive parenting style.

When arranging the environment, or 'staging' communicative situations, parents can make use of the range of strategies outlined in Box 6.1. Whenever setting the occasion for communicative behaviour, it is important that the child be given enough time to initiate or respond to the situation. Asking parents to pause and count silently to ten, while looking expectantly at their child, is a good way to help them to wait for the child to respond. These communicative opportunities may also create ideal times for the parent to elaborate on the child's behaviour, thereby extending the interaction and building more complex behaviours.

Identifying specific routines and situations during their day where parents can arrange the environment to elicit communicative behaviour can ensure that this strategy is fully utilised. This might include putting just one or two highly desired objects in the house in a place where the child can see them, but they are out of reach.

Routines in particular can be used as a context for using sabotage or silly situations. Children with ASD are often motivated to complete an established routine, so interrupting that routine can be one way of enticing the child to communicate. There are, however, some important considerations when using this strategy. Interrupting or changing routines needs to be done with sensitivity and respect for the child's tolerance of changes in routine, as the intention is not to trigger behaviour problems or cause undue frustration. Furthermore, putting objects out of reach or in containers that can't be opened may elicit requests for help but, if overused, could undermine the child's independence and also lead to frustration. An approach should be encouraged that includes moments throughout the day when the child is enticed to communicate, balanced by times of lower demand.

---

**A FATHER TALKS ABOUT ARRANGING THE ENVIRONMENT**

He really loved looking at the photo albums, and we would put those up on the high shelf, so that when he wanted to have a look at them, he would have to say, 'Get the photo albums,' so it was a real way of forcing him to ask to bring them down. (Quote from Paul, father of Peter)

---

There are many advantages to encouraging parents to use environmental arrangement in the home, whether this involves a behavioural or developmental orientation. The strategies are easily implemented by parents, increase parental awareness of opportunities for communication, encourage parents to notice the communicative attempts of their child, and occur in natural contexts where the child can experience natural consequences from his or her communicative responses and initiations.

## Offering Choice

Learning to make choices is an essential part of every child's development, but there are additional reasons why choice-making is important for children with ASD. Allowing a child to choose which activity he or she would like to do, or what toy he or she would like to play with, can be a powerful means of increasing the child's motivation, interest, and engagement in the activity or toy. Research has shown that even when a young child with ASD is given a limited choice between two toys, his or her engagement with the chosen toy is significantly higher than if someone were to give the child a toy (Reinhartsen, Garfinkle, and Wolery, 2002). There is also evidence to show that child choice can reduce the occurrence of problem behaviours in children with ASD (Peck *et al.*, 1996). The other major benefit of offering choice is that it can create the need for a child to communicate. A child who prefers to drink juice can be automatically given a cup of juice at mealtimes or when thirsty. Alternatively, the child can be shown two cups, one with juice and the other with milk, and asked, 'Which one, juice or milk?' The child is thus encouraged to communicate by requesting either juice or milk. The requesting opportunity is embedded in a naturally occurring situation, and the child is more likely to communicate in this situation, being offered something highly motivating (the juice) when he or she is thirsty.

There are many occasions during the day when children can be offered choices. Mealtimes are ideal because they are usually a time when the child will be especially motivated to communicate, because of being thirsty or hungry. Several food and drink options can easily be presented, but a choice of plates to eat from and cups to drink from can also be incorporated, particularly if the child has a strong preference based on size, colour, or shape. Choice can be embedded into just about any situation, from toy play through to bedtime and bathtime routines. It is simple to implement and can be a very effective way of increasing the number of communicative opportunities throughout the day.

## Imitation

Imitation is important for learning and is also an important part of social communication, so it is not surprising that previous research has demonstrated a close relationship between imitation, play, and language development (Sigman and Ungerer, 1984). Imitation is one of the areas affected by ASD that contributes to the overall difficulties children with this disorder have in establishing and maintaining synchronous, reciprocal interactions with others. Imitation has been a key element of behavioural and developmental social-pragmatic interventions, and is a widely adopted practice in early intervention for young children with ASD (Ingersoll, 2010b).

Typically developing children are able to respond to being imitated, and to initiate imitative sequences with their mothers, from around nine months of age (Nadel and Pezé, 1993). Being imitated tends to stimulate interest toward the imitator – so a child is encouraged to be socially interested when a parent imitates him or her. The child is then more likely to imitate the parent in this context. According to a number of studies reported in the literature, children with ASD demonstrate impairments in imitation skills (Dawson and Adams, 1984; Rogers and Bennetto, 2000). In toddlers with ASD the frequency of imitative behaviours is decreased, and in older children the accuracy of imitative movements is impaired (Rogers and Bennetto, 2000). Impaired theory of mind and executive functioning, dyspraxia, as well as difficulty planning, executing, and sequencing movements, have all been explored to gain a better understanding of the imitation skill deficits of children with ASD.

For parents of children with ASD, imitating and encouraging imitation can facilitate joint engagement with their child, enhance face-to-face interaction, and increase social responsiveness (Dawson and Galpert, 1990; Lewy and Dawson, 1992). Landa and colleagues (Landa et al., 2011) recently published the results of a randomised controlled study of the effects of an early intervention for children with ASD which directly targeted socially engaged imitation, joint attention, and affect sharing. Socially engaged imitation was defined as imitating the actions of others while also making eye contact with them as a sign of social connectedness. The researchers were able to show that the amount of imitation increased as a result of the intervention. In another randomised controlled trial, Ingersoll (2010a) taught imitation skills to children with ASD using Reciprocal Imitation Training (RIT), a naturalistic imitation intervention implemented while children are playing. This study was also able to demonstrate gains in elicited and spontaneous imitation skills following intervention, for the children who received the RIT intervention. These are important findings because they demonstrate the capacity of some children with ASD to develop imitation skills with appropriate intervention. This highlights the importance of parents imitating the actions of their children and encouraging their children to imitate.

Parents need to imitate and be imitated by initiating actions and encouraging imitation on the part of the child. Synchronous imitation appears to be more powerful than delayed imitation, eliciting more social behaviour from the child being imitated (Nadel and Pezé, 1993). Synchronous imitation is a bit like being a mirror to the child's actions. This can be achieved by having duplicates of toys and other objects, so that the parent can imitate the child's actions simultaneously. Once again, imitation can be done in the context of play and embedded in daily routines. As with all the strategies discussed in this chapter, once the parent understands the importance of imitation and is familiar with how to imitate, it is most beneficial to include imitation within a range of naturally occurring situations throughout the day. This increases the number of times when imitation may occur within natural contexts that are motivating for the child.

---

**A MOTHER TALKS ABOUT IMITATION**

It's not a regular occurrence, like every day at a certain time we say, 'Okay, time to imitate.' It's just as the day goes through we just take notice of what he's doing. He might have a stick and be drawing in the sandpit with the stick and making little figures or something. So we can go up there and draw with him, and do the same as he's doing. And he feels like we're involved in his world, which is just wonderful, because often he doesn't want to be involved in our world, so if we can go and join in with him, then he'll want to join back with us. (Quote from Katherine, mother of Ryan)

---

## TURN-TAKING

Turn-taking emerges at the age of between 6 and 12 months and is evident in social games played by infants and toddlers, such as pat-a-cake (Hall, 2009). Turn-taking is inherently social and builds on joint engagement behaviours. The social nature of turn-taking, the involvement of imitation in some turn-taking activities, the necessity to wait for a turn, to share and reciprocate, make turn-taking a complex skill to acquire, particularly for children with ASD. Taking turns is essential in many social contexts and is fundamental to engaging in conversations with others. Children who are unable to share and take turns will find difficulties when interacting with peers, since it is likely to impede social interactions.

Parents are well placed to introduce children to turn-taking through joint engagement and responsive interactions focused on the child's interests.

*For example, a mother might sit on the floor with her son while he is playing with toy cars, place each one at the top of a plastic ramp, and let go, so that the car runs down the slope to the ground. The mother can then pick up the car after the child has done this a few times and say, 'My turn,' imitating the child's behaviour by placing the car at the top of the ramp and letting go. When it reaches the bottom she can hand the car to the child and say, 'Your turn.' She can do this occasionally and quickly, so that the child has little time to wait until it is his turn and so that he gets many more turns than does his mother. Gradually, the amount of waiting time can be increased, together with the number of turns taken by the mother. Once this pattern is established, it may be possible to involve a sibling who is prepared to wait and take turns on a schedule that leads to a successful interaction for both children.*

It is not a good idea to introduce turn-taking for the first time with a sibling or same-age peer, as sharing and waiting for a turn for both the child with ASD and the sibling or peer may be too difficult to control. Turn-taking can be integrated into natural contexts when the child is engaged in preferred activities, and visual cues can help to signal whose turn it is and assist the child to know when to take a turn and when to wait.

---

A FATHER TALKS ABOUT TURN-TAKING

I think we're making some advances with turn-taking, just by trying and trying and trying again. I think that's what you have to do, and to reinforce the fact that if one of them [the child with ASD and sibling] waits for a short time, their turn will come. So, to give an example, both of them love to have stories read to them. But they really want the story to be read to them exclusively and we can't do a story reading all together. So we have to insist on this sort of routine, that Dad reads a story to Cathy (Peter's sibling), and then he reads a story to Peter. And to be honest it's been very hard to get that message across, but I think we are starting to turn the corner... Peter knows now that if he sits and waits patiently, his turn will come. (Quote from Paul, father of Peter)

---

## CONCLUSION

When a child is first diagnosed with ASD, parents are often keen to know what they can do to help their child's development, and can play a critical role in the first few months when they are usually busy investigating and accessing educational and therapeutic services for their child. Typical daily routines and activities provide wonderful opportunities to embed opportunities for children to learn and practise social communicative behaviours. In this chapter we have described a number of key parenting strategies that can readily be applied in the home setting and provide a framework for other strategies that we will describe in the following chapters on communication, behaviour, play, and sensory issues.

Chapter 7

# About Communication and Behaviour

## INTRODUCTION

Communication characteristics are considered to be central to the understanding of ASD and to the development and implementation of effective treatments (Prizant and Wetherby, 1993). In addition, ASD is associated with a high frequency of behaviour problems (Dunlap, Robbins, and Darrow, 1994; Matson *et al.*, 1996). Some of these behaviour problems are likely to be related to the failures and frustrations associated with attempts made by children with ASD to communicate. Many problem behaviours are a form of communication, and by understanding what the child is trying to communicate through this behaviour, it is possible to help him or her to learn alternative and more appropriate ways to express specific needs. In this chapter we will consider ways in which children with ASD may communicate differently from their typically developing peers, what triggers and contexts may give rise to problematic behaviours, and how parents can enhance communication and prevent or decrease problem behaviour in the home.

## ABOUT COMMUNICATION

To understand the nature of communication impairments in children with ASD, it is first necessary to consider some key concepts.

Communication involves an interactive process between at least two people whereby messages are sent (*expressive* communication) and received (*receptive* communication). The way in which a message is sent is referred to as the communicative *form*. The form may be a conventional gesture such as a wave, or it may be speech. There are also non-speech forms and less conventional forms that may be used, particularly by children with ASD and communication impairments. We shall return to this when we consider the communication characteristics of children with ASD.

In addition to the form of communication, the message has a communicative *function* and social use, and this is known as *pragmatics*. Some communicative functions are about regulating the behaviour of others, like making a request of another person to give a desired object. Other behaviour regulation functions are, for example, protesting and rejecting. There are also communicative functions that are more social in nature, such as making a comment or requesting information about something. In typically developing children, these functions appear to emerge concurrently.

The emergence of communication skills in the typically developing child appears to progress in an orderly and predictable sequence from non-purposeful, reflexive behaviour, to purposeful, intentional, and ultimately symbolic communication (Reichle, Halle, and Drasgow, 1998). That is, the infant moves from babbling, crying, and random hand movements to more controlled and deliberate actions such as reaching, pointing, and shifting eye gaze from a parent to an object. With these deliberate actions, the infant more frequently intends to communicate with others, using these behaviours to convey a message. Over time, the behaviours become more sophisticated until the child is able to use words, which are symbols for ideas, objects, and events.

The intention to communicate (*intentionality*) usually begins to emerge around nine months of age, and, while a critical milestone, there has been debate in the literature about how to determine the achievement of this milestone. This is because intentionality is an internal state, and must be inferred by the communication partner, who may interpret a child's behaviour as communicative when possibly it was a reflexive behaviour with no communicative intent. In fact, Elizabeth Bates theorised that when adults interpret preintentional infant behaviour as communicative, this contributes to the child's development during the prelinguistic period (Bates, Camaioni, and Volterra, 1975). Various definitions and behavioural indicators of intentionality have been proposed. Wetherby and Prizant (1989) proposed the following criteria as indicators of intentionality:

- alternating eye gaze between goal and listener

- persistent signalling until the goal is accomplished or failure indicated

- changing the signal quality until the goal has been met

- ritualising or conventionalising the form of the signal within specific communicative contexts

- awaiting a response from the listener

- terminating the signal when the goal is met

- displaying satisfaction when the goal is attained, or dissatisfaction when it is not.

If strictly applied, these criteria may over-exclude children with ASD as intentional communicators, taking into account, for example, the difficulties these children have with eye gaze and with frequency of communicative breakdowns (Iacono, Carter, and Hook, 1998; Keen, 2003, 2005). Despite these difficulties, a primary goal of many communication interventions for children with ASD is for them to achieve more intentional and symbolic forms of communication that will result in greater clarity and capacity for communication.

## IMPACT OF ASD ON COMMUNICATION

In Chapter 1 we introduced the concept of joint attention. We discussed that deficits in joint attention are a core feature of ASD and one of the early signs that a child may have the disorder. Joint attention skills have a social function, and refer to the behaviours required to co-ordinate attention in a triadic relationship involving the child, an object, and another person (Mundy, Gwaltney, and Henderson, 2010). The lack of joint attention is typical of the way in which children with ASD tend to communicate in order to regulate the behaviour of others (e.g., leading an adult by the hand in order to get the adult to retrieve something from a high shelf which the child can't reach). The communicative functions most commonly seen in young children with ASD are therefore requesting and protesting, since communication is less often used by children with ASD for social purposes, which include communicative functions such as showing and commenting. It is thought that impairments in joint attention are fundamental to ASD and have a significant impact on later language development (Wetherby, Prizant, and Schuler, 2000).

In addition to impairments in joint attention, children with ASD also have difficulty acquiring conventional and symbolic forms of communication (Wetherby *et al.*, 2000). This includes limitations in the use of speech and gesture. The example given above of a child leading an adult to an object is an example of a type of physical or contact gesture on which the child may rely, instead of drawing on more conventional gestures such as pointing. Children with ASD who have limited or no speech often come to rely on nonverbal (sometimes referred to as prelinguistic) behaviours to communicate. There has been recent research interest in the assessment and enhancement of these prelinguistic communicative behaviours, which we will discuss further in this chapter (Keen, Sigafoos, and Woodyatt, 2000, 2001; Kublin *et al.*, 1998; Yoder *et al.*, 1994).

Reliance on prelinguistic behaviours appears to increase the risk of these children experiencing communication breakdowns (Alexander, Wetherby, and Prizant, 1997; Keen, 2003). A breakdown occurs when a child attempts to communicate but the communication partner (e.g., parent) ignores, misinterprets, or in some way doesn't understand the child's communicative message. Communication partners may overlook or misinterpret the child's communicative message due to the subtle or idiosyncratic way in which the child attempts to convey that message. When faced with a breakdown, most children will attempt to repair that breakdown by repeating the original communicative form or changing it in some way. To repair a breakdown, a child needs to recognise that the adult has not understood his or her message, and then must show persistence in trying to send the message again.

During the prelinguistic stage, typically developing children have been found to rely on gesture and repetition to repair breakdowns, but as verbal competence increases, they use more modifications (Alexander *et al.*, 1997). While the repair strategies used by typically developing young children in the prelinguistic stage have been investigated (Golinkoff, 1986), there has been little research into the use of repair strategies by children with ASD, even though they are more likely to experience communication breakdowns (Keen, 2003). They also exhibit higher rates of problem behaviours than their typically developing peers (Dunlap *et al.*, 1994). Problem behaviours are those actions that significantly interfere with the quality of life of individuals engaging in these behaviours, and those around them (Zona, Christodulu, and Durand, 2005). They may include behaviours that are hurtful to the individuals themselves, or to others, or behaviours such as yelling and screaming, which are generally disruptive. These behaviours can have a significant impact on the child's quality of life, often restricting their access to learning opportunities and their participation in activities of daily living. The child's family is also impacted by these behaviours, sometimes resulting in social isolation and family breakdown (Lucyshyn, Dunlap, and Albin, 2002).

It has been suggested that some of these problem behaviours may be a kind of repair strategy used when a child with ASD has used a less problematic form of communication that has been unsuccessful.

*A child may, for example, see a cake on the kitchen bench and request a piece by patting his mother's leg. The mother is busy in the kitchen and doesn't notice the child tapping her leg. There is a breakdown in communication in that the mother has overlooked the child's attempt to make a request. The child then repeats his original behaviour (patting mother's leg) but also screams. This is an example of a repair strategy, using repetition and an addition (the scream). The mother now hears the child, notices the cake on the kitchen bench, assumes this is what the child wants, and hands him a piece of cake.*

In this example, the child's problem behaviour (screaming) can be seen to have a communicative function (requesting), but it also acts as a repair strategy which proves effective and is therefore likely to be reinforced. Reinforcement increases the likelihood of the screaming behaviour occurring again within this context in the future.

Problem behaviours may arise in a range of different contexts and may represent different communicative functions. For example, they may serve the function of gaining attention, protesting, or requesting. Essential to preventing or reducing the frequency and severity of problem behaviour is identification of what communicative function the behaviour may serve. An intervention can then be developed to replace the behaviour with a more appropriate form that serves the same function. The replacement of problematic or idiosyncratic forms of communication will be discussed in more detail in the remainder of this chapter.

## HELPING PARENTS TO FACILITATE THEIR CHILD'S COMMUNICATION

Parents play a critical role in the development of their child's language and communication skills. Parents of children with ASD may often find it difficult to understand and interpret their child's behaviour because of the communication impairments outlined earlier in this chapter. In particular, when children rely on idiosyncratic or problematic behaviour to communicate, their communicative attempts may be misunderstood or overlooked, and this can lead to frustration for everyone in the family.

A comprehensive assessment and intervention programme focused on the core impairments of ASD is highly recommended and, in keeping with a trend toward diagnosis earlier in the child's development, it is highly desirable that intervention commences as soon as possible following diagnosis. In Chapter 10 we discuss the variety of interventions available for children with ASD and their families, and the challenges parents face in evaluating and selecting an appropriate intervention for their child.

It may take parents some time to select an intervention, and there may also be waiting lists for some programmes. During this time, parents are keen to know how they can better communicate with their child. There are many ways in which we can help parents to gain a better understanding of their child's communication skills and to quickly improve communicative interactions in the home prior to the introduction of a more comprehensive intervention.

### Communication Assessment

A good starting point for parents is to identify the range of communicative forms and functions their child uses, and this can be facilitated by using a parent-friendly assessment tool such as the Inventory of Potential Communicative Acts (IPCA; Sigafoos *et al.*, 2000; see appendix to this chapter). The IPCA was originally developed as an interview-based assessment tool to systematically gather information about behaviours that parents or teachers believe children use to communicate. A series of 53 questions probes information about communicative forms associated with ten different communicative functions.

The information gathered through the interview is summarised with the help of a matrix that shows the behaviours thought by the parent to be communicative, mapped against the various communicative functions they represent (Keen, Woodyatt, and Sigafoos, 2002). While designed as an interview tool, the IPCA can be used in a questionnaire format so that parents can complete the questions independently. The communication profile of the child that results from administering the IPCA assists parents to identify and recognise the diverse behaviours the child may use for different communicative functions. This can help them to interpret the child's behaviour, and can also provide a platform for identifying communicative behaviours that can later be shaped into more symbolic and conventional forms.

Table 7.1 presents an example of a section of the IPCA for the function of reject/protest, completed by the parent of a three-year-old girl with ASD. The behaviours considered by the parent to be communicative for the function of reject/protest include a range of behaviours that are problematic, such as screaming and throwing things.

**Table 7.1 Examples from the IPCA function of reject/protest**

| Reject/protest | Behaviours | Examples |
|---|---|---|
| **What does the individual do if...** | | |
| he or she is required to do something he or she doesn't want to do. | Grimaces, vocalises, throws things. | |
| he or she doesn't like something. | Moves away, throws objects. | Doesn't like play dough. |
| a favourite toy/food is taken away. | Screams, pulls away from me, tries to resist. | Likes water and sand play; jumping on the trampoline; swing. |

Table 7.2 provides an example of a section of the IPCA completed by the same parent for the function of requesting (an object). The behaviours considered by the parent to be communicative for the function of requesting include reaching, vocalising, 'pointing', and looking at objects. The child may also pull the adult toward the object or activity she wants.

**Table 7.2 Examples from the IPCA function of requesting an object**

| Requesting an object | Behaviours | Examples |
|---|---|---|
| **Please describe how the individual lets you know if he or she wants...** | | |
| an object (e.g., toy, book). | Reaches, vocalises. | Books interest her, but must be in her sight, wouldn't request them otherwise. |
| more of something. | Approaches object/ activity, 'points', looks at it, pulls me back to activity. | Loves music, if it stops, will approach machine and point. Pulls me back to water play activity if she wants more. |

These examples of communicative forms illustrate the range of unconventional behaviours that children may use to communicate. The main goal of intervention is to move the child toward more symbolic forms of communication that can more readily be understood by others. It is useful to think about different intervention pathways that might be appropriate in this context, based on the existing communicative forms used by the child (Sigafoos, Arthur-Kelly, and Butterfield, 2006). Based on the doctoral work of the first author, Figure 7.1 shows a number of intervention options that can be considered, and each of these will be described in more detail below.

## Intervention Pathways

In the first instance a decision must be made about whether the existing communicative form is problematic or socially inappropriate. Replacement would be an appropriate option in this case. Throwing objects and screaming, shown in Table 7.1 for the function of reject/

protest, would be obvious examples of communicative forms that should be replaced by more appropriate behaviours. Other behaviours, such as reaching, may limit the child's communication when an object is out of sight and, at times, be socially inappropriate. In this case, the child would benefit from learning to point to, touch, or exchange a symbol of the object (e.g., a line drawing or picture), instead of reaching. Use of a symbol would expand the child's communication options, and is more age-appropriate as the child gets older.

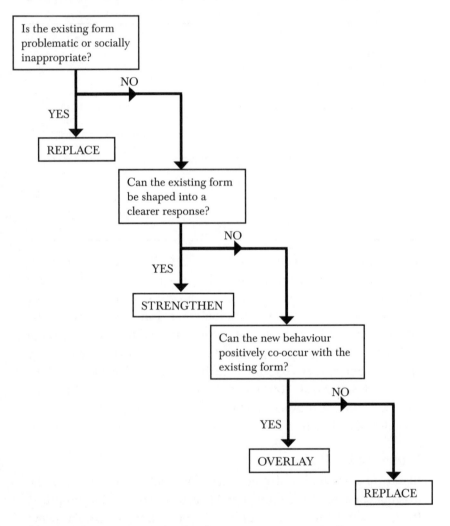

*Figure 7.1 Intervention options related to existing communicative forms*
*Reproduced from Keen, 2001.*

If existing forms were assessed as being appropriate but unclear, then the degree to which an existing behaviour could be shaped into a clearer form of communication should be considered. For those that could be shaped into clearer communicative forms, the intervention option would be one of strengthening the existing form. In the examples given in Table 7.2, when this child wants more of something, she does a number of things, including looking at the object and 'pointing'. In further discussions with the mother, it was clear that the child used these behaviours inconsistently, and that the pointing action was unclear and more like a gross hand movement than a point. Strengthening the looking and pointing behaviours may provide a useful focus for intervention in this case. Shaping the hand movement into a point and achieving greater consistency in the use of this behaviour would help to make this communicative form easier to identify and interpret. This context may also provide an opportunity to work on joint attention behaviours that utilise the existing behaviour of looking, and encourage shifts in eye gaze between the object and the parent.

Overlaying or pairing the existing behaviour with an additional communicative form may be an option when the existing form is unclear but appropriate.

*Consider another child, Tom, who occasionally looks at his parent as a form of greeting. Looking at someone when greeting is both appropriate and desirable, so this behaviour would not be targeted for replacement. As Tom tends to avoid eye contact with people, strengthening the behaviour of looking might be less successful than choosing to introduce another behaviour that can serve the same function. In working with Tom, we decided to teach him to wave, a form of greeting that would be easier for others to recognise. We began by physically prompting him to wave and reinforce this behaviour, gradually fading out the physical prompts until he could use the behaviour independently. At times, waving co-occurred with looking, so that both behaviours were reinforced. Tom learned to wave but there was also an increase in looking when he greeted someone.*

This showed that a new behaviour could be learned and the existing behaviour didn't interfere with this learning. It is important to consider whether an existing form may compete with the acquisition of a new form (as may happen with a problematic behaviour), and ensure that the replacement pathway is used in these cases. For Tom, however, the outcome was positive in that he learned to wave and also showed an increase in the use of looking when he greeted others.

## Home-based Strategies

The assessment strategies and intervention pathways described in the previous sections help parents to consider particular communicative behaviours they may wish to work on at home. In Chapter 6 we described a number of parenting strategies that can be used when trying to enhance social communicative interactions in the home. A number of these strategies are particularly important for achieving improved communication in the home because they help to create communicative opportunities (e.g., environmental arrangement; offer choice) and provide alternative and augmentative forms of communication (e.g., visual supports).

### Communicative Opportunities

Children with ASD may be reluctant communicators and there are many ways of arranging the child's environment that can either encourage or discourage communication. Earlier in this chapter we stated that children with ASD are more likely to communicate for the purpose of behaviour regulation than for social purposes. Put another way, they are more motivated to let you know when they want something than to share or comment on something. If their needs and wants are anticipated and automatically met by their parents, they have little reason to communicate. Increasing the opportunities throughout the day when the child needs and is motivated to communicate provides the context for learning and practising new communicative forms. Let's return to the IPCA examples in Table 7.2.

*The child (Judith) reaches and vocalises when she wants an object. Based on the intervention pathways approach, we decide to teach Judith to exchange a photograph of the object she wants. As a first step, we prepare photographs of items in which she often shows interest. These can then be introduced whenever she makes a request. Through the use of techniques such as prompting and reinforcement, she can be taught the steps involved in making the picture exchange. One of the difficulties, however, is that when learning a new skill, repetition is very important, and Judith doesn't spontaneously make many requests throughout the day. It is possible to create many opportunities by arranging the child's environment so that desired items are out of reach, or in containers that can't be opened without help. This sets the occasion for a request and creates a teaching opportunity where the picture exchange can be used and reinforced.*

In Chapter 6 we gave examples of offering the child a choice of drink, utensils, and food as another way of creating these opportunities. Photographs can easily be prepared and placed in front of two cups containing different types of drink. The child can be asked which one they would like and prompted to exchange the photograph for the preferred drink. The home can be a useful context for creating motivating situations to teach the child to exchange photographs, making use of strongly preferred items, whether food, drink, toys, or activities. The opportunities can be embedded in daily routines, when the child is more likely to be highly motivated.

## Augmentative and Alternative Communication

Augmentative and Alternative Communication (AAC) refers to either temporary or permanent compensations that enable an individual with severe communication impairments to communicate (Beukelman and Mirenda, 2005). *Compensations* can involve symbols, aids, strategies, and techniques that the individual uses to enhance their communication. *Symbols* are representations of concepts and can include photographs, manual signs, line drawings, printed and spoken words, objects, remnants of objects, and so forth. *Aids* are objects or devices that can be used to send or receive messages, such as communication boards and voice-activated speech generating devices. As information and communication technologies (ICTs) have flourished over the past decade, communication aids have become more accessible, compact, portable, and less expensive. Where previously specialist equipment was required, some individuals are now able to make use of generic devices such as iPhones™ and iPads™, which provide a range of useful applications.

The development of a comprehensive communication system following a detailed assessment of a child's existing communication skills is best achieved with the help of a speech pathologist who specialises in ASD and can identify suitable communication systems that will best match the needs of individual children. However, parents are well placed in the early days following diagnosis to introduce visual supports in the home to enhance communicative interactions between the child and the family. Some parents may initially be reluctant to make use of visual supports if they fear that the child may come to rely on these forms of communication, which may then interfere with language development. A recent study should help to allay these fears. Romski and colleagues (Romski *et al.*, 2010) studied the language performance of 68 young children with developmental delays and vocabularies of fewer than ten words, who were randomly assigned to one of three parent-coached language interventions. The interventions differed in that one group received only spoken language, while the others received one of two types of augmented communication interventions. Previous research has found that AAC intervention doesn't hinder the development of speech, but these studies have generally considered older groups of children (Millar, Light, and Schlosser, 2006). The study by Romski and colleagues involved children aged between 21 and 40 months, and they found that augmented language interventions did not hinder, but actually helped, speech production abilities of the children. The children who had received the augmented communication interventions produced more spoken words than children in the speech language intervention.

Visual supports appear to be particularly beneficial for children with ASD. The spoken word is transient: once uttered, there is no trace. Visual supports remain and can be looked at repeatedly, which places less demand on memory. It is also thought that individuals with ASD have a strength in visual processing over auditory processing, which further strengthens the argument for using visual supports (Quill, 1997). When using visual supports, it is important to consider the developmental level and existing communication skills of the child relative to the type and level of symbol. The level of symbolic representation can be thought of as a hierarchy ranging from the actual object, which is the most concrete, to the spoken word, which is the most symbolic form of representation. In Chapter 6 we looked at an example of visual supports where Joan and her son Thomas were going shopping and the car keys acted as a cue for Thomas to understand that they were going somewhere in the car. Without this cue, he was unable to understand his mother's instruction. In a similar way a parent might hold up a bath towel while telling a child who is watching television that it is time to go and have a bath. These examples illustrate how an object can symbolise an activity through association. This differs from, for example, holding up an apple and asking the child if he or she would like one. An example of a hierarchy progressing from the most concrete to the most symbolic form is given in Figure 7.2.

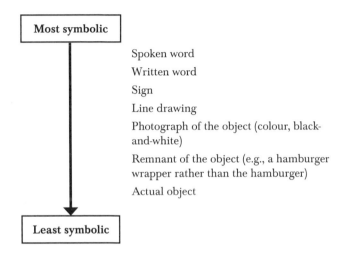

*Figure 7.2 Hierarchy of symbolic forms*

Line drawings are less concrete than photographs but can provide greater flexibility. The most commonly used line drawings are Picture Communication Symbols (PCS) which can be downloaded through a computer software programme called Boardmaker (Mayer-Johnson, 1981). An example of these symbols is shown in Figure 7.3.

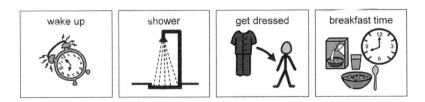

*Figure 7.3 A Sample of Picture Communication Symbols*

*The Picture Communication Symbols © 1981–2011 by DynaVox Mayer-Johnson LLC. All Rights Reserved Worldwide. Used with permission.*

## Introducing Photographs or Line Drawings

If children are ready to progress from actual objects to photographs, these can readily be produced in the home, using a digital camera. This facilitates producing photographs of a consistent size and quality. When introduced, the photographs should be paired with the objects they represent, so that the child can learn the association between the photograph and the object. It is best to start with just a few colour photographs and to concentrate on one communicative function – preferably requesting, because, as noted previously, this function is one of the earliest children acquire. It also enables immediate reinforcement to occur when the child makes a request using the new communicative form. Beginning to teach this skill using a highly preferred item means the child is likely to be very motivated to exchange the photograph for the object, as in the following example.

*Stephen's favourite food is toast with peanut butter. He has this each morning for breakfast. Michael (Stephen's dad) decides to teach Stephen to request toast using a photograph during breakfast, so that the learning will take place within a naturally occurring situation and when Stephen is usually hungry. He sits facing Stephen at the breakfast table and places a photograph of a piece of toast with peanut butter in front of him on the table. He cuts up Stephen's toast into eight pieces and puts them on a plate on the table, but out of Stephen's reach. Michael asks Stephen, 'What do you want?' while showing him the plate. Michael then guides Stephen to pick up the photograph and give it to him. Michael immediately gives Stephen a piece of toast, saying, 'You want toast'. It is important always to pair the photograph with the name of the object, so that the child is hearing the word simultaneously with using the photograph to make a request. Because Michael cut the toast into eight pieces, he is able to repeat these steps eight times, so there are many opportunities to practise requesting using the photograph. He reduces the amount of guidance he gives Stephen as his son becomes more independent in making the exchange.*

Effective ways of teaching children with ASD to use photographs or line drawings to communicate is an area that has attracted considerable research interest. This led to the development of a detailed training technology for this purpose called the Picture Exchange Communication System (PECS; Bondy and Frost, 1994). PECS involves a highly structured teaching format, based on principles of ABA, where pictures are exchanged for desired objects, and consists of six phases. (Each phase also includes the generalisation of learned behaviours across different settings and communicative partners, which is an important component of any learning.) During the first two phases of PECS, the child doesn't need to understand that the picture symbolises the object, as the child is taught to make a simple exchange. In later phases, symbolic representation awareness is necessary, as the child must be able to discriminate between a picture of the desired object and a distracter symbol. Research has indicated that PECS is generally an effective intervention to increase the communicative function of requesting for children with ASD (Flippin, Reska, and Watson, 2010; Preston and Carter, 2009).

## Visual Schedules

So far we have considered visual supports as a means to enhance communicative interactions between the child with ASD and others. Visual supports can also be used to teach specific skills and to assist with the sequencing of routines, activities and events. A visual schedule can help children to learn and recall the steps involved in a particular task, or to know what order things will occur in their day. Figure 7.4 shows an example of this type of visual schedule.

Visual schedules can be constructed using actual objects, remnants, photographs, PCS, or words, depending on the child's level of understanding and development. It is helpful to be consistent concerning the direction in which the schedule needs to be read (i.e., from left to right or from top to bottom), and to be careful not to include too many items on the schedule. As shown in Figure 7.4, there may be as few as two items in a schedule. If using a daily schedule similar to the one for Dylan in Figure 7.4, the child can remove the symbol for each activity when it is completed and put the symbol in a 'finish' box. These procedures have been developed and implemented as part of the Training and Education of Autistic and Related Communication Handicapped Children programme (TEACCH; Mesibov, Shea, and Schopler, 2005). This educational programme was developed in the USA and makes extensive use of visual supports to help organise the child's learning environment and to teach social, communication, and academic skills throughout the school day.

*Figure 7.4 A visual schedule*

So far in this chapter we have considered the impact of ASD on communication, and ways of using different strategies and techniques to enhance communication skills of children with ASD. In the process, we have looked at the use of the IPCA to identify communicative behaviours, and the introduction of visual supports to teach children more symbolic forms of communication. In the next section, we discuss some communicative forms that can be problematic, and how the strategies we have already discussed can help in addressing these problem behaviours.

## MANAGING PROBLEM BEHAVIOURS

One of the most significant challenges facing parents of children with ASD is the high rates of problem behaviour evident in this group of children. They exhibit higher rates of problem behaviour than children with other types of developmental disabilities (Dunlap *et al.*, 1994). These problem behaviours can have a significant impact on the quality of life of the child and his or her family (Lucyshyn *et al.*, 2002). Problem behaviours can vary significantly within and between children and may range from mild behaviours that can be disruptive, such as spitting and screaming, to severe and seriously concerning behaviours, such as self-injury, aggression, and property destruction.

Sigafoos *et al.* (2006), have outlined various reasons why problem behaviours may occur among individuals with developmental and physical disabilities:

- biological factors (certain syndromes are associated with particular behaviours, e.g., stereotypic handwringing in children with Rett's Disorder)

- psychological factors (psychiatric or mental health disorders which may increase frequency or intensity of problem behaviour)

- medical factors (certain types of epilepsy, illness)

- environmental factors (e.g., an impoverished environment)

- learning factors (reinforcement of problem behaviour, increasing the likelihood that it will recur).

In dealing with problem behaviours, a multi-component approach is recommended which combines the teaching of new skills, making changes to the environment, and modifying the consequences for positive and negative behaviours (Carr and Carlson, 1993). For parents, this will generally involve structuring child and family routines at home and in the community, and enhancing the child's communication skills using approaches discussed in this chapter. A psychologist who specialises in ASD can make a valuable contribution here, being trained to assess the behaviour and then use the assessment data to develop a suitable, individualised, multi-component intervention.

It is important to consider that many problem behaviours may serve a communicative function. Problem behaviours that are a form of communication can potentially be replaced with communicative forms that are more appropriate or acceptable but serve the same function as the problem behaviour. This approach to problem behaviour is known as functional communication training (FCT) and has been shown to be effective for children with problem behaviours (Donnellan *et al.*, 1984; Mirenda, 1997). The effectiveness of FCT relies on accurate assessment of the underlying communicative function being served by the problem behaviour. A functional assessment must inform the intervention.

*Let's consider a child with ASD (Sandra) who screams when prompted to use a fork to eat her dinner. There may be many reasons for Sandra's behaviour, but for this example we will consider only two. First, she may enjoy the attention she gets at mealtime when being fed by her mother, and her screaming may be motivated by seeking her mother's attention. Second, she may not like using a fork to eat because she finds it too difficult, in which case the motivation for her screaming may be avoidance. If we accept the first explanation, that screaming is motivated by attention, we may intervene by providing attention in other ways (e.g., sitting beside her), but continue to encourage the child to use the fork herself. If we accept the second explanation, however, this strategy would probably lead to an escalation of the child's behaviour, because she is still finding the task of eating with a fork too difficult. We may, in this case, make the task easier by giving her a spoon, stabilising the bowl, or providing finger food while she is learning to manage the fork herself. Again, these strategies are unlikely to decrease the screaming if this behaviour is motivated by seeking attention.*

Although somewhat simplified, this example serves to illustrate the importance of matching intervention strategies to the communicative function of the problem behaviour.

It is only since the 1980s that we have come to understand that problem behaviour can be a form of communication. Prior to this time, interventions often relied on the use of punishment and extinction of problem behaviour. While this approach sometimes led to a reduction in the behaviour, it wasn't always successful. On occasions, the target behaviour might cease, only to be replaced by behaviour that was more severe and concerning than the original behaviour. We now understand that if you punish or eliminate a child's problem behaviour without addressing the underlying communicative function, the child is likely to find an alternative behaviour to communicate their message, and this behaviour may also be problematic. Many problem behaviours appear to be motivated by communicative functions that commonly include gaining and maintaining attention, gaining and maintaining access to preferred objects or activities, escaping and avoiding non-preferred objects or activities, and self-stimulation (Durand and Crimmins, 1988; O'Neill *et al.*, 1990). A particular problem behaviour may actually serve more than one communicative function, and there may be more than one behaviour serving a particular function, which can make the assessment task more complex.

Functional assessments of problem behaviour usually involve interviewing people who know the child well, and direct observations of the child, to determine what happens before (antecedents) and after (consequences) the problem behaviour occurs. The information collected in this way can help to identify potential triggers for the behaviour and what might be rewarding/reinforcing or maintaining for the behaviour. We need to search for patterns in the information we collect that will determine what communicative functions are associated with the particular behaviour. Sometimes the communicative function may remain unclear, and in this case we may need to 'test' different hypotheses. In the example of Sandra above, a simple test to determine the likely function of her behaviour when eating with a fork would be to try briefly each of the two different interventions suggested, and see if either one results in less screaming.

Having identified the probable communicative function of a problem behaviour, the next step is to teach an alternative communicative form that can serve the same function. Below are some factors to consider when replacing a problem behaviour with another communicative form:

1.  Ensure that the replacement behaviour serves the same function as the problem behaviour.

2.  Provide opportunities for the individual to practise the replacement behaviour. Ensure that the replacement behaviour, when initially introduced, is reinforced every time until it is well established.

3. The replacement behaviour must not require more effort than the behaviour that it is to replace. If it requires more effort, the child is more likely to resort to the 'easier' (problem) behaviour to meet his or her needs.

4. The replacement behaviour must be reinforced, and that reinforcement must be at least as frequent and immediate as the reinforcement that the problem behaviour received. If the old behaviour is more successful in meeting the child's needs, then why would he or she use the replacement behaviour?

5. Learning and practising the replacement behaviour can be more effective when the person is highly motivated.

In a way, it helps to think of the problem behaviour and the replacement behaviour as being in competition with each other. You want to try to give the replacement behaviour all the advantages, and to pay as little attention as possible to the problem behaviour. When choosing a replacement behaviour, the strategies discussed earlier in this chapter can serve as the basis for selecting communicative forms that are most appropriate for the individual child. The IPCA can be used to identify existing communicative forms that are preferred by the child, and the use of AAC techniques, particularly visual supports, can provide a means of introducing forms that may be easier for the child to acquire and use in place of the problem behaviour.

## CONCLUSION

We began this chapter by describing the components of communication and how ASD impacts on these various components. Impairments from an early age in the development of joint attention contribute to ongoing difficulties in the acquisition of intentional and symbolic forms of communication. Many children rely on unconventional or idiosyncratic behaviours, some of which may be problematic. Through the use of AAC strategies and FCT interventions, we described how parents can learn to encourage and enhance the communication skills of their child with ASD, and deal with some of the problem behaviours that might arise.

# Inventory of Potential Communicative Acts

## BACKGROUND

The Inventory of Potential Communicative Acts (IPCA) is based on three years of research funded by the University of Queensland and the Australian Research Council. It was developed by Jeff Sigafoos from the University of Tasmania and by Gail Woodyatt, Deb Keen, Kathleen Tait, Madonna Tucker, and Donna Roberts-Pennell from the University of Queensland. To date, the research and field testing have involved more than 30 children with developmental disabilities and severe communication impairments. Current research is examining the validity of the IPCA for intervention purposes. At the present time, the instrument can be used for gathering descriptive information on communicative behaviours.

The IPCA is designed to be completed by educators, therapists, family members, or other people who know the individual (the child) well enough to serve as useful informants. As a general rule of thumb, anyone who has known and cared for the individual for at least six months could complete the IPCA. The IPCA seeks to identify any potential communicative acts that might be used by an individual for any of ten different communicative functions.

A *potential communicative act* is defined as any behaviour that you think the individual uses for communicative purposes. These behaviours might include vocalisations, body movements, facial expressions, breathing patterns, challenging behaviours, or stereotyped movements.

They might also include more symbolic forms of communication, such as speaking some single words, producing a few manual signs, or using a picture-based communication board. In completing the IPCA, you are encouraged to identify all behaviours that you have observed the person using while communicating with others.

With the IPCA, the specific meaning that a person is attempting to communicate through a particular behaviour is referred to as the *communicative function*. The IPCA seeks information on ten distinct functions. Under each of these ten functional categories, a number of more specific communicative functions are included. Again, this list of specific communicative functions is not exhaustive, and you are encouraged to include other specific messages or purposes that the person has been observed to express. Space is provided for you to record examples of other specific functions.

## DIRECTIONS

The IPCA consists of a series of questions that are designed to identify the behaviours that a person uses to communicate. In completing the device, you are asked to list behaviours that you have observed the child using for a number of specific communicative functions. The IPCA also asks you to provide a concrete example of the circumstances under which the person has been observed using the behaviour to communicate. These examples should be as detailed as possible. In writing your examples, please provide information about *when*, *where*, and *how* the behaviour occurs.

If the person does not seem to express one of the specific functions, then you should write *Does not do this* in that section. For example, the first question asks you to *Describe how the person greets you/others*. For this question, you may have noticed that the child greets you by making eye contact, smiling, and extending his or her arms outward. Your specific example might be something such as *When I first see her in the morning and say 'Hello,' she always looks at me, smiles, and reaches out her arms*.

## SCORING GRID

There is a scoring grid at the end of the inventory. The scoring grid is designed to provide a visual summary of the information documented on the IPCA form. First of all, you would list the person's behaviours in the blank spaces in the first ('Behaviours') column of the grid. Completing the scoring grid involves shading in those cells corresponding to the behaviours and functions you have identified, using the IPCA. For example, if the IPCA reveals that a person uses the behaviour of reaching to make a choice, then the cell that corresponds to the intersection of this behaviour and the relevant function would be shaded in. If an individual does not exhibit a particular behaviour/function combination, then that cell is left blank.

Once all of the identified behaviour/function cells have been filled in, the scoring grid can be used to give an indication of the extent of a person's communicative repertoire. Scanning the completed scoring grid from top to bottom, for example, will provide an overview of the different behaviours that the person uses to communicate, and scanning from left to right will indicate the range of communicative functions exhibited by the individual. A more detailed summary of the information from the IPCA will come from examining individual cells, as they indicate exactly what behaviours an individual uses to communicate a specific function.

A summary of the information from the IPCA can be shared among educators, therapists, family members, peers, and other relevant individuals to ensure that all communication partners are aware of the behaviours that the individual uses to communicate and what these behaviours mean when they occur in a particular context. When all communication partners are aware of the information collected in the IPCA, there is a much better chance that the person's communication attempts will be encouraged, acknowledged, and reacted to appropriately.

# INVENTORY OF POTENTIAL
# COMMUNICATIVE ACTS[1]

Date: _____

Name of the individual: _____

Name of the informant: _____

Informant's relationship with the individual: _____

☐ Teacher ☐ Parent ☐ Other _____ (specify)

How long have you know this individual? _____ years _____ months

Individual's date of birth: _____

Diagnoses: _____

---

1 Inventory of Potential Communicative Acts (IPCA) on pages 138–151 reproduced with permission from *Enhancing Everyday Communication for Children with Disabilities* by Jeff Sigafoos, Michael Arthur-Kelly, and Nancy Butterfield. Copyright © 2006 Paul H. Brookes Publishing Co., Inc. All rights reserved.

## Social Convention

Please describe how the individual...

| Items | Behaviours | Examples |
|---|---|---|
| 1. Greets you/others | | |
| 2. Indicates farewell to you/others | | |
| 3. Responds to his or her own name | | |
| 4. Other | | |

## Attention to Self

Please describe how the individual...

| Items | Behaviours | Examples |
|---|---|---|
| 1. Gets your attention | | |
| 2. Seeks comfort | | |
| 3. Requests a cuddle/tickle | | |
| 4. Shows off | | |
| 5. Other | | |

## Reject/Protest

What does the individual do if…

| Items | Behaviours | Examples |
|---|---|---|
| 1. His or her routine is disrupted | | |
| 2. He or she is required to do something that he or she doesn't want to do | | |
| 3. He or she doesn't like something | | |
| 4. A favourite toy/food is taken away | | |
| 5. An adult stops interacting with him or her (e.g., stops playing) | | |
| 6. Other | | |

## Requesting an Object

Please describe how the individual lets you know if he or she wants…

| Items | Behaviours | Examples |
|-------|-----------|----------|
| 1. An object (e.g., toy, book) | | |
| 2. Something to eat | | |
| 3. More of something | | |
| 4. Television or music | | |
| 5. Other | | |

## Requesting an Action

Please describe how the individual lets you know if he or she wants or needs…

| Items | Behaviours | Examples |
|-------|-----------|----------|
| 1. Help with dressing | | |
| 2. Help with a game | | |
| 3. To go to the bathroom | | |
| 4. Someone to come/ be near | | |
| 5. Other | | |

## Requesting Information

Please describe how the individual lets you know if he or she wants…

| Items | Behaviours | Examples |
|-------|-----------|----------|
| 1. Clarification (e.g., if he or she doesn't understand something you said) | | |
| 2. Information about something (e.g., the name of something) | | |
| 3. Other | | |

## Comment

Please describe how the individual lets you know if he or she…

| Items | Behaviours | Examples |
|---|---|---|
| 1. Is happy, pleased, enjoying something, or excited | | |
| 2. Is unhappy, sad, or anxious | | |
| 3. Is bored or disinterested | | |
| 4. Finds something funny | | |
| 5. Is frightened or surprised | | |
| 6. Is in pain or feels sick | | |

7.  Is angry or feels
    frustrated
    _____    _____
    _____    _____
    _____    _____

8.  Is tired
    _____    _____
    _____    _____
    _____    _____

9.  Other
    _____    _____
    _____    _____
    _____    _____

SAMPLE

## Choice-making

Please describe how the individual…

| Items | Behaviours | Examples |
|---|---|---|
| 1. Makes a choice between two or more objects (e.g., foods, drinks, toys) | | |
| 2. Chooses what he or she wants to do | | |
| 3. Chooses when to start or stop an activity | | |
| 4. Other | | |

## Answer

Please describe how the individual…

| Items | Behaviours | Examples |
|-------|-----------|----------|
| 1. Reacts when someone talks to him or her | | |
| 2. Tells you 'yes' in response to a question | | |
| 3. Tells you 'no' in response to a question | | |
| 4. Other | | |

## Imitation

Please describe how the person imitates or attempts to imitate the following communicative actions of others…

| Items | Behaviours | Examples |
|---|---|---|
| 1. Another's speech (e.g., sentences, single words, vocalisations) | | |
| 2. Head nod 'yes' | | |
| 3. Head nod 'no' | | |
| 4. Shrugging shoulders | | |
| 5. Pointing | | |
| 6. Other | | |

## Scoring Grid

|  |  | | | | | | | | | | | | | | | | | | | |
|---|---|---|---|---|---|---|---|---|---|---|---|---|---|---|---|---|---|---|---|---|
| Request action | other | | | | | | | | | | | | | | | | | | | |
| | near | | | | | | | | | | | | | | | | | | | |
| | toilet | | | | | | | | | | | | | | | | | | | |
| | game | | | | | | | | | | | | | | | | | | | |
| | dress | | | | | | | | | | | | | | | | | | | |
| Request object | other | | | | | | | | | | | | | | | | | | | |
| | TV or music | | | | | | | | | | | | | | | | | | | |
| | more | | | | | | | | | | | | | | | | | | | |
| | food | | | | | | | | | | | | | | | | | | | |
| | object | | | | | | | | | | | | | | | | | | | |
| Reject/protest | other | | | | | | | | | | | | | | | | | | | |
| | adult | | | | | | | | | | | | | | | | | | | |
| | take | | | | | | | | | | | | | | | | | | | |
| | dislike | | | | | | | | | | | | | | | | | | | |
| | do | | | | | | | | | | | | | | | | | | | |
| | routine | | | | | | | | | | | | | | | | | | | |
| Attention to self | other | | | | | | | | | | | | | | | | | | | |
| | shows off | | | | | | | | | | | | | | | | | | | |
| | cuddle | | | | | | | | | | | | | | | | | | | |
| | comfort | | | | | | | | | | | | | | | | | | | |
| | get attention | | | | | | | | | | | | | | | | | | | |
| Social convention | other | | | | | | | | | | | | | | | | | | | |
| | name | | | | | | | | | | | | | | | | | | | |
| | farewell | | | | | | | | | | | | | | | | | | | |
| | greet | | | | | | | | | | | | | | | | | | | |
| | Behaviours | | | | | | | | | | | | | | | | | | | |

| | | | | | | | | | | | | | | | | | | | |
|---|---|---|---|---|---|---|---|---|---|---|---|---|---|---|---|---|---|---|---|
| **Imitate** | other | | | | | | | | | | | | | | | | | | |
| | point | | | | | | | | | | | | | | | | | | |
| | shrug | | | | | | | | | | | | | | | | | | |
| | no | | | | | | | | | | | | | | | | | | |
| | yes | | | | | | | | | | | | | | | | | | |
| | speech | | | | | | | | | | | | | | | | | | |
| **Answer** | other | | | | | | | | | | | | | | | | | | |
| | no | | | | | | | | | | | | | | | | | | |
| | yes | | | | | | | | | | | | | | | | | | |
| | reacts | | | | | | | | | | | | | | | | | | |
| **Choice-making** | other | | | | | | | | | | | | | | | | | | |
| | start | | | | | | | | | | | | | | | | | | |
| | wants | | | | | | | | | | | | | | | | | | |
| | two or more | | | | | | | | | | | | | | | | | | |
| **Comment** | other | | | | | | | | | | | | | | | | | | |
| | tired | | | | | | | | | | | | | | | | | | |
| | angry | | | | | | | | | | | | | | | | | | |
| | pain | | | | | | | | | | | | | | | | | | |
| | fright | | | | | | | | | | | | | | | | | | |
| | funny | | | | | | | | | | | | | | | | | | |
| | bored | | | | | | | | | | | | | | | | | | |
| | sad | | | | | | | | | | | | | | | | | | |
| | happy | | | | | | | | | | | | | | | | | | |
| **Request info** | other | | | | | | | | | | | | | | | | | | |
| | info | | | | | | | | | | | | | | | | | | |
| | clarification | | | | | | | | | | | | | | | | | | |
| | **Behaviours** | | | | | | | | | | | | | | | | | | |

Chapter 8

# About Play

## INTRODUCTION

Play is often considered a window to children's development as well as being a sensitive barometer of a range of developmental difficulties (Restall and Magill-Evans, 1994). Research has shown that the play of children with ASD is significantly different from that of age and developmentally matched peers, indicating that it is not just developmental age that impacts on children's play, but that children with ASD experience additional challenges to the development of their play skills (e.g., Dominguez, Ziviani, and Rodger, 2006; Libby *et al.*, 1998; Skaines, Rodger, and Bundy, 2006). The picture of play in children with ASD is complicated by the presence of the multiple challenges discussed in Chapter 2 and expanded upon in this chapter. These include:

- sensory sensitivities and preferences

- poor motor skills and planning

- difficulties with communication and social interaction

- cognitive issues such as rigidity, inflexibility, theory of mind, weak central coherence

- restricted interests and preoccupations.

This chapter will first address each of these areas and describe how they influence children's play. The second section of the chapter will address how to assist parents to facilitate their children's play alone, with siblings, with parents, with peers, and in a range of contexts.

# IMPACT OF ASD ON CHILDREN'S PLAY

## Sensory Issues and Play

When we observe children with ASD playing, sometimes their sensory issues influence the types of play they choose. Children who are oversensitive to tactile sensations might avoid playing with objects of certain textures or sensations, like glue, sand, and wet grass. On the other hand, children who are under-responsive to certain sensory stimuli may actively pursue sensory input to stimulate their nervous system. For example, they may be constantly mouthing toys, or seeking to play with sand or dirt in the garden (Dodd, 2005). Alternatively, children who are undersensitive or under-responsive to sound may make humming noises while they play, which may sound socially inappropriate to their playmates, but may help them stay focused while playing.

## Cognitive Issues and Play

The cognitive inflexibility of children with ASD may lead to the use of repetitive and ritualistic play routines. This is why many children with ASD have limited play repertoires.

*For example, Charlie is three years old and likes to play with his Thomas the Tank Engine™ toys, watches Thomas the Tank Engine™ and Bob the Builder™ videos, and likes to play on the computer. He has some favourite cars and trucks that preoccupy him for long periods of time, and a few favourite books. When he plays with his toy vehicles, he specifically lines them up in different lines, sometimes according to colour and sometimes according to whether they are cars or trucks or motorbikes. He dislikes his lines being disturbed. When he plays with one car on its own, he lies on the floor with his face on the ground and the car at eye level, pushing it backwards and forwards and making a 'brumming noise', or holds it up in front of his face and spins the wheels around. He loves being out in the garden, wandering around and watching insects that most people can't see.*

ASD may also interfere with the child's development of pretend play (i.e., this is when the child pretends to be someone or something else, such as a superhero like Batman or Spiderman, or acts out a scene such as playing tea parties with teddybears and dolls, or going to the doctor). Pretend play requires high levels of abstraction and representative thinking, which is difficult for children with ASD, particularly when they have limited language and communication abilities. Limited imagination can lead to repetitive play and a lack of observable pretend or symbolic play. Symbolic play refers to acting 'as if' something is the case, when in reality it is not. Play is very important in cognitive development, especially for supporting the transition from concrete to symbolic thinking (El'Konin, 1999). While typically developing children begin to show preference for pretend play from around three years old, children with ASD may struggle to engage in pretend play even at a much older age.

During childhood, play provides an avenue for early learning about concepts, the world, and social conventions and roles. The aloof and restricted play of many children with ASD provides them with fewer and less rich opportunities to learn about their world. Audet (2004) described three related cognitive components that negatively impact the play of children with ASD: ideation, problem-solving, and representational thought. Although these can be addressed separately, they are closely integrated during play.

Difficulties with ideation can lead to the restrictive, repetitive play sequences seen in children with ASD, such as lining up cars, attention to parts of objects such as car wheels rather than the whole car, and repetitive actions with toys or objects, such as pushing cars backwards and forwards. This ritualistic or repetitive use of toys tends to replace imaginary or pretend play, and downplays the need for problem-solving or representational play. Poor problem-solving (due, for instance, to cognitive inflexibility and/or poor praxis) can also lead to a lack of diversity or variety in play, hence the child may resort to repetitive and stereotypical play responses. Lack of representational or abstract thought also reduces the ability to engage in imaginative play (Craig and Baron-Cohen, 1999).

Often children with ASD engage in constructional or functional play rather than representational/symbolic or pretend play, the latter of which is cognitively and socially more complex (Desha, Ziviani, and Rodger, 2003; Libby *et al.*, 1998). In part this may be attributable to receptive or expressive language difficulties; poor motor skills, praxis, and even imitation may pose hurdles to the development of this level of play (Mostrangelo, 2009). There is generally a paucity of symbolic play in children with ASD compared to matched controls

(Sigman and Ungerer, 1984; Stone *et al.*, 1990). Further, Desha *et al.* (2003) found that children with ASD spent a considerable amount of time in non-play (e.g., wandering around, observing or watching, or engaging in stereotypic behaviour related to their body or objects), when observed in both structured and unstructured clinical play settings.

## Motor Issues and Play

While motor and co-ordination difficulties are not a core impairment of ASD, some children experience difficulties with motor planning and co-ordination that can impact the quality of movements in gross motor play, and their precision in fine motor play. First, these children may have difficulty with construction. For example, when presented with wooden blocks, they may struggle with putting the objects together in new and different ways, and so prefer to stack the blocks up repetitively. Second, grading or calibration (the ability to vary the intensity of movement) can be difficult for some children with ASD. For instance, when handling electronic toys, they may appear to be rough and use intense force to manipulate the toy when only gentle touch is needed. Third, timing and sequencing can be challenging. In other words, it can be tricky for them to perform motor tasks at the appropriate time and in the correct order. Co-ordination difficulties also can cause frustration in fine motor play, such as threading beads or assembling small puzzles.

## Social and Communication Issues and Play

Social interaction difficulties and delayed communication can impact the development of friendships during play, leading to playing alone. Playing alone can result in less experience with social play, giving and taking, conversations, and development of advanced interactive play scripts. Lack of problem-solving and social skills can cause frustration during group play. Children with ASD tend to prefer solitary play to group or cooperative play. While they may prefer to play alone, they may also want to engage in play with others but lack the ability to integrate the complex mix of social, cognitive, motor, and communicative demands required in these situations (Wolfberg, 1999). Hence, providing opportunities for these children to become competent in play in socially integrated settings and natural play contexts is critical.

## Playfulness

Children with ASD have been found to be less intrinsically playful than typically developing children (Muys, Rodger, and Bundy, 2006; Skaines et al., 2006). In these studies, children with ASD were less playful compared to typically developing children, even when accounting for developmental age. Both groups of children were slightly more playful in a structured environment with adult facilitation and play support, indicating that adult support can enhance play performance. Each child's playfulness is believed to be a stable aspect of the child's personality and a construct that holds consistently across raters, situations, contexts, tasks, materials, and time. Playfulness has been defined as the internal disposition to play, and is understood as a quality of the child's play rather than simply the child's skills in performing specific activities (Bundy, 1997). Bundy's Model of Playfulness (Bundy, 2003) depicts playfulness as determined by intrinsic motivation, internal control, freedom to suspend reality, and framing.

Clinicians and researchers have primarily focused on teaching play skills and incorporating toys that elicit different types of play (Beyer and Gammeltoft, 2000; Bundy, 1997). There is some evidence to support the effectiveness of these interventions, and a small amount of research suggesting that playful adults facilitate playfulness in children with ASD (Reed, Dunbar, and Bundy, 2000). For adults to be playful with their children, it is best to encourage play within natural environments (e.g., on the floor as opposed to seated at a desk). As discussed in Chapter 6, in order to encourage playfulness, adults need to learn to read their children's social cues and to follow their leads, giving them choices and opportunities to engage in activities in which they appear interested (Rigby and Rodger, 2006). To be playful, it is also important for adults to feel relaxed and enjoy the play times spent with their children, rather than being in a hurry to finish playing.

## TYPES OF PLAY INTERVENTIONS

While the play of children with ASD is compromised, it is possible to improve their spontaneous play skills (e.g., Kok, Kong, and Bernard-Optiz, 2002; Sherratt, 2002; Skaines et al., 2006). Play intervention can be broadly classified as 'behavioural' or 'developmental'. Behavioural interventions use strategies based on ABA (Baer, Wolf, and Risley, 1968). These approaches emphasise the learning of specific play skills. Behavioural interventions are generally adult directed, although some interventions are peer-mediated, and may include play goals that involve learning skills such as imitation and language.

An example of developmental approaches is the DIR or Floortime model (Wieder and Greenspan, 2003). These approaches emphasise the child's strengths and interests, using these to expand and develop play. Because developmental approaches allow the child to lead the interaction, they appear more playful in nature. With either approach, adults in the child's environment have a critical role. In behavioural intervention the adult's role is one of training, while in developmental interventions the adult's role is in facilitating play as a play partner who is able to shape or scaffold play behaviour (e.g., Kok *et al.*, 2002; Sigman and Ungerer, 1984; Skaines *et al.*, 2006). The latter is more the focus of this chapter because the strategies emphasised in this book are oriented more towards a developmental relationship that professionals can use to assist parents to engage positively with their child with ASD.

## HELPING PARENTS TO FACILITATE THEIR CHILDREN'S PLAY

In this section, we address how to assist parents to facilitate their children's play alone, with siblings, with parents, and in a range of contexts. We talk about how play can be extended, using the child's special interest(s), and how sharing and turn-taking can be facilitated while playing with peers. To begin with, we need to consider what level the child is at developmentally.

### Developmental Level of the Child

Although the diagnosis of ASD is characterised by impairment in social interaction and communication, as well as by restricted, repetitive and stereotyped behaviour, interests and activities, the constellation of symptoms exhibited in children with ASD varies considerably (American Psychiatric Association, 2000). On the same note, the nature of their play engagement is highly individualised and may be influenced by the child's developmental level, intellectual ability, and characteristic manifestations of the disorder, such as lack of creativity and motivation (Desha *et al.*, 2003). Therefore, when considering the facilitation of play, it is important to determine the child's developmental level in a range of abilities (e.g., intellectual, language, motor, creativity).

By considering children's developmental level and skills, one can provide them with their preferred play objects, and consequently succeed at engaging with them. In a study involving observations of 24 preschool children with ASD, it was found that preferred play objects tended to be those that offered play experiences that suited the child's developmental level and skill base (Desha *et al.*, 2003). For example, children with impaired intellectual functioning may prefer gross motor play items and infant toys. This is because gross motor play items are less demanding in a cognitive sense and provide immediate gratification (e.g., movement), while infant toys produce sounds and movement with minimal effort.

Parents may sometimes feel pressured to provide age-appropriate toys and types of play for their children, according to their chronological age. This can happen when they compare their child with ASD with his or her typically developing peers and feel the need to get their child to play what the others at that age are playing. This can also occur when they choose toys according to the ages that are indicated on commercial labels on toys. It is important to reassure parents that the purpose of providing toys is to engage the child in play, both alone and with others. Chronologically age-appropriate toys may not necessarily be developmentally age-appropriate for the child. Therefore, it is more fruitful to provide toys according to the stage the child is at developmentally, and use the toys to encourage some form of social interaction, regardless of whether or not the toys are chronologically age-appropriate. However, when there is a significant disparity between the child's developmental and chronological age, it is important to find a toy or object that is similar in function but more chronologically age-appropriate.

## Consideration of the Child's Likes and Dislikes

Children's play preferences across ages, gender, and developmental status vary, and these variables influence children's play (Case-Smith and Kuhaneck, 2008). For example, with typically developing children, rough-and-tumble play increases from three to five years of age, and then decreases from five to seven years of age, with an increase in preference for video and computer games (Case-Smith and Kuhaneck, 2008). It is important to understand each child's play preferences and facilitate play using what he or she likes.

Depending on their developmental status, children with ASD may display different play preferences. Some may prefer simpler, lower play demand activities such as rough-and-tumble play and object exploration, while others may begin to develop interests in pretend play. Although typically developing children display a significantly higher preference for games involving social interaction, many children with ASD also enjoy playing with friends. Likewise, they may develop interest in pretend play at an older age. To determine play preferences of the child with ASD, one can begin by providing a wide range of toys with properties that enable the child to play with them in a variety of ways, depending on his or her level of functioning. Parents generally have a clear idea about the child's likes and dislikes, and are an important source of information about their child's play preferences in different settings.

Sometimes parents of children with ASD are unsure of their children's play preferences. In this case, professionals can advise them how to provide their child with a suitable range of different play activities. Together they can observe whether he or she is more interested in exploratory play (e.g., banging toys, observing bubbles), constructive play (e.g., building with blocks, puzzles), rough and tumble play (e.g., tickling, throwing and chasing ball), pretend play (e.g., dolls and action figurines), or structured play (e.g., computer games).

Apart from identifying play preferences, it is also important to understand what the child dislikes. The sensory issues experienced by some children with ASD can influence the types of play chosen and those avoided. For example, children with difficulty in touch processing, otherwise known as tactile defensiveness, may be oversensitive to light touch, either from adults or other children (Dunn, 1997). As a result, a tactile-defensive child may be very reluctant to participate in social games such as 'Musical Chairs', where there is a high chance that other children may bump into or touch him or her (Lim and Chen, 2010). Children who are tactile defensive may also avoid certain textures, and be reluctant to play in the sand or with materials such as glue (Ziviani, Boyle, and Rodger, 2001). A child who experiences difficulties with auditory processing may exhibit sensitivity to certain volumes or pitches of sound (Moyes, 2001). These children can have difficulty playing in loud, confusing places like a noisy childcare centre or kindergarten. These insights help parents to understand why it is that children dislike particular play environments (e.g., playground near a busy road or train station), and particular play experiences (e.g., finger paint).

There are two approaches that could be followed here. The first is to determine whether the child needs to be systematically exposed to particular play experiences and environments to desensitise them to any particularly overwhelming sensory features. This is usually only recommended if the child really needs to engage with a particular environment or play experience. For example, if the child is overwhelmed by an older sibling's loud play with friends when they visit, he or she may need to be systematically exposed to this, given the need to learn to get on with all people in the household. A quiet withdrawal space may be created at home, such as a cubbyhouse or tent, which is quiet and cosy, with cushions and books and calming activities. This allows the child to retreat from the noisy environment. The second approach is to avoid experiences and environments that are overwhelming for the child. For example, the parent could provide a paintbrush so that the child does not have to use fingers to paint at playgroup. The provision of simple choices, such as paintbrush versus fingers, helps give the child more control over the situation, in this case to enjoy the creativity of painting without the pressure of doing so in a particular way.

## Using the Child's Special Interests

Children with ASD quite often have special interests. Some children may have a general special interest such as vehicles or dinosaurs, while others may have a very specific one such as Bob the Builder™. Some parents have been told to avoid the child's special interest to prevent him or her being 'too obsessed' with it. In most cases (if not harmful in some way to the child or others), instead of avoiding it, parents can make use of the child's special interest to engage the child in play related to this interest, and introduce more varied toys, or varied ways of playing with the object of interest.

---

### A FATHER TALKS ABOUT HIS SON'S SPECIAL INTEREST

So I remember, he still does it, plays around with the CD player. Your natural tendency is to try to explain to him that we should put a CD on and we should listen to the music, 'cos that's what we do... But he of course is interested in the buttons and looking at the numbers and the lights. So once I let go of the need to have him listen to it the way I do, and actually got in and enjoyed watching the numbers go up and down, and pressing the buttons, it was great, because we learnt about numbers, he's really good at counting now.

---

There is a tendency for children to engage with play objects to which they have been exposed through toy industry advertising and media. In a study that involved preschool children with ASD, there was clear preference for the Thomas the Tank Engine™ toys (Desha *et al.*, 2003). It is suggested that if toys from popular television series are appealing and enhance motivation for play, it may be worthwhile harnessing the power of these characters to help improve a child's play. For example, parents can use Thomas the Tank Engine™ toys to further develop pretend play and help their child with ASD extend the story line in their play. Instead of removing the stimulus that the child is fixating on, they can exploit that stimulus for other purposes (Luthman, 2010). The child's interest in Bob the Builder™ may allow the parent to engage the child with construction activities, such as building blocks into towers, houses, walls, and space ships, and so progressing from lining up blocks. A Bob the Builder™ toolkit could be used to support roleplay and other building/construction themes. Use of the preferred toys/objects for other purposes, such as letting a child wear a Spiderman outfit to improve self-care skills, provides, for example, opportunities for undressing and dressing.

When the child has limited interest in toys but prefers other objects such as pieces of wool or straws, these can be developed by demonstrating other things that can be done with these objects. For example, straws can be glued on paper to make shapes, or joined together to make a wand, and then the child can be introduced to standard construction toys that have straws and/or connecting pieces that can be used to make other objects. Straw play may expand to magnetic sticks, pickup sticks, pipecleaners, and ice lolly sticks (see Figures 8.1–8.4).

*Figure 8.1 Pile of straws*

*Figure 8.2 Magnetic connecting toy (similar to straws)*

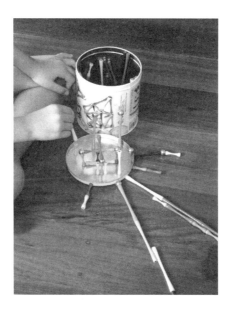

*Figure 8.3 More advanced construction with magnetic straws*

*Figure 8.4 Pick-up sticks*

Playing with straws can be developed by incorporating playdough with straws, sticks, or candles to make a cake, and then involving imagination to enact a birthday party; or use playdough to represent an animal farm or zoo (with the animals surrounded by a fence made of ice lolly sticks in dough; see Figures 8.5–8.9).

163

Children who enjoy the sensation of having grains of sand run through their fingers can be introduced to different ways of playing with sand – for example, using a sieve in the sandpit to collect the larger grains of sand; filling up a bottle to make maracas; building a sandcastle, or sticking different coloured sand on a piece of cardboard to form a picture. The objective is to introduce the child to different ways of playing with a non-toy object, beyond the limit of repetitive play.

*Figure 8.5 'Birthday cake' with straws*

*Figure 8.6 'Birthday cake' with candles*

*Figure 8.7 'Birthday cake' with toy animals*

*Figure 8.8 'Birthday party'*

*Figure 8.9 'Zoo' (note the fence)*

## Useful Play Strategies for Parents

It may be useful to teach parents the following strategies to help them successfully engage their young children with ASD in playful interactions.

### Joining In: Follow and Join

Adults often succeed better in engaging the child with ASD in play when they follow the child's lead. Engaging in child-directed play involves observing, following, and joining in. By allowing the child to take the lead, adults create a comfortable, stress-free play space for the child. Provided that the chosen play is safe, it is often useful to step back, observe the play in a non-judgemental manner, and consider how one can follow and join in the play. Imitation, as we discussed in Chapter 6, can facilitate learning and social communication, and can be a useful strategy to foster play. For a start, parents can imitate what the child is doing, rather than redirect the play; allow the child to lead, but extrapolate on ways to encourage interaction during play (Luthman, 2010).

*For example, Samuel, who has ASD, enjoys lining up cars. It is easy to regard Samuel's play as repetitive, and hence stop him. Instead, Samuel's mother observed his play and considered creative ways of joining in. On the first day, she joined in the play by passing more cars to Samuel, one at a time, to extend the line of cars. With each car she passed, she made the sound 'vroom, vroom'. Samuel soon imitated the sound and continued lining up the cars. In this way Samuel's mother successfully led him into doing some imitation, by taking his lead. On the second day, she did the same as before, except that she would playfully pass him a block instead of a car, once in a while. When Samuel looked up at her, not wanting the block, she would laugh and say, 'Silly! Blocks, not car!' and pass him a car instead. Soon Samuel found this funny and laughed along each time she handed him a block. By gently joining Samuel in his play she coaxed him to accept her as a playmate, instead of viewing her attempts as intrusive.*

The example above illustrates how parents can join in a seemingly monotonous and repetitive play activity, and engage the child by following child-directed play. As adults we may not be used to creative play, and can be stuck with ideas about how to have fun in a repetitive game. Therefore, it is worth observing the child and first considering how one could participate in the play in a fun, yet non-intrusive manner, before joining in. It is tempting to teach the child what to do and instruct the child how to play differently. Sensing that an adult is attempting to change his or her play, the child may get frustrated with the intrusion, and this in turn may lead to problematic behaviour. Play should be self-chosen and intrinsically motivating (Bundy, 1997), and so attempts to regimentally instruct a child 'how to play' should be avoided. This is why following and joining in is encouraged, as it allows children with ASD to continue their play with items that intrinsically motivate them. This approach is consistent with the responsive parenting style introduced in Chapter 1.

It is important to emphasise to parents that not every attempt to join in will be successful. In the event of a failed attempt, one can simply watch and show interest in what the child is doing by commenting on it (e.g., 'Oh, I see, this is how you do it.'). After all, it is about joining in and following the child's lead rather than joining in and changing the child's play (at least, not at first). The key is to be patient, keep innovating, and not get discouraged.

### *Extending Play through Scaffolding*

'Scaffolding' is the provision of sufficient external adult support to achieve learning. In doing so, adults mediate a child's attempts to take on new learning. Adults can scaffold the play of children with ASD by helping them to learn new concepts or develop more interaction by extending their play. Once parents identify the child's likes and dislikes, they can engage the child more in liked forms of play, and slowly extend that play. For instance, a mother noticed that her child was very interested in watching bubbles. She began the play session by blowing bubbles, followed by encouraging her child to take turns with her in blowing bubbles. She then extended the play by getting her child to poke the bubbles that she pointed to, with the intention to improve the child's joint attention. On another play occasion, she encouraged her child to imitate her actions, such as clapping or stepping on the bubbles.

There are various ways to teach children how to extend their play. One is the 'hand over hand' method, also known as patterning. For many children with ASD, seeing or hearing what they are required to do can be very confusing, or it may not mean very much to them.

'Patterning' describes the process in which someone else helps the child to perform a task by physically moving the child's body through that task. The child often learns best by actually physically performing the task with the help of an adult. For example, patterning can be used to teach a child how to throw and catch a ball. The steps involved in patterning are as follows:

1.   The patterning adult stands behind the child.

2.   The patterning adult places the child's hand in the appropriate position (reaching out at a level to which the ball will be thrown) and then the adult places his or her own hand over the child's.

3.   The adult carries out the process of catching and throwing with another adult opposite, ensuring all the time that the child's hands are under his or her own. The child is therefore performing the task as well.

4.   The adult standing opposite talks to the child as the actions are performed and gives encouragement throughout (e.g., 'Good catch!' 'Good throw!').

*Demonstration*

For children who have fairly good joint attention, adults can extend the child's play through demonstration. Adults often need to use their voices and actions creatively to get the child's attention in order that he or she can watch the demonstration. For example, a child may be repetitively stacking blocks. A mother may want to show the child how the blocks can be arranged into different patterns, such as a train or an aeroplane. In order to do so, she needs to attract the child's attention to watch what she is doing, for example, by imitating the sound of a train or plane engine in the process, and to encourage the child to do the same. The essence of effective demonstration is to attract the child's attention to watch the adult demonstrate. Therefore, the therapeutic use of self is important, where adults have to change their volume, pitch, and body posture such that the child is keen to watch, and is interested to try the extended play.

### Forward and Backward Chaining

Another way to teach a child to extend play is through 'chaining'. Chaining involves linking a series of related behaviours into a more complex, composite behaviour. Chaining involves a task analysis, which is the breaking down of a task into its component elements. There are two types of chaining – forward and backward. In forward chaining, we begin by teaching the first element in the chain and progress towards the last element in the chain. Once the child performs the first element satisfactorily, let him or her perform the first and second element, and reinforce the effort. Continue this process until the child learns the entire task.

*For example, a father is trying to extend the pretend play of his child with ASD. He wants to introduce the sequence of feeding the teddybear breakfast. First, he teaches the child to feed the bear with a spoon. Once the child masters that, he teaches the child to feed the bear, followed by giving it a drink from a cup. Next, the father teaches the child to feed the bear, give it a drink, and then clean the bear's mouth with a handkerchief. In this way, the pretend play sequence is slowly extended through forward chaining.*

The second type of chaining is backward chaining. In backward chaining, the child is taught the final step first. The adult prompts through all of the steps up until the last, at which point the adult will pause and wait for the child to finish the task on his or her own. As the child masters that step, the adult introduces the second-to-last step, and so on.

*A good example is teaching a child to complete a five-piece puzzle. To backward chain this play task, the adult inserts the first four pieces and then presents the task, complete except for the last piece, and prompts the child to insert it. Praise the child for completing the puzzle. After the child can successfully do this a number of times, the adult then guides the child to complete the puzzle by inserting the fourth and fifth pieces. These steps are repeated until the child has learnt to complete the entire puzzle independently. Prompts may include visual cues, such as pointing to a puzzle piece, or verbal cues, such as 'Next one' to encourage the child to pick up another piece. Through backward chaining, the child with ASD can learn to extend his or her play.*

## Generalising Play Skills

Quite often a child with ASD may be keen to play with one toy, but will only do it in a certain fixed way, or in one context only. Therefore it is important to teach the child how to generalise his or her play. This can be done by introducing the same type of play activity in different settings, or by modifying the play a little at a time.

*For instance, Gordon, who has ASD, enjoys watching his therapist blow bubbles. His parents help him generalise this interest by blowing bubbles with him at home, in the garden, and at his grandparents' place. They introduced different types of bubble pipes and wands to Gordon. With this interest, they encourage Gordon to play with bubbles in the bath at bathtime.*

By means of generalising his or her play, the child learns that a particular game can be played in different ways and in different settings.

## Encouraging Sharing and Turn-taking

It is difficult for children with ASD to keep their attention on a shared activity with others. They can easily be distracted by extraneous stimuli in the surrounding environment. In addition, they may also have their own ideas as to what the interaction is about. To participate successfully in a game, it is important for them not only to focus during their turn, but also to be involved in the game while the other players are having a turn (Lim and Chen, 2010).

For children with ASD, it helps to set up in advance a physical environment where visual cues tell them where the game is to take place (Gammeltoft and Nordenhof, 2007). To limit naturally the area in which the game takes place, it is useful to set it up around a table and chairs, or on a mat on the floor. Each chair will mark a place for a player. Having the table and chairs at the corner of a room where there is less noise and fewer visual stimuli (e.g., open window) can help minimise distraction by external stimuli. Playing around the table helps the children keep their attention on the common area. Alternatively, other play areas can be set, up using play mats, rugs, bookcases, or a taped area on the floor.

Children with ASD can find it difficult to take turns. It helps to use visual cues such that the play sequence can be easily understood. If each child is given a number, the child with ASD can be cued visually regarding the order of play, to make the game work as intended. By visualising the order from the beginning, the child is less likely to go off and do his or her own thing (Gammeltoft and Nordenhof, 2007). To help the child understand whose turn it is, a cap worn on the head can be used as a clear marker to show who is taking the present turn. The cap is passed on to the next player when it is his or her turn.

Sharing is an important social skill that enables a child to play well with other children. It can be a difficult skill to learn for children with ASD, as they often become very attached to a certain toy. It is not uncommon for them to react aggressively (e.g., bite, hit, or kick other children) in an effort to protect their favourite things. To encourage a child with ASD to share, one can introduce the concept gradually. Children with ASD can be very literal in their understanding of what we say. When asked, 'Give Sam your toy,' the child with ASD may think that he has literally to give away the toy and that he is not going to get it back. When we ask children with ASD to share toys, it is important to explain to the child that the toy will be given back. To begin with, it may be helpful to facilitate the child's experience of sharing with a timer, so that he or she understands that sharing toys is only temporary and that it can be a pleasant experience. Explain clearly what the child is required to do – for example, 'Give your toy to Sam and you can have it back when the timer rings.' Gradually, as the child with ASD understands the concept of sharing, he or she will be willing to share for a longer period of time and without the need of a timer.

With a more verbal child, social stories can be used to introduce sharing. Social Stories™ are stories written individually for a child that clearly describe challenging social situations and provide suggestions about how to behave (Gray, 2010). The goal of a Social Story™ is to increase the child's understanding of a specific social situation and to offer alternative, appropriate responses to it. To teach a child how to share, an adult may write a Social Story™ relating to sharing. The adult can either read the Social Story™ to the child or get the child to read it before entering a situation where sharing is anticipated. Social Stories™ can be an effective way to teach these children, as they are based on the strengths of children with ASD; they are visual, situation-specific, and offer explicit information (Quirmbach *et al.*,

2009). Social Stories™ are customised for individuals – in other words, they are written according to the specific difficulty faced by the child with ASD.

Gray (2010) defines a number of sentence types (e.g., descriptive, perspective, directive, affirmative) that can be used to write Social Stories™. For example, descriptive sentences are used to explain when and where a situation occurs, who is participating, what will happen, or why the person should behave in a certain way. Depending on the difficulty experienced by the child, Social Stories™ can be tailored to help improve a particular behaviour. An example based on the principles of writing Social Stories™ is included in Table 8.1.

### Playing with the Nonverbal Child

With a nonverbal child, it may be useful to begin engaging the child with toys that are simple and less verbally or intellectually demanding. Play materials that demonstrate cause and effect (e.g., pop-up and musical toys) and involve easily repeatable actions (e.g., blowing bubbles) are engaging and can capture the child's attention. Quite often, a nonverbal child may have impairments in joint attention (see Chapter 2). Joint attention is an early developing social communicative skill that involves two people actively sharing attention with respect to an object or event and monitoring each other's attention to that object or event (Jones and Carr, 2004). Once the child is engaged, the adult can become more involved both in the play and in making responses to the toy and the child's reaction. For example, with cause-and-effect toys, the adult can clap and praise the child for causing the effect in the toy. The adult gets the child to notice his or her actions in relation to the toy (e.g., 'Look, you did it,' or 'You made the music start.'). Through engaging with a toy that the child is interested in, the adult enters the shared play space with the child.

For the nonverbal child to be engaged in a series of games, it can be helpful to organise the play session with games in different boxes (such as shoe boxes). Depending on the attention span of the child, two to three games can be incorporated in a play session of ten minutes. For example, one could start with a shape-sorting activity, followed by a game of dressing the teddybear, and end with a puzzle. Place the materials for each different activity in a separate box. In a play session, organise the toys so that it is clear which materials belong together, how they should be used, and where each game starts and ends. If the start and finish of the game is unclear, at some point the child with ASD may feel lost and lose interest in the game. Being clear about which materials belong together and when the game starts and ends helps the child to understand that when the toy or game is packed away in the box, it goes away under the table and another box can come out. This builds anticipation, expectation, and opportunities for requesting more, or another game.

**Table 8.1 Example of a Social Story illustrating various sentence types**

| Sentences in the story | Type of sentence |
| --- | --- |
| I love playing with the train set. | Descriptive |
| I like to join the train tracks. | Descriptive |
| Sam likes to play with the train set, and sometimes he asks me, 'Can I have some train tracks, please?' | Perspective |
| I can lend Sam some train tracks. | Directive |
| Now I have some train tracks, and Sam has some train tracks, we can join the tracks for the train to run on. | Descriptive |
| We are sharing the train set. | Descriptive |
| It is fun to share toys with my friend. | Affirmative |

With a nonverbal child, it is helpful to create short, playful sessions during different daily activities. Back-and-forth communication can take place when parents engage in playful interactions with their children. Greenspan and Wieder (2009) describe the concept of opening and closing circles of communication. This can be done with any item or activity that is safe and of interest to a child. In an example raised by Greenspan and Wieder (2009), instead of stopping a child who is interested in opening and closing doors, adults can use this as an opportunity for a two-way communication with the child. The father could block the door with his foot so that it can't open easily. He can ask if the child wants to open the door and wait for the child to respond. When the child does respond with a nod or some other gesture, the two-way communication begins. The father can then hold the child's hand and try to push it open. He can indicate that the door is too heavy and they need the mother's help, and consequently they approach the mother to join in. The three of them can continue this task of opening the door in different ways, and in the process engage the child in some form of playful interaction.

To engage the child in play, parents can also be playfully obstructive (Greenspan and Wieder, 2009). What this means is that when the child with ASD wants to play with his or her favourite toy or engage in repetitive stimulation (e.g., spinning), parents can obstruct the child playfully and attempt to engage him or her in some form of interaction. For example, when Johnny chooses to run around the living room repetitively, his father could playfully extend his hand to block his way and say, 'Ticket please!' As Johnny tries to push him away, the father can say, 'Here you go, door open,' while slowly retracting his hand. He does this repeatedly in a playful manner, sometimes with a silly face, sometimes with a higher pitch, or an 'Uh oh!' After a while, Johnny realises that this is a game that they are playing together. While he continues to run around, he stops each time, looks at his father and responds in one way or another, such as laughing and gesturing. The same idea can apply when a child wants to take his favourite toy. The mother can playfully put it above the child's reach (by rearranging the environment) and offer to help the child reach for it. The mother can carry the child forward, backward, and sideways from the toy, each time interacting with the child to ask if they are getting closer, so as to encourage some interaction, whether verbally or in the form of gesture, from the child.

### Playing with the Verbal Child

Children with ASD who have verbal skills are quite often able to play games that involve simple rules, when they are well supported. Although they may be keen to participate in games, they may struggle with different aspects, such as taking turns or dealing with losing a game. Various research studies have demonstrated that stories are effective for improving the game-playing skills of children with ASD (e.g., Kuoch and Mirenda, 2003; Quirmbach et al., 2009). A child who frequently tantrums after losing a game may need a Social Story™ written to explain winning and losing, and how to cope with losing a game.

Sensory stories are developed to target specific occupations such as play, which are difficult for a child to engage in due to sensory modulation disorders (Marr and Nackley, 2010). Unlike Social Stories™, sensory stories do not attempt to teach abstract ideas or concepts. Instead, sensory stories include an explanation of the context, the steps for a targeted occupation (e.g., getting a haircut), and suggested sensory strategies that the child may consider using during the targeted, challenging occupation (Marr and Nackley, 2010). If a child with ASD is having difficulty in playing as a result of sensory issues, sensory stories may be useful. For example, if the child is sensitive to noise and gets overwhelmed when playing in a noisy environment, actions that provide calming sensory input (e.g., giving yourself a hug) can be included in the story, or suggestions for removing him or herself to a calm place can be incorporated. Sensory issues are discussed further in Chapter 9.

### Extending Play when Alone

While some children with ASD spend a lot of time playing alone and may not wish to engage with others, there are some who have limited capacity to play alone. When left alone, these children are at a loss what to do – they may fuss for attention or occupy themselves with repetitive actions, such as climbing up a sofa and jumping down from it repeatedly. Parents often identify goals for helping these children play alone for an extended period, so that they can get on with chores such as preparing dinner or collecting clothes from the washing line. To encourage spontaneous and independent play, a key phrase to remember is 'Catch them being good' – in this case, playing alone. The aim is to increase the length of time the child can safely play alone. On finding the child with ASD spontaneously playing with a toy, the adult rewards the child with praise. Alternatively, the adult can join in the play, to indicate to the child that he or she can attract the adult's attention by playing independently without instruction (Young, Partington, and Goren, 2009). The amount of time the child plays independently is systematically increased before rewarding him or her with praise or positive attention.

Visual cues and a timer can also be used to help the child with ASD extend the time spent playing alone. Some children with ASD may have limited ideas about what they can play, and many of them may not have good concepts of time (i.e., one minute may feel like a long time). Once parents have introduced a few types of games the child can play (e.g., puzzle, shape sorter, building blocks), they can take photos of these toys and make them into little cards. A 'visual list of things to play' can be created by sticking three or four photo cards on the wall, explaining to the child that these are the toys they can play with at any time they choose. Parents can then instruct the child to play for a short period of time alone (e.g., five minutes), until the timer goes off. The child is provided with positive reinforcement, such as a sticker, when he or she manages to play independently until the timer goes off. As the child manages some 'play alone' time, the length of time is gradually increased, and the child is included in planning the 'visual list of things to play'. One should also aim to increase the child's interests so that he or she has more variety of toys and games to play with. When playing together, parents can take the opportunity to introduce more new games and increase the child's interests. Once the child has learnt to play with the new toy or game, he or she can include that activity during the 'play alone' time.

### Facilitating Play with Siblings

Siblings of a child with ASD play an important role in the child's life. Within someone's lifetime, the people who will know him or her the longest are neither the parents, nor the spouse, but rather the siblings. Parents sometimes feel it is important not to 'overburden' siblings with responsibilities for a child with ASD. While it is sensible for parents to be wary of making too many demands, siblings need to be involved in the family's challenge of helping the child with ASD grow and develop (Greenspan and Wieder, 2009). Siblings of a child with ASD can make things easier for the family by being involved. On the contrary, they can also make things more difficult for the family if they do not understand the situation and become resentful, jealous, and vie for attention in a disruptive way. Therefore, it is of utmost importance to explain to siblings about the condition of ASD, the situation the family is in, and the very special role that siblings can play. This needs to be done carefully, as appropriate to the siblings' ages.

There are some useful resources that explain the condition of ASD to siblings. For example, *My Brother is Different: A Parents' Guide to Help*

*Children Cope with an Autistic Sibling* by Barbara Morvay (2010) and *Living with Autistic Spectrum Disorders – Guidance for Parents, Carers and Siblings* by Elizabeth Attfield and Morgan Hugh (2006). To explain the condition to younger children, books such as *All About my Brother* by Sarah Peralta (2002) or *My Brother is Different: A Book for Young Children who Have a Brother or Sister with Autism* by Louise Gorrod (1997) may be helpful. For older children, try *Views from our Shoes: Growing up with a Brother or Sister with Special Needs* by Donald J. Meyer (1997).

It is important to empower siblings of children with ASD, praise them for their effort to play with the child, and reinforce how well they play with the child. In doing so, siblings can feel that they are in a unique position, or even see themselves as very special people the child with ASD likes to play with.

It is also important for these siblings to meet other children whose siblings have ASD. There are various sibling support groups that can provide guidance and support for siblings of children with ASD. (ASD-specific organisations frequently have sibling support groups.) These support groups are committed to enhancing the well-being of siblings of children with ASD. They organise events such as recreation camps and educational programmes to help siblings relate to one another, and to understand the condition of ASD. Empowering siblings through praising their efforts to play with the child with ASD, as well as providing avenues for support, can help siblings to enjoy this unique role.

When parents draw siblings into the effort to help the child with ASD, siblings feel included. This can be done by facilitating play with siblings. If the siblings are older, the parents can coach them on how to play with the child with ASD. As described above, the parents can demonstrate and teach the older siblings how to playfully obstruct the child with ASD (Greenspan and Wieder, 2009) or extend play in other ways. Once the older siblings have learnt how to play with the child with ASD, they can do this spontaneously, or with prompting, while the parents are busy with household chores.

During family play times or outings, parents can give opportunities for each child to take the lead, so that the typically developing children can be motivated to join in and have fun with the parents and other siblings. The leader chooses the activity and the parents try to bring the child with ASD into the game as much as possible. When it is time for the child with ASD to lead, parents can take cues from what he or she is interested in doing. For example, when the child with ASD is jumping around aimlessly, parents can make this into a game where everyone in the family can jump together. This can be extended and changed slightly by getting siblings to suggest different ways of jumping or moving. Family time, where everyone plays together, is also an opportunity for younger siblings and children with ASD to play together.

Although it is understandable that parents caring for a child with ASD may have little spare time, it is suggested that spending some time each day with the siblings without challenges will enable them to take the lead and demonstrate the play they are good at (Greenspan and Wieder, 2009). This could be in the form of sports, for example, or more complicated card games which would be hard for the child with ASD to join in with.

### Playing in the Community

Children play everywhere. When helping parents to facilitate their children's play, it is imperative to consider contexts beyond the home. Other places in the community where children commonly play include parks, playgrounds, and friends' homes. Children's play can be influenced by the goodness of fit between the child's interest and abilities, the characteristics of the play activity, and the environment (Rigby and Rodger, 2006). Professionals can assist parents to identify what is engaging in a child's play, and what is supporting the play in one setting, and how to apply this knowledge to another (Rigby and Rodger, 2006). For example, if it is identified that the child plays better in a quiet, non-distracting environment, parents can choose to take the child to a playground at a less busy time of the day, or select a playground that is situated away from a noisy road.

Ritualistic patterns of behaviour in ASD have impacts on children's play when they are out and about in the community. Quite commonly, children with ASD may be afraid of unfamiliar environments, such as a friend's house. They may be distressed if familiar routes are not followed when out in the community – for example, taking a different route to the playground (Dodd, 2005). With these different concerns, trips out into the community can be fear-inducing for them. For children to feel playful, they need to feel that the environment is safe. Steps can be taken to help these children become familiar with an environment, so that they can feel comfortable to play.

When introducing a new environment (e.g., a friend's house, or new park, or playground), adults can prepare the child by showing him or her photographs of the place. Depending on the language ability of the child, the adult should also explain the purpose of visiting the place, and how long they will be there for. Providing more information about the trip allows the child a clearer expectation of what is going to happen. It is also ideal that parents bring along familiar toys that the child is interested in, to play with in the unfamiliar environment. This also promotes sharing, as the child can bring toys to share at the friend's house.

When possible, it is useful to set routines, such as having play dates on a certain day of the week, at a regular time, and at a particular place. This provides an opportunity for the child to socialise, and helps the child focus on play rather than trying to cope with too many new environments and new situations each time a play date occurs.

In the playground, some children with ASD find swings and slides frightening. A fear of heights and movement may be related to vestibular processing difficulty, but it could also be due to a fear of a new, unfamiliar experience. Due to poor motor planning, some children with ASD may also find it hard to control the movement required to use swings and slides. Therefore, such experiences can be terrifying, as children may not feel in control of the swing. What appears fun for typically developing children may be distressing for children with ASD. It is essential that adults introduce these new experiences gradually and in a non-threatening manner. Let the child with ASD spend some time observing someone else play, before letting him or her have a go. Instead of putting the child at the top of the slide and pushing him or her down to have a go, parents can first let the child experience the slide sitting on the adult's lap. Teach the child how to control the movement (e.g., by placing your hand along the slide to slow down the motion, or teaching the child how to 'pump' the swing).

With the swing, let the child feel the gentle movement, and help the child get down off the swing before reaching the stage where he or she is distressed. Children who enjoy counting may feel more in control if adults count the back-and-forth motion of the swing. One can help the child extend the length of time on the swing by extending the count – for example, 'Let's see if you can stay on the swing until I count to 20 this time round!' Alternatively, do it with a song: 'Let's stay on the swing until we finish singing "Baa, baa Black Sheep"'. Introducing distraction (such as counting or singing), eases the child into the new experience of staying on the swing.

To help a child get comfortable with height, one can encourage the child to climb up to get an item that he or she likes. For instance, place a sticker of Thomas the Tank Engine™ at the third step of the ladder, so that the child is motivated to climb two steps to get it. Once he or she has succeeded, increase the challenge by placing the sticker on the fourth step, and so on. The keys to success in helping children with ASD familiarise themselves with playground equipment are gentle introduction, motivating them to have a go, and helping them feel in control.

As children grow to enjoy the playground, parents often have a different set of problems – getting them to leave. Children with ASD tend not to like change without warning (Dodd, 2005) and this includes getting them to change activities (such as leaving the playground). Helping the child transition from one activity to another involves preparing him or her for the change. If the mother decides that it is time to leave the playground and head to the supermarket, she will need to inform the child ahead of time so that he or she can anticipate the change. Young children have poor concepts of time, so telling them 'Five more minutes' may not mean anything. Useful transitioning strategies include counting (e.g., 'Five more rounds of going down the slide and we are going'), use of a timer (either a visual timer or one with sound), and use of visual cues (e.g., helping the child put the playground picture card in the 'Finish' envelope, and showing the child the supermarket or home picture card).

The community offers a vast number of opportunities and environments for children with ASD to play, socialise, and learn. Getting children with ASD to play in the community takes time and effort. Professionals need to assist parents to set goals, have realistic expectations, and a timeframe for this to happen. If playing in a new environment does not occur on the first time, it is important to reassure parents not to give up, but rather to have a break and try again. The end result of getting the child with ASD to engage playfully outside the home will be worthwhile and fulfilling.

## CONCLUSION

In this chapter we have discussed how and why children with ASD may play differently from their same-aged peers. We have described a range of strategies that parents can use to engage in playful interactions with their child with ASD. These strategies enable the parent to engage with the child with ASD, to extend their play, to assist them to play alone, with others, and with siblings, and to assist them with a range of different types of play in different contexts. Professionals working with parents at or around the time of diagnosis can work with parents to help them learn these strategies, which can be used at home in their everyday lives.

Chapter 9

# About Sensory Issues and their Management

## INTRODUCTION

It is well documented that children with ASD frequently experience idiosyncratic responses to sensory stimuli, though the reason for this is unknown (Baranek, 2002; Bogdashina, 2003; Gal, Cermak, and Ben-Sasson, 2007). This was discussed in some detail in Chapter 2, which provided information about the nature of ASD. The aim of this chapter is to outline some management strategies that may help parents with their children's sensory issues at home, in the community, and in early childcare settings. It may be necessary for readers to refer back to Chapter 2 to revise definitions of terms used to describe sensory processing issues.

## HELPING PARENTS MANAGE SENSORY ISSUES

The sensory systems can have significant negative impacts on children's behavioural and emotional responses to everyday situations. Sensory problems have been found to be significant areas of concern for parents of children with AS and other ASDs (Smith-Myles *et al.*, 2000) when responding to the Sensory Profile (Dunn, 1999), a parent-report tool that focuses on children's responses to various types of sensory stimuli in everyday settings. Difficulties with discrimination of sensation (knowing its characteristics) are also common. For example, children may have difficulties with auditory discrimination that prevents them from focusing on what is necessary (such as a parent's instruction to do something). This can occur at home when a parent's instruction competes with background noise, such as the television or another conversation happening at the same time. They may also have difficulty discriminating tactile qualities (e.g., texture) and may be overly responsive to differences in texture. One of the most important aspects of managing sensory issues is to help parents to better appreciate and understand the impact of various sensations and sensory aspects of the environment on their individual child within his or her family context. A recent finding of atypical sensory processing in 94 per cent of adults with ASD suggests that these sensory issues can persist well into adulthood (Crane, Goddard, and Pring, 2009).

Given that these issues are likely to continue into adulthood regardless of our interventions, it is important that parents and carers initially, and children as they become older, understand their sensory processing needs and their impact on daily life. As Dunn (2001) stated, 'Sensory processing patterns are reflections of who we are: These are not a pathology that needs fixing' (p. 617). As an aspect of 'who we are' they need to be appreciated and understood. Various authors have found that parents of children with sensory processing issues value information that leads to better understanding of their children's behaviour (Cohn, Miller, and Tickle-Degnen, 2000; Dunstan and Griffith, 2008). In order to do this, professionals may utilise a range of information exchange strategies (see Chapter 5) such as information booklets, individual discussions, group discussions, and web resources to provide parents with information about the body's major sensory systems (visual, auditory, tactile, gustatory, olfactory, vestibular, kinaesthetic), and how children with ASD might be more or less sensitive to these sensations. See Chapter 2 for a more in-depth discussion of sensory systems and the impact of ASD.

Occupational therapists understand children as individuals at the body structure/functions level in terms of sensory, motor, cognitive/ perceptual, and affective functioning. They know about children's activities and their development in the areas of play, self-care, school work, and the importance of transitions in light of families' daily routines. They also have expertise in understanding the impact of the environment (both sensory and physical) on children's performance, as well as how to modify, adapt, alter, and adjust the environment to support the child's optimal functioning. Hence if you have an occupational therapist in your team or have access to one, he or she is likely to be able to assist you to support parents in this area.

## Provision of Specific Sensory Input

Sometimes specific sensory input can be provided to children with the aim of helping regulation of the central nervous system. Although provision of some calming (e.g., deep touch or pressure) or alerting sensory input (e.g., jumping on a trampoline or scooter boarding into pillows) may have a short-term impact on behaviour or task engagement, to date there is little evidence to support interventions that claim to have a long-term impact on the way the nervous system processes sensory stimuli (Rodger *et al.*, 2010).

The Wilbarger Deep Pressure and Proprioceptive Technique (Wilbarger and Wilbarger, 2002), which requires a rigorous programme of brushing the child's body during the day, using a surgical brush, along with a sensory diet (sensory activities interspersed throughout the day) aims to change the way the central nervous system processes sensory input. Segal and Beyer (2006) found children's responses and parents' perceptions of the effectiveness of the programme to be highly variable. Some families have reported that intensive sensory programmes (many of which have frequent and time-specific schedules) can be overly burdensome, while others have concerns about the social stigma associated with sensory approaches used in school or community settings, since this adds to the perception that these children are different (Segal and Beyer, 2006). Intensive sensory programmes currently lack strong empirical support (Rodger *et al.*, 2010). The approach outlined in Chapter 10 to guide the selection of interventions is recommended if this type of programme is considered by parents.

Therapies relying on sound as the intervention modality, such as Auditory Integration Training® and Therapeutic Listening® are sometimes advocated by professionals, despite being insufficiently supported by evidence (American Speech and Hearing Association, 2004; National Autism Centre, 2009). Although a recent study on Therapeutic Listening® (Hall and Case-Smith, 2007) reported some positive findings, the study was limited by small sample size, lack of a control group, and lack of independent evaluation. Hence parents and professionals need to be aware of the evidence surrounding such programmes before recommending or embarking on these with families (see Chapter 10). Issues such as the time, resources, and cost involved, and the sustainability of managing a structured timetable of regular intervention, need to be carefully considered, especially if these further limit children's participation in everyday home and kindergarten activities. Professionals can assist children and their families to problem-solve and learn a range of self-management strategies to address a range of issues including sensory overload, transitions between tasks, the establishment of functional routines, and self-regulation of behaviour. Long-term it is thought that development of self-regulation strategies is more appropriate to assist with the management of sensory issues than provision of direct sensory input to alter the child's nervous system. The following section provides suggestions to assist parents manage some sensory issues commonly experienced at home and in the community (e.g., playground and shops).

## MANAGING THE SENSORY ENVIRONMENT AT HOME AND IN THE COMMUNITY

Many autobiographical accounts (e.g., Temple Grandin, 1995) and some preliminary evidence suggest that people with ASD find it easier to perform daily life tasks in environments that are less challenging from a sensory perspective. Parents may observe aspects of the environment that lead to difficulties such as avoidance, non-compliance, overt distress, or challenging behaviour. Parents may note (1) who is present at the time and (2) the features of the environment (visual, noise/sounds, smell, time of day) that cause their child distress, and determine whether there are any emergent or repeated patterns in relation to this behaviour or distress (Rodger and Ziviani, 2011). For example, parents often comment that loud noises, such as vacuum cleaners or mowers at home, or the noise of the hand dryer in public toilets, upset their child. It might therefore be possible to plan for house cleaning or gardening to occur when the child with ASD is at kindergarten/childcare or visiting grandparents, and toilet stops might need to be arranged beforehand. Other overwhelming sensory experiences at shops include odours such as intense chemical smells outside hair and beauty salons, or strong smells such as popcorn cooking.

While one option is to avoid environments that are overwhelming, this is not always possible, so the next best option is to prepare the child for what to expect when visiting the environment, and to help them with a coping strategy or to develop solutions (e.g., use of an iPod™ with familiar music to screen out noise while out shopping). Cognitive self-regulation programmes such as 'sensory stories' (Marr *et al.*, 2007) enable development of sensory strategies by children with ASD. Sensory stories can help prepare children for what they might experience, and to learn how to regulate or modulate their own sensory systems. This is important in terms of developing long-term self-management strategies likely to be required throughout their lives.

## Using Sensory Stories

Sensory stories might be helpful for children who are either under- or over-responsive to specific sensory stimuli, leading to non-functional routines and negative behaviours. Individual coping or self-regulatory strategies that are effective for the child can be incorporated into the story so that it is customised for the child and his or her preferences (Marr and Nackley, 2006). As with standard Social Stories™ (Gray, 2000), the sensory story is read to the child, or the child reads it for him or herself prior to the experience that challenges the sensory systems being encountered.

Sensory stories have a similar sentence structure and story style to Social Stories™, and are read frequently to prepare the child for challenging sensory situations. In using sensory stories, the aim is to identify contextual factors that impede the child's participation, to teach children to utilise self-directed sensory strategies, and to establish performance patterns or habits that foster participation.

There are two key types of sensory stories, namely those that employ *inhibitory sensory input* (such as using deep pressure or firm touch), and those that aim to *minimise sensory input* from the environment (such as using headphones to drown out other disturbing noises).

There are a number of components to a sensory story (Marr and Nackley, 2006):

1. introduction to the targeted experience

2. identification of the potential negative sensory input during that experience

3. acknowledgement that the experience can be unpleasant or uncomfortable

4. strategies that can prepare the child for the experience

5. outlining the steps of the experience and the strategies to be used during the experience

6. strategies at the conclusion of the experience

7. ending the story on a positive note.

A series of single case studies (Marr, Gal, and Nackley, 2006; Marr *et al.*, 2007; Sherick, 2004; Shepard, Knoop, and Telarole, 2008) have demonstrated positive outcomes for children with ASD using sensory stories related to a range of self-care routines. Some of the positive outcomes from these studies have included: no longer tantrums at bedtime; sleeps better; trying new foods; staying calm for the shower from the first day; wants to brush teeth more; asking parent to wash hair (previously would hit and scream); willing to have nails cut with therapist; and changing into pyjamas more easily.

It is suggested that sensory stories might be more appropriate than Social Stories™ if:

1. the child has a sensory processing challenge that influences activities and participation

2. the activity in question has challenging sensory features that need to be addressed

3. challenging behaviours are associated with the activity and these have a sensory basis

4. sensory features of the environment can be modified to optimise the child's participation, and the child needs to learn some sensory strategies to cope better.

(Marr and Nackley, 2010)

## Managing Sensory Issues within Self-care Routines

Many aspects of self-care are influenced by symptoms experienced by children on the autism spectrum. Issues with sensory over- and under-responsivity may influence such things as bathing and nail cutting, and difficulties with performing self-care tasks are frequently reported and prioritised by parents as goals for intervention (Rodger, Keen, and Braithwaite, 2004). At home sensory stories can be used for sensory challenges within self-care routines, such as bathing, combing hair, cleaning ears, eating, getting dressed, nail care, showering, sleeping, brushing teeth, and washing hair (Marr and Nackley, 2006).

*Sleeping*

Many children with ASD have high rates of sleep problems; approximately two-thirds of children with ASD are estimated to exhibit sleep difficulties at some point during childhood (Richdale and Schreck, 2009). These difficulties may be related to difficulties with transitions, an overly rigid bedtime routine which does not work when one component is missing, dysfunctional routines and rituals, inability to shut out distracting sensory stimuli (e.g., the noise of the traffic outside, the light coming through the doorway), difficulties with communication, making it impossible to communicate fears, feelings, and sensory discomfort relating to falling asleep. However, sleep difficulties may also stem directly from sensory issues. As in the case of many young children, this can be related to fear of the dark, fear of being alone, having difficulty with self-calming and modulation to enable rest, the texture of bedlinen and pyjamas, and not feeling secure in bed.

Children with ASD are likely to benefit from a regular bedtime routine that incorporates calming activities. Because events such as brushing teeth can be stressful, it is often useful to complete this straight after dinner rather than wait until just before bedtime. Routines before bed are important. For example: story time while lying or sitting on the bed, lights off and night light on, restful music or taped story, kiss goodnight, then door closed. The nature of the routine will vary in different families, depending on other family members and their routines and children's preferences. Some children need to be tucked into bed snugly or to have pillows placed so that they feel secure in bed, and others have preference for certain pyjamas and types of bedding (e.g., soft flannelette vs. cotton sheets, woollen blankets vs. comforters or duvets). Attention to these sensory features of bedlinen, clothes for bed, and the environment (e.g., bed position, room lighting, gentle music or taped story) can make the transition to sleep easier.

Some children are exceptionally sensitive to light, so sleeping when there is even a very dim light on could be very difficult for them. Putting up thick, light-blocking curtains might assist. Similarly, some parents have found that their children can be woken by very slight sounds at night. Sometimes even a computer left on standby can be enough to disrupt sleep. Earplugs, or music playing on headphones, could also be used to block out noise for those children who are comfortable with wearing these. Touch sensitivity is extremely common in ASD. Some children may experience certain types of touch as physical pain. Labels on bedclothes and different materials can also be uncomfortable. Attention to nightwear can help (National Autistic Society, 2010a).

Children with ASD may not be able to articulate their need to unwind and relax, and may feel more anxious and confused around bedtime. Relaxation techniques that include attention to sensory experiences can be helpful.

- Massage; direct skin contact can be uncomfortable for some children with ASD, but for some a gentle foot, hand, or scalp massage in the right environment might help the child to calm down before going to bed.

- Introducing an hour's quiet time before the child's bedtime can help the whole household settle and relax. Parents may consider switching off the television or computer and instituting a bedtime story reading routine.

- Physically exhausting children in the afternoon is a good way of ensuring that they sleep. Many children with ASD enjoy rough-and-tumble play, and although this may seem to be the opposite of the points made above regarding quiet time at the end of the day, it might help some children.

- Some parents have found formal relaxation aids, such as music and reduced lighting (e.g., a lava lamp) in the bedroom can be helpful.

Considerations for developing a bedtime routine include asking parents:

- Is it possible to eat dinner at the same time each night?

- Does this happen already?

189

- Is this quite late in the evening or quite early?

- Is it possible for the child with ASD to have a bath at the same time each night?

- Is there anything about the child's routine that can only be done in your home?

If the routine needs to be altered, it can then be explained visually (see information on visual schedules in Chapter 7). It may be that the timetable needs to be more detailed, so that the child is told exactly what to do when going to bed – for instance, draw the curtains, get into bed, turn light off, lie down, pull cover up. It may also be worth setting aside time to prepare for the next day in the routine. This could include getting the schoolbag ready or making a list or timetable of things that need to be done the next day (National Autistic Society 2010a).

## *Eating*

The types of problems related to eating behaviour for children with ASD include restrictive eating, selective or picky eating, food refusal, and food neophobia (i.e., unwillingness to try new foods; Martins and Young, 2008; Williams, Gibbons, and Schreck, 2005). The factors related to these eating problems are difficult to define, but are multifactorial, including physiological and behavioural factors (Schlundt, 1995). As anecdotally stated in most studies, sensory preferences play a dominant role in influencing eating patterns among children with ASD (Bogdashina, 2003), especially for those who have oral and/or olfactory hypersensitivity (Bennetto, Kuschner, and Hyman, 2007; Blakemore *et al.*, 2006). Taste, colour, texture, and the appearance of foods might affect the food acceptance of children with ASD (Johnson *et al.*, 2008; Schreck and Williams, 2006; Williams, Dalrymple, and Neal, 2000). In addition, some researchers have even found that the brands and packaging of foods could influence the dietary intake of children with ASD (Cornish, 1998). Restrictive, repetitive, and stereotyped behaviours among children with ASD might also be one cause for their narrow selection of food items (Ozonoff, South, and Miller, 2000). This is because children with ASD are likely to insist on sameness with respect to those foods eaten (Delfos, 2005; Ritvo, 2006). Lack of variety in foods, rigidity about only eating specific foods presented in certain ways (e.g., toast or bread cut in fingers, not triangles, or bananas peeled vs. unpeeled), and issues managing foods with different textures, particularly those that require chewing, are very common in children with ASD. Some children will eat only white foods (e.g., bread, popcorn, marshmallows, mashed potato, and puffed rice cereal), and no fruit and vegetables, resulting in a diet that is likely to lack nutritional value. Parents are often exasperated by children's restricted intake (Herndon *et al.*, 2009; Schmitt, Heiss, and Campbell, 2008). The lack of variety and unwillingness to try new foods may be a result of oral tactile over-responsivity and/or cognitive rigidity, which leads to specific routines being set up with respect to what is eaten. Difficult behaviour at mealtimes may occur for a range of reasons, which are summarised in Box 9.1.

## Box 9.1 Possible reasons for eating difficulties at mealtimes

- Not wanting to sit for meals (no social eating experiences).

- Sniffing and inspecting food (their own and others').

- Taking food from others' plates.

- Gorging food, hoarding food in their mouth.

- Gagging on food or vomiting food they don't like.

- Obsessive placing of food on their plates (e.g., no different types of food touching).

- Specific cutlery, crockery or position at the table.

- Eating only using fingers.

- Refusal of new foods.

*Adapted from Tonge and Brereton, 2010.*

Introducing new foods often requires considerable negotiation and rewards. For instance, giving a child her favourite foods only after something new has been tasted is a tactic that works for many families. Many parents of children with ASD have their children on vitamin/mineral supplements and sometimes protein-based drinks to ensure they have sufficient nutritional intake. Consultation with family doctors and dieticians is useful for children with very restricted intakes (Schmitt *et al.*, 2008). Many children show increased willingness to try new foods as they get older. However, many children with ASD still have strong food preferences related to food colours and textures, which persist into adolescence and beyond. Box 9.2 summarises ideas that may be helpful to address fussy eating habits and food refusal.

### Box 9.2 Suggestions for food refusal and fussy eating

- Limit food/drink which is calorie empty or nutritionally unhealthy (junk food).

- Offer appropriate serving sizes (not too much on the plate).

- Make food attractive – try different shapes and colours (e.g., cut bread into TellyTubby™ or Thomas the Tank Engine™ shapes).

- Offer new foods early in the day (not when child is tired or already full).

- Offer different/new foods when child is hungry/thirsty.

- Involve child in food preparation if possible.

- Grind vitamin and calcium supplements finely then add to food (e.g., can mix into peanut butter, jam, vegemite, or marmite without altering the taste).

- Put vegetables in the blender and add them to preferred foods (e.g. spaghetti Bolognese) – they disappear and do not change the texture of the food you add them to.

- Have a preferred toy at hand so that the child plays with this rather than the food.

- If the child persists in wanting to drink formula or milk, he or she will usually grow out of this habit, and in the meantime it remains an excellent food source (but remember that milk/formula is just a small component of a balanced diet and is not sufficient on its own for a growing child).

*Adapted from Tonge and Brereton, 2010.*

Consultation with occupational therapists or speech pathologists may be required if children experience extreme oversensitivity with gagging, spitting, and vomiting on introduction of new foods.

## Grooming and Hygiene

Grooming (e.g., cutting nails, washing and cutting hair, and brushing teeth) may be problematic in children with ASD due to unpleasant sensory experiences related to these activities. While this sometimes improves with age, they can be problematic for some years. Finding a sympathetic hairdresser who is willing to take time, taking little trips to the hairdresser to desensitise the child to the experience (e.g., just going and sitting on the chair or mother's lap and tolerating having the cape put around the neck), and easy-to-manage hairstyles, can be helpful (Rodger and Ziviani, 2011).

Difficulties with brushing teeth and nail cutting are often caused by sensory over-responsivity. Experimenting with regular vs. electric toothbrushes, types and tastes of toothpaste, applying toothpaste on an adult finger and placing it in the mouth over gums and teeth as a form of desensitisation are sometimes helpful. As stated earlier, family routines where, for example, all children have the same teeth brushing time and can watch other siblings, can help. Use of visual symbols or pictures and Social Stories™ that illustrate a sequence of dinner, then brushing teeth, then something fun like story time, can help prepare children for the transition from one task to another.

## Bathing and Washing

While many typically developing children find bathing fun and relaxing, children with ASD can find this a stressful time. There are many sensory experiences that they have to deal with when taking a bath. For example, changes of temperature when undressing, and getting in and out of the water; water dripping into the eyes during hair washing; smell of soap and shampoo, and texture of towels when drying. It is important to observe the child in detail and analyse which part of the bath process is making him or her uncomfortable. If the child is unsettled during the drying process, experimenting with towels of different textures and sticking to the one that the child likes best may be helpful. Children who are sensitive to smell may prefer to use soap and shampoo that are fragrance-free.

Some other tips for managing bathing and hair washing include the following.

- Recognise the child's sensory sensitivities, such as for loud noises. Do not let the water go down the plug-hole (or flush the toilet) until the child has left the room; adjust the temperature in the bathroom so that there is not a stark contrast between warm water in the bath and cold air in the bathroom; have a bath instead of a shower if the physical sensation of shower water on the skin is uncomfortable.

- Use of Social Stories™ about where the water goes down the plug-hole, or why it makes a noise, can also be helpful. Social Stories™ can also be useful for explaining why people have baths or explaining other social aspects of behaviour (e.g., modesty/privacy or transitions between activities).

- Use of a shield during hair-washing to keep water from running down the child's face is one example of the kind of problem-solving approach needed.

### Toileting

Toileting seems to be an area of difficulty for many young children with ASD for a myriad of reasons, including sensory issues. For some children, sitting on the toilet seems insecure, with legs dangling in the air. Others are fearful of the loud noise of the toilet flushing, or the noise of the bowel movement hitting the water (Rodger and Ziviani, 2011).

Some children with ASD can find bowel movements very frightening and not understand what is happening. When teaching bowel control, sometimes sitting on the toilet with the nappy on but with a hole cut in the bottom can help. Then slowly cut away the nappy each time until the child is able to go without the nappy at all. This feeling of security around their waist will, in turn, enable them to feel relaxed enough to poo on the toilet. Others appear to have difficulty with the control and planning of the breathing and pushing actions required.

Many behavioural toileting programmes exist which rely on rewards and consequences, and these may be helpful. Once again, visual picture stories of the toileting process, such as pants down, sit on toilet, feet on stool or floor, pushing, wiping, flushing, pants up, washing hands, can be of assistance. Ensuring the child has a step-up stool to place feet on, so that they are not dangling in the air but stable, can help the child feel more secure. Wheeler (2004) provides a comprehensive guide with toilet training tips for parents of children with ASD, and a myriad of case examples.

It is important to note that not all toileting issues are sensory in nature, and a systematic approach to toilet training that draws on strategies that have been found to be effective is important. These strategies are based on behavioural principles that we described in Chapter 1 and include the following:

1. baseline monitoring to identify patterns of urination

2. toilet visits based on that pattern or a predetermined schedule

3. increased fluid intake to increase frequency of urination and practice

4. use of prompts to request toileting, using pictures, language, or signs

5. fading of prompts over time

6. reinforcement for appropriate toileting behaviours.

(Ellis, 1963)

Another useful strategy that can be used is video modelling. Keen, Brannigan, and Cuskelly (2007) assessed the effectiveness of an animated toilet training video with five young boys with ASD. These children had proved to be particularly resistant to toilet training efforts, and all previous attempts at toilet training had been unsuccessful. It was thought that the inclusion of visual materials (i.e., a toilet training video), in conjunction with the usual approaches to toileting outlined by Ellis (1963), would assist the children to learn because of the visual processing strengths of children with ASD (Quill, 1997). The video used in the study ('Tom's Toilet Triumph') was developed by the Intellectual Disability Services Council in South Australia in association with Minda Incorporated (2001).[1]

---

1   This can be purchased at the following url: http://shop.service.sa.gov.au/site/page.cfm?content=search_results.cfm&mode=single&product_id=5335

The video featured animated characters (there is a male and female version) following the sequence of steps involved in toileting, accompanied by simple verbal instructions. A set of picture cue cards was also used. The researchers found that when usual teaching strategies were used in conjunction with the toileting video, the children were able to learn more of the steps involved in toileting. Some of the children also used the toilet more frequently, even though they were not fully toilet trained by the end of the study. Not all the children showed sustained improvement in their toileting but the video did assist some of these boys who were incontinent at the start of the study.

Toilet training requires effective habit training for children who may lack awareness, not understand the significance or meaning associated with physical sensations, be limited by decreased or absent physical sensations, or may have tried toilet training unsuccessfully before. Taking the child to the toilet at set times throughout the day, and requesting the parent to keep a chart of times each day and successes, is advised. It is important to help the child feel relaxed enough while sitting on the toilet to open their bladder and bowels. Having the tap running in the background can assist the child to wee, and blowing bubbles or blowing up a balloon can help the child to open the bowel. Sometimes having a toy to handle or a book to read can be useful, both to keep your child on the toilet and to relax him or her. Your child should be able to sit comfortably on the toilet with hips and knees flexed at a 90-degree angle and with feet flat on a secure object. Children who lack awareness or sensation may have to be taught a strategy like counting to ten before getting off the toilet in order to avoid accidentally weeing on the floor (National Autistic Society, 2010b).

The bathroom needs to be a calm, relaxing, structured environment in order to encourage independence and success with the complete toileting routine. Structuring the bathroom and removing all distractions can help your child understand expectations and reduce distractions. Making the bathroom as comfortable as possible, adding foot supports, side rails, reduced lighting, switching off the fan, and having a smaller toilet seat, can all help reduce anxieties and sensory over-responsiveness. Helping parents to be aware of (and avoid) strongly scented hand soap or liquid wash, scented toilet paper, and the sound of an extraction fan that comes on automatically with the light, can all assist in providing a bathroom environment that does not overload the child's senses (National Autistic Society, 2010b).

*Dressing*

Not all children with ASD have difficulty with the task of dressing in itself. However, some children do have difficulty with planning the movements and sequence of dressing. They may be assisted by visual schedules. For some children, issues related to the textures of clothes (e.g., having preferences for certain soft, comfortable shirts that must be laundered each night to be ready for the next day; disliking the feel of labels sewn into seams or at the neck) can influence what is worn and when. Some children seem to be very sensitive to having any clothes on their body, and remove their clothing at home as soon as they can do so. In winter, some children with ASD are known to wear summer-weight clothes and appear not to feel the cold. This can cause tantrums when parents want to dress them more warmly for outings. Many do not tolerate wool or scratchy materials close to their skin, preferring fleece or other soft fabrics. Hats, gloves, scarves and heavy coats can feel intolerable to some children. Fortunately there is a considerable variety of warm, lightweight fabrics available. Rather than attempting to desensitise the child to particular fabrics, it is better to work with clothes that match their sensory preferences and choices (within reason). Children who are irritated by seams in the socks can wear their socks inside-out. Sensory stories may be written to reinforce the type of clothing appropriate for particular seasonal or climate conditions.

## MANAGING THE SENSORY ASPECTS OF PLAY

The picture of play in ASD is complicated by the presence of multiple challenges, as described in Chapter 2 and Chapter 8. Sensory sensitivities, poor motor planning, and difficulties with social interaction or cognition can all interfere with the development of play and playfulness. For instance, sensory issues can impact on the types of play chosen (e.g., children might avoid certain textures like play dough, glue, sand, and wet grass). Figures 9.1–9.5 illustrate a range of messy play experiences that most young children readily engage in at home and at kindergarten, but which might be challenging for children with ASD if they have sensory sensitivities.

Cognitive inflexibility may lead to the use of repetitive, ritualistic play routines. It may also interfere with the development of pretend play. Lack of problem-solving and social skills can cause frustration during group play. Lack of imagination can lead to repetitive play, and no observable pretend or symbolic play. Motor planning and co-ordination difficulties can impact on the quality of movements in gross motor play and precision in fine motor play. Social interaction difficulties and delayed communication can impact the development of friendships during play, leading to playing alone. In turn, playing alone can result in less experience with social play, giving and taking, conversations, and development of interactive play scripts (Rodger and Ziviani, 2011).

Children with ASD need opportunities to play in a variety of environments with different sensory properties, such as sandpits, water play, rolling and tumbling on grass, playgrounds with wooden apparatus, plastic apparatus, tyres, swings, ropes, and climbing frames. Sometimes this requires a gradual introduction to new sensory experiences and some desensitisation such as sitting on the edge of the sandpit playing with sand running through their fingers before sitting in the sandpit itself.

Children who are overwhelmed by noisy playgrounds may benefit from going to playgrounds initially at less busy times, so that they are not so overwhelmed by the shrieks, chatter, and laughter of other children, as well as having other children in close physical contact, scrambling up and down the apparatus or sliding down the slide close behind them. This lets parents help children to master the play equipment, novel situations, and movement sensations on new apparatus, before addressing the sensory aspects of noise and close proximity to other children at busier times.

*Figure 9.1 Playing with messy dough*     *Figure 9.2 Cooking as messy play*

*Figure 9.3 Messy play in dirt with pretend cooking set*

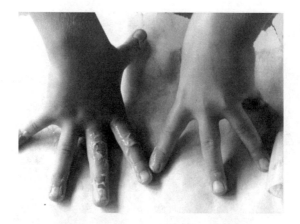

*Figure 9.4 Playing with finger paint*

*Figure 9.5 Gardening as messy play*

## TROUBLESHOOTING SENSORY ISSUES WITHIN CHILDCARE ENVIRONMENTS

Apart from the home environment, children with ASD often spend a large amount of time in childcare environments. In this section, childcare environments include kindergartens, preschools, and day-care centres. Parents may be at a loss in terms of what to do to address the child's sensory issues within these childcare environments as they are not physically present to observe what actually occurs. It can be frustrating for them to hear the teachers' concerns about their child's behaviour, which may not be the same as behaviours observed by the parents at home. For example, one parent reported that 'the teacher complains that my son hums constantly at childcare, but he doesn't do that at home'. Such concerns may lead to miscommunication between the teachers and parents, as well as mistrust regarding how the teachers are managing the child. The following section provides information that can help parents to troubleshoot sensory issues that may arise in childcare environments with the child's teachers or aides. It will begin with considerations when selecting a childcare centre.

## Selecting the Right Childcare Environment

Apart from logistical considerations such as distance from home and costs, there are other factors to consider when selecting a childcare centre. Sensory difficulties can be impacted by a range of variables, such as the amount of structure present, methods of instructional delivery, changes in routine, adult personalities involved, and the amount of rest (Smith-Myles *et al.*, 2000). When possible, it is ideal for parents to choose a childcare centre that is situated at a quiet location (e.g., away from a busy road, flight paths). This helps prevent children with ASD who have auditory hypersensitivity from being constantly distracted by noise, and may facilitate restful naptime and more settled behaviour.

A childcare centre that has separate classrooms or discrete corners or areas is also likely to be less noisy and overwhelming than one with an open plan concept. When children with ASD fail to filter out background noises, they will have difficulty following instructions and may be viewed as uncooperative (Lim and Chen, 2010). Children with ASD thrive on routine and learn better in a stable, predictable environment. Therefore, a childcare centre that has a more structured and organised programme may be more suitable for the child with ASD compared to a centre that is focused more on self-directed learning and tends to be less structured. More will be discussed in relation to routines in a later section of this chapter (see 'Transitions', pages 204–205). Childcare centres that use visual supports and schedules to enhance instructional delivery are also recommended.

## Sensory Issues within the Childcare Environment

Despite efforts to select the most ideal childcare, children with ASD can still experience various challenges within the childcare environment. While parents do not have any absolute control over the sensory aspects of childcare environments, they have a wealth of information about their child and how he or she responds to a range of sensory experiences. This information can be very useful for early childhood teachers/childcare workers to assist them with managing the child with ASD at kindergarten/childcare and minimising potential distress. The child's reaction of being overwhelmed by sensory experiences may sometimes be similar at home and at early childcare environments. In situations where the child with ASD is universally overwhelmed and avoids sensation across contexts (e.g., avoids sticky fingers), strategies that have been trialled successfully at home can also be implemented within the childcare environment.

However, recent research has suggested the home and school contexts also reflect sensory circumstances that are unique to each environment (Brown and Dunn, 2010). Therefore, parents and teachers may report different sensory-related behaviours presented by the child. For example, in a quiet family the parents may not have observed many reactions from the child to auditory stimuli, as compared to the teacher who observes him or her in a noisy classroom environment. Hence, it is necessary for professionals to use contextually relevant assessments to identify the presence of sensory processing difficulties. The *Sensory Profile School Companion* (commonly referred to as the *School Companion*; Dunn, 2006) was developed for children aged 3 to 11 years to enable the teacher to report on the child's responses to daily sensory experiences in the classroom. To gain a comprehensive view of the child's sensory processing, occupational therapists and other professionals may use these tools. By doing so, the professional can assist the parent in determining which situations are most overwhelming for a child and planning for more effective interventions.

As children with ASD are highly influenced by the environment, it is desirable to observe their behaviour in the natural setting (Tomchek and Case-Smith, 2009). Assessment of this allows for analysis of the child's typical behaviour and performance in functional everyday activities that are a familiar part of his or her daily routine (Tomchek and Case-Smith, 2009).

One tool that can be used to obtain useful information about the child's sensory processing and its impact on a child's ability to perform expected activities in the classroom is *Questions to Guide Classroom Observation* (Kienz and Miller, 1999). It contains a series of 38 questions that guide professionals in observing the child within the classroom setting. These questions address the following areas: child; task; physical environment; social context; cultural context. This observational assessment assists the professional in analysing the child's behaviour, the tasks in which he or she performs, and the environment (Smith-Myles *et al.*, 2000). This tool is commonly used alongside other formal or informal measures.

The following section helps professionals to help parents to work with teachers, or professionals to work directly with teachers, to troubleshoot sensory issues that may occur during different parts of the day in childcare environments.

*Indoor Time*

In childcare environments, children spend some of their day indoors in the classroom and other parts of the day outdoors, which requires the child to transition between environments. There are various activities that take place within the classroom that the child with ASD may consider to be noisy. This includes circle time where children sit and sing together, as well as activity times where children go to different stations of their choice and engage in free play. Although most people find children's singing delightful, it is not uncommon for the child with ASD to find the music and singing loud, noisy, and consequently overwhelming (especially if certain instruments such as maracas or bells or tambourines are used). As a result, the child may engage in behaviours that appear to be uncooperative (e.g., cover ears, hum loudly) or disruptive (e.g., cry, shout). This can also happen during free play where children are playing and talking loudly within the enclosed space. Teachers may find it peculiar that, whereas most typically developing children enjoy these occasions, the child with ASD can have difficulty coping. Therefore, it is important to explain to teachers the different sensory processing difficulties experienced by the child with ASD so that they can find ways of helping the child cope.

There are various strategies that can be explored with regards to noisy indoor environments. One option is to explore the use of headphones or earplugs so that the noise is less overwhelming. Another option is to set up a cubby house at the back of the classroom – an area with dimmer lights and cushions, into which the child can retreat and rest for a while when overwhelmed, and maybe listen to calming music through headphones while resting on a beanbag cushion. During music time, the teacher can gradually increase the sound level by getting the children to begin by singing softly to slow, gentle music, before moving on to louder, fast tempo singing. Children may be slowly introduced to loud instruments such as the tambourine. For example, children with ASD often manage better when they are in control of the instrument and volume. They may, however, need to be systematically introduced to the tambourine at a time when other children are not present, and be brought gradually into a music group with a range of instruments.

## Transitions

Children with ASD have difficulty coping with things that are new and unpredictable, and so changes to activities or routines can create confusion and anxiety (Dodd, 2005). The transition from one activity to another tends also to be the time when the child with ASD encounters new or different sensory experiences. One example is when the noise level increases in the classroom as all children pack up their toys and get ready for outdoor play. Another example is when the child moves on from drawing to sandpit play, where he or she comes into contact with a new texture. Therefore, transitions can be a stressful time for children with ASD.

As mentioned earlier in this chapter, when selecting a childcare centre for the child with ASD, it is recommended to choose one that has a routine that is stable and predictable. Establishing a routine helps foster a feeling of independence and security (Dodd, 2005). A sense of security leads to a decrease in stress and anxiety, which helps the individual to accept minor change (Dodd, 2005). When children with ASD feel secure, they are less likely to become overwhelmed by sensory experiences. Routine helps them learn to predict the new or different sensory experiences that will occur with the transition, and to become more prepared for them. For example, the child may learn to cover his or her ears or put on headphones as the classroom becomes noisier during the transition period.

Routines should be presented visually, as this is the format that is most easily understood by the child with ASD, and to minimise anxiety for the child when change occurs, the visual routines and sequences can be modified to reflect the change. Letting the child anticipate the change ahead of time provides the opportunity for him or her to process the information and get ready for the change. Using an egg timer plus a visual aid to give advance notice that a change will occur in two minutes can assist the child in learning about the timeframes for changes.

During transitions children often wait in line for their turn, to go inside or outside. For instance, they may be waiting in line to move from indoors to outdoors, or for a turn to wash their hands before snack time. As young children wait in line, they can stand very close to one another and are likely to bump into each other. A child with ASD who is tactile defensive may not tolerate the close contact with other children, and may get upset when touched unexpectedly by someone. One strategy to minimise this discomfort is to have the child stand either at the beginning or at the end of the line. Another strategy is to have the child hold the door open for the rest of the class by leaning his or her back against the door (Smith-Myles *et al.*, 2000).

### Outdoor Play

As children with ASD make the transition from a more structured indoor environment to outdoor play, they experience a different set of challenges. Children with ASD may have difficulty processing kinaesthetic information about movement, space, gravity, and balance (Dodd, 2005). Children who are hypersensitive tend to be easily overwhelmed by unpredictable movements. They appear to be in distress when their feet leave the ground and may be worried about falling. They may be hesitant to access playground equipment such as swings and slides (Smith-Myles *et al.*, 2000). With poor motor planning, some children appear physically clumsy, and may appear to be at a loss as to what to do in the playground (Trecker and Miller-Kuhaneck, 2004). Teachers can encourage a child to try different playground equipment by providing supervised practice and allowing the child to direct the movement to the degree that he or she tolerates

– for example, controlling how high to pump the swing (by doing this himself, or learning a phrase like 'enough swing' to indicate the height that she is comfortable with) rather than the teacher pushing the child (in which case he or she has no control over the height; see Chapter 8).

Children with ASD who are hyposensitive may actively seek intense sensory experiences by spinning, jumping, and crashing to stimulate their sense of movement (Dodd, 2005). During outdoor play these children can appear to be taking excessive risks and playing 'dangerously'. They are constantly on the go, and some will seek opportunities to fall without regard for personal safety (e.g., climb up a slide and jump down). Quite commonly children who are hyposensitive have high pain tolerance (Mailloux and Roley, 2004). As a result they may continue to hurt themselves without learning from the feedback received from injuries associated with previous falls. These children have difficulty registering the qualities of movement and require intensive supervision to prevent them from hurting themselves. Teachers who do not understand these sensory issues may want to limit or restrict the child at outdoor play. However, these hyposensitive children often crave excessive movement in order to stay alert and organised (Dodd, 2005). Instead of limiting their movement, teachers can provide safe challenges for them during outdoor play. They can let a child participate in organised gross motor activities, such as an enclosed trampoline, wheelbarrow races, tug-of-war, or plan for obstacle courses that include jumping, pushing, pulling, and hanging by the hands (Smith-Myles et al., 2000).

If a child with ASD appears to be unsettled or fussy after outdoor play, checking his or her footwear may be in order. During outdoor play it is easy for dirt or sand get into the shoes, but children with ASD may not tolerate sand or dirt in shoes and may react negatively, while having difficulty in expressing their discomfort. If so, it may be worth making it part of the routine, after outdoor play, to check shoes or washing hands and feet.

Children with ASD frequently need visual supports to assist with transitions, as well as settling time after outdoor play to enable them to regroup, calm down, and be ready for indoor play or story time.

## CONCLUSION

This chapter has described some of the sensory processing issues that are experienced by children with ASD. It has presented a number of assessment tools that can be used by professionals to determine a child's responses to sensory stimuli, both at home and in early childhood environments. It is important to analyse engagement and participation in everyday activities from a sensory processing perspective. Such evaluation provides parents and teachers with an understanding of the sensory and motor underpinnings of the child's choices and capabilities when participating in daily life.

Considering the child's sensory processing difficulties helps to reframe the interpretation of problematic behaviours and mannerisms, hence allowing effective management strategies to be generated. Sensory issues do not necessarily need a specific sensory solution, such as providing a particular type of sensory input. Changing the parameters of the task or activity, or features of the environment, can also help the child participate more easily.

This chapter has outlined some management strategies that may help parents with their children's sensory issues at home, in the community, and in early childcare settings. With suggestions about how to modify, adapt, alter, and adjust the environment, professionals can assist parents to support the child's optimal functioning. Through supportive, pertinent guidance, and suggestions of practical strategies for managing sensory issues, professionals can provide hope for an improved quality of life for children with ASD, as well as their families.

Chapter 10

# Early Intervention Options and Choices

## INTRODUCTION

A great deal of attention has been paid over the past 40 years to developing treatments and intervention practices that will lead to better behavioural and developmental outcomes for children with ASD. To this end there has been extensive research investigating some of these interventions to evaluate their efficacy. It is vital for us to know which practices are most effective, and which children are likely to benefit from particular intervention practices. Without this knowledge, we are at risk of losing valuable time on interventions that are not effective – or, even worse, on interventions that may be harmful or impede development.

Despite developments in treatment approaches, there has been a continued proliferation of controversial treatments whose proponents claim high rates of success, or even cure, in the absence of evidence. Anecdotal accounts from parents who have used these treatments may be offered as indicators of efficacy, and can be very persuasive to parents in search of help for their child. However, in order to test whether these interventions are truly effective, they must be exposed to well-structured research studies.

Parents and professionals face a complex challenge when trying to select evidence-based interventions for children with ASD. They may be well aware of the importance of selecting appropriate and evidence-based interventions, but how do they go about making these choices? How do they know which ones work best for particular children? Without evidence, there is no way of knowing whether an intervention or treatment approach will improve outcomes beyond developmental maturation that could normally be expected to occur over time in the absence of any ASD-specific intervention.

Research evaluating the efficacy of interventions has struggled to keep pace with the number of treatments available, and the speed at which they are introduced to the marketplace. The results of an internet survey of 552 parents of children with ASD conducted by Green and colleagues (2006) found that 108 different treatments were being used, or had been used in the past, by at least one parent. Parents also reported using, on average, seven different treatments at the time of the survey. The results of this study serve to illustrate the range of interventions available, and the challenges for parents when faced with so many different treatment options.

## TREATMENT OPTIONS

The research that has been undertaken on treatments and interventions for children with ASD requires close scrutiny to gain an understanding of the strength of scientific evidence associated with a variety of different intervention practices. This has been particularly challenging as new approaches continue to be presented which claim much but have not been fully researched, and where the research 'gold standard' of using randomised control led trials to evaluate existing interventions is extremely difficult to implement. These difficulties include the ethical and moral issues of allocating children to a non-treatment control group to provide comparison between the effects of receiving a particular intervention, and receiving no intervention. Large-scale studies comparing different intervention approaches are very complex, time-consuming, and costly, as researchers must ensure that interventions which are to be compared are implemented with fidelity, and that children receiving the interventions are matched on key criteria such as chronological and mental age, language, and symptom severity. The large number of intervention practices available and being accessed by families who frequently combine different interventions simultaneously further extends these challenges.

Where evidence does exist for certain intervention practices, the evidence may be limited to children who have certain characteristics.

These may include chronological and mental age, IQ, symptom severity, and language level. For example, a recent review of music interventions for children with ASD found that, with the exception of two adolescents, all the studies reviewed had involved children under the age of 12 years (Simpson and Keen, 2011). This has an impact on the generalisability of the study findings to children who fall outside this age range. While this review found some evidence that music may facilitate learning under particular circumstances, these findings can't be assumed to apply to adolescents or adults.

A number of articles recently published in peer reviewed journals have synthesised the available evidence on various intervention approaches. Odom and colleagues recently reviewed Comprehensive Treatment Models (CTMs) and Focused Intervention Practices (FIPs) for children with ASD (Odom *et al.*, 2010a; Odom, Collet-Klingenberg, Rogers, and Hatton, 2010b). CTMs are manualised programmes delivered in very prescribed ways with interventionists trained in the particular approach. They are designed in a comprehensive and holistic way to address the developmental and learning needs of children with ASD, and generally target the core impairments of ASD: socialisation, behaviour, and communication. Of the 30 CTMs reviewed by Odom and colleagues (2010a), most were considered to provide only weak evidence of efficacy.

FIPs are 'designed to produce specific behavioural or developmental outcomes for individual children with ASD' (Odom *et al.*, 2010a, p. 425). These practices include a range of ABA techniques that have an established history of use with people with developmental disabilities, including ASD. For example, task analysis, reinforcement, prompting, modelling, and shaping, are techniques that would be included here as focused intervention practices. None of these practices could be conceptualised as an intervention per se, but rather as building blocks that, when combined, may lead to better learning and behavioural outcomes.

It is not feasible in this chapter to review the range of individual treatment options that have been developed for children with ASD. What follows is a brief description of some of the better known approaches, and specific examples of these approaches that parents may come across as they face the difficult task of deciding which intervention they believe will be most appropriate for their child.

## Therapists

Given the diversity within the population of children diagnosed with ASD, and the nature of the core impairments associated with the disorder, a multidisciplinary approach to assessment and treatment is generally recommended. Professional groups including occupational therapists, speech pathologists, and psychologists are frequently called upon to provide unique perspectives on the child's learning, communication, play skills, and behaviour.

### Speech Language Therapy (SLT)

SLT is concerned with development and enhancement of communication skills, although professionals may also assist with related issues, such as eating. Treatment varies, depending on the child's developmental level, skills, and communication difficulties, which, in ASD, may range from an absence of speech to praxis issues (e.g., dyspraxia, a motor planning disorder that can affect oral development). SLT may therefore involve working on the mechanics of speech, the social meaning of language, the use of gesture, or other aspects of communication.

### Occupational Therapy (OT)

Occupational therapists are concerned with the relationship between the child (and his or her characteristics), the child's occupational roles (e.g., player, self-carer, student/learner), and various external or environmental factors. The main goal is to build on the child's strengths, minimise, overcome, or compensate for weaknesses, and improve the child's participation in life roles at home, school, and in the community. Children may be seen individually or in small groups, at a clinic, home, or in early childhood centres. Both occupational therapists and speech pathologists provide input to multidisciplinary teams in early intervention contexts to support children's development of communication, play, self-care, and social skills.

## Behavioural Approaches

In Chapter 1 we introduced ABA and discussed the fundamental concepts that underpin this approach. There are many treatments for ASD that are based on or draw from an ABA framework. Examples are given below of some primarily behaviourally-based programmes.

Many programmes for children with ASD are based on the principles of ABA but emphasise different techniques. These principles include the control or manipulation of antecedents and consequences to increase or decrease the occurrence of target behaviours. Programmes are generally highly structured, and techniques such as task analysis, prompting, chaining, and reinforcement are used to increase or decrease specific skills and behaviours that are targeted for intervention. In addition, behavioural approaches are data-driven. Data on the child's performance of a target behaviour or skill are gathered during training to provide information about the child's learning and progress toward goal attainment.

*Lovaas Programme*
Sometimes the term 'ABA' has been incorrectly used as synonymous with the Lovaas Programme, named after its founder Ivar Lovaas (Lovaas, 1987). This programme is, however, a particular application of ABA, drawing on the underlying principles to implement an intervention specifically designed for children with ASD. This particular programme is manualised and demands a high level of intensity (30–40 hours per week). It is delivered by individuals who have been trained and certified in the techniques, and is usually conducted in the child's home with parental support and involvement. The programme is highly structured, and involves one-on-one training. The unit of instruction for teaching selected behaviours or skills in this approach is the discrete trial. Each trial consists of gaining the child's attention, presenting a stimulus, response from the child, and feedback to the child following the response (Heflin and Alaimo, 2007). Following a brief interval during which the trainer records information about the child's performance, the trial is repeated. An intervention session consists of mass trials. This process of massed discrete trials is generally referred to as Discrete Trial Training (DTT).

*Pivotal Response Training (PRT)*
PRT is based on the concept that there are pivotal behaviours that affect a range of other behaviours. Proponents of this approach argue that the primary impairment in ASD is a qualitative impairment in social communication (Koegel *et al.*, 1999a; Koegel *et al.*, 1999b). The aim of PRT is to increase the child's motivation to engage in social

interactions by targeting communicative initiations, self-regulatory behaviour, and responses to interactions involving multiple cues. Improvements in these pivotal behaviours are believed to lead to improvement in related behaviours that are not directly targeted for intervention.

### Training and Education of Autistic and Related Communication Handicapped Children (TEACCH)

TEACCH is a special education programme based on 'structured teaching' (Schopler, Mesibov, and Hearsey, 1995). TEACCH classrooms are highly structured, with predictable routines and extensive use of visual supports. An organised and structured environment that incorporates visual supports is believed to play to the processing strengths of children with ASD. Furthermore, it is thought to reduce anxiety and stress that arise from having to manage environments that may be overstimulating and unpredictable.

### Picture Exchange Communication System (PECS)

PECS is a communication system involving the exchange of picture symbols with a partner (Bondy and Frost, 1994). It was originally developed for use with preschool-age children with ASD who had little or no functional speech. It has since been more widely used by children and adults with a variety of diagnoses who have difficulty acquiring speech (Bondy and Frost, 2009). Learning to use PECS involves a training protocol consisting of six phases:

1. exchange

2. distance and persistence

3. discrimination

4. building sentences

5. responding

6. commenting.

Children commence at the first phase, which teaches the basics of requesting.

## Developmental and Relationship-based Approaches

Developmental or relationship-based approaches emphasise the importance of being child-centred, following the child's lead, building on the child's interests and strengths, and using naturally-occurring situations as teaching contexts.

### Floortime (Developmental Individual Difference Relationship Model or DIR)

Developed by Stanley Greenspan in the 1980s (Greenspan and Wieder, 2000), Floortime focuses on enhancing emotional and intellectual development in six key areas:

1.  self-regulation

2.  intimacy

3.  two-way communication

4.  complex communication

5.  emotional ideas

6.  emotional thinking.

Floortime takes a very child-centred, developmental approach. Adults, particularly parents, use natural contexts (e.g., playing with the child on the floor) to follow the child's lead and make use of the child's interests to engage him or her in more complex interactions. The adults are guided by the child's developmental level, interests, and strengths to build social and emotional competence.

### Relationship Development Intervention (RDI)

RDI was developed by Steve Gutstein to provide parents with tools to remediate their child's deficits in the core social-emotional impairments in ASD (Gutstein and Whitney, 2002). It is primarily a developmental approach that involves systematically building motivation and teaching skills, using the child's current developmental level as a starting point for intervention.

## Hanen 'More Than Words'

'More Than Words' is a programme developed by the Hanen Centre, a government-funded agency in Canada. The programme involves training parents of children with ASD to use their child's everyday activities as a context for learning, particularly in the area of communication. It draws on principles of ABA, but also emphasises the use of naturalistic contexts and activities to embed the teaching of functional skills and to enhance social interactions.

## Social Communication/Emotional Regulation/ Transactional Support (SCERTS)

SCERTS is an intervention that focuses on the development of child-initiated communication in naturalistic contexts, and the application of functional and relevant skills across different settings and with a variety of partners (Prizant et al., 2004). It draws on social-pragmatic approaches to language acquisition, the use of environmental arrangement, and the development of behaviours to support self-regulation.

## Other Approaches

In additional to interventions that are primarily behavioural or developmental in their approach, there are interventions that have been derived from causal theories of ASD that have a more biological basis. There is limited research support for many of these approaches.

## Sensory Integration Therapy (SI)

SI is based on sensory integration theory, which relates to the neurological process of integrating and interpreting sensory stimulation received from the environment. SI claims to assist in the organisation and processing of sensory input, such as touch, deep pressure, and vestibular input. The focus is on improving the child's central nervous system's ability to integrate and process incoming information. Many of these therapies are not supported by robust research evidence (Rodger et al., 2010). Specific skill acquisition is not the target of this intervention; rather, improved sensory integration is the desired outcome. This outcome is difficult to measure. On the other hand, interventions focusing on enhancing the match between the child, the task, and the environment, aim to adapt the task/activities and/

or the environment in order to assist children to manage the sensory overwhelm they often experience. The latter approach does not attempt to change the child's nervous system per se, rather it aims to adapt the task or environment (or both) to enable the child to function effectively (Rodger *et al.*, 2010).

## Gluten-free, Casein-free Diet (GFCF)

Theories that diet may cause or exacerbate the core impairments of ASD have been proposed since the 1950s. The GFCF diet is based on a theory that people with ASD have difficulty digesting food proteins, particularly those related to casein (found in milk) and gluten (found in wheat). This causes a release of chemicals which enter the nervous system and cause an increase in opioid activity in the brain, leading to autistic behaviour. Exponents of the diet argue that by excluding foods containing gluten and casein, the behaviours associated with ASD will decrease.

## SELECTING INTERVENTIONS

Given the current limited state of scientific evidence available to inform choice of intervention for parents, it is helpful to consider a set of guidelines to use with parents who are faced with decisions about which intervention to choose for their child. Some have suggested that we should approach any new treatment with hopeful skepticism (Hall, 2009). In the early stages following diagnosis, parents are generally very motivated to do everything they can to help their child, and may be keen to try new and often untested treatments. Providing parents with a framework within which they can weigh up the pros and cons of a treatment approach can assist them in making an informed decision.

A good starting point with parents is for them to apply the following tenets of 'best practice' developed by Prizant and Rubin (1999), and Roberts and Prior (2006).

- Intervention approaches should be individualised to match a child's current developmental level and his or her profile of learning strengths and weaknesses.

- Intervention for young children should be based on our current knowledge of child development.

- An intervention approach should directly address the predominant core characteristics of ASD, also referred to as ASD-specific curriculum content.

- Systematic instruction and generalisation strategies should be incorporated.

- The learning environment should be highly structured and supported.

- Supported transitions between settings and activities should occur.

- A functional approach to behaviour management should be used.

- Intervention approaches should demonstrate a logical consistency between their long-term goals and teaching protocols.

- Intervention approaches should be derived from a range of sources.

- Families should be involved.

## Questions Parents Can Ask

In addition to these tenets of best practice, we used a set of questions in our workshops with parents, derived from the research literature, to help them determine the efficacy of treatment approaches they might consider (Keen *et al.*, 2010; Keen *et al.*, 2007). These questions can assist parents in making considered judgements about the efficacy of early intervention approaches, and how a treatment may fit with their particular child and family situation.

1. What are the expected outcomes (e.g., what skills are targeted, how much improvement is expected, and over what time period)?

2. For whom does the programme work best (e.g., child's age, ASD severity, IQ, etc.)?

3. What evaluation methods have been used to assess the treatment outcomes?

4. What objective evidence is there of effectiveness (e.g., controlled studies, results published in peer reviewed journals)?

5. How much time will be involved for the child, the family, and others (hours per week, duration)?

6. How much will it cost and over what period of time?

7. Is there any family involvement?

8. What demands and pressures will this place on family life (e.g., child, siblings, parents)?

9. Are there any risks associated with this programme?

Parents can also benefit from additional information and resources about treatment approaches, such as websites and other written material that give a rating of the level of evidence available to support interventions they may be considering. Some government agencies and ASD organisations around the world have provided guidelines for selecting evidence-based practices by classifying intervention practices according to the approach taken and the level of scientific evidence available to support their efficacy. Level of evidence for a particular intervention practice is generally assessed by considering the total number of studies that have been conducted, the number of participants, and the quality, rigour, and outcomes of each study.

In Australia, the Raising Children Network website provides just one example of a set of guidelines for ASD intervention practices which is available to parents and professionals (Raising Children Network, 2011). The Raising Children Network rating system is based on work undertaken by the National Autism Centre in the USA through the National Standards Project. Interventions are classified under the headings: behavioural, developmental, therapy-based, medical, family-based, combined, alternative, and other. Each intervention practice receives a research rating.

To illustrate the way in which interventions may be evaluated and rated, we have taken each of the interventions described in this chapter and provided information about their respective ratings. Table 10.1 provides a list of the interventions and shows the ratings they have been given, based on three different sources: the Raising Children Network website and two review articles, one by Simpson (2005) and the other by Odom *et al.* (2010a).

The Raising Children Network website (Raising Children Network, 2011) rates interventions according to the following scale:

- Established: research shows positive effects.

- Promising: some research shows positive effects, more research needed.

- Yet to be determined: not enough research available.

- Ineffective/harmful: research shows that this approach is ineffective or can be harmful.

The Simpson (2005) review utilises a similar scale, where a practice rated as 'scientifically based' must have significant and convincing empirical efficacy and support. A 'promising' practice has efficacy and utility but needs additional objective verification, while those with 'limited supporting information' lack objective and convincing supporting evidence. 'Not recommended' practices are those that lack efficacy and that may be harmful.

The rating system used by Odom and colleagues (2010a) considers five different dimensions for each intervention, rather than providing one overall rating. Each dimension is rated on a scale from zero, which is the lowest possible rating, to the highest rating of five. The dimensions rated are as follows:

- Operationalisation: the degree to which procedures and programme content are specified sufficiently for the programme to be replicated (e.g., through a manual).

- Fidelity: a measure of the degree to which the programme is replicated accurately with reliability and validity.

- Replication: take-up of the programme by others independent of the original developers.

- Outcome data: amount and quality of evidence of efficacy, with the highest ratings given to interventions that have experimental, peer reviewed journal articles which analyse the efficacy of the programme.

- Quality: critical evaluation of the research methodology used in determining the efficacy of the intervention.

- Additional studies: complementary evidence from studies conducted on focused intervention practices that are a component of the intervention being rated.

An examination of the interventions described in this chapter and rated according to the three different sources used for this exercise reveals some level of agreement across the rating systems. DTT (see 'Lovaas Programme' on page 212) and PRT received the highest ratings among the interventions reviewed and were considered to have a convincing body of evidence supporting the efficacy of those programmes. A second group of interventions, which includes TEACCH, PECS, Floortime, and RDI, is considered to show promise, although more research is required to support the efficacy of these interventions.

A number of the interventions listed in Table 10.1 were not rated, making it difficult to determine from these sources the efficacy of these interventions owing to the absence of evidence. None of the interventions discussed in this chapter were rated as ineffective, harmful, or not recommended – but such interventions continue to exist. Facilitated communication (FC) is one such example (Biklen, 1992). Using this approach, a child with ASD spells out words on a keyboard or other device while a facilitator physically supports the child's hand, wrist, or arm. Advocates of this programme believe that the physical support, provided by a facilitator who establishes a trusting relationship with the child they are assisting, overcomes barriers to communication caused by motor and other difficulties. Studies that have independently evaluated FC as a communication technique have generally found the facilitator to be responsible (although not consciously) for words apparently produced by the individual with ASD they are supporting (Hall, 2009).

## CONCLUSION

Ultimately, parents will arrive at their own decision about which intervention they wish to pursue for their child. Based on previous research, we know that they are likely to try a number of different approaches. Providing information to parents about the efficacy of interventions and principles of good early intervention practice, as described in this chapter, can significantly assist in their decision-making, and may help them to avoid the more questionable approaches that promise much but deliver little to children with ASD and their families.

Table 10.1 Ratings of treatment approaches

| Intervention approach | Raising Children Network website[1] | Simpson (2005) | Odom et al. (2010a) (Operationalisation/Fidelity/Replication/Outcome data/Quality/Additional studies) |
|---|---|---|---|
| Speech Language Therapy | Not rated | Not rated | Not rated |
| Occupational Therapy | Not rated | Not rated | Not rated |
| Lovaas Programme | Not rated | Not rated | 5/4/5/5/3/5 |
| DTT[2] | Established | Scientifically based practice | Not rated |
| Pivotal Response Training | Established | Scientifically based practice | 4/3/5/4/2/5 (as per the erratum to original article) |
| TEACCH[3] | Promising | Promising practice | 3/3/5/5/2/2 |
| PECS[4] | Promising | Promising practice | Not rated |
| Floortime | Promising | Limited supporting information | 5/3/5/4/2/0 |
| RDI[5] | Promising | Limited supporting information | 5/3/0/4/2/0 |
| Hanen 'More Than Words' | Not rated | Not rated | 2/0/1/3/NA/2 |
| SCERTS[6] | Not rated | Not rated | 5/0/0/0/NA/4 |
| SI[7] | Yet to be determined | Promising practice | Not rated |
| GFCF[8] | Not rated | Not rated | Not rated |

1 http://raisingchildren.net.au/parents_guide_to_therapies/parents_guide_to_therapies.html
2 Discreet Trial Training
3 Training and Education of Autistic and Related Communication Handicapped Children
4 Picture Exchange Communication System
5 Relationship Development Intervention
6 Social Communication/Emotional Regulation/Transactional Support
7 Sensory Integration Therapy
8 Gluten-free, Casein-free Diet

# References

## CHAPTER 1

Aarons, M., and Gittens, T. (1992). *The Handbook of Autism: A Guide for Parents and Professionals.* New York, NY: Tavistock and Routledge.

Alberto, P.A., and Troutman, A.C. (2006). *Applied Behavior Analysis for Teachers* (7th ed.). Upper Saddle River, NJ: Pearson.

Aldred, C., Green, J., and Adams, C. (2004). 'A new social communication intervention for children with autism: Pilot randomised controlled treatment study suggesting effectiveness.' *Journal of Child Psychology and Psychiatry 45,* 1420–1430.

American Psychiatric Association (2000). *Diagnostic and Statistical Manual of Mental Disorders* (4th ed.). Washington, DC: APA.

Baer, D.M., Wolf, M.M., and Risley, T.R. (1968). 'Some current dimensions of applied behavior analysis.' *Journal of Applied Behavior Analysis, 1,* 91–97.

Begun, A. (1996). 'Family Systems and Family-centered Care.' In P. Rosin, A. Whitehead, L. Tuchman, G. Jesien, A. Begun and L. Irwin (eds), *Partnerships in family-centered care: A guide to collaborative early intervention.* Baltimore, MD: Paul H Brookes.

Bettelheim, B. (1967). *The Empty Fortress.* New York: Free Press.

Davey, K. (2002). 'Diagnostic experiences and empowerment in parents of children with Autism Spectrum Disorder.' Unpublished thesis. University of Queensland, Brisbane.

Dempsey, I., and Keen, D. (2008). 'A review of processes and outcomes in family-centered services for children with a disability.' *Topics in Early Childhood Special Education, 28,* 42–52.

Duker, P., Didden, R., and Sigafoos, J. (2004). *One-to-one Training: Instructional Procedures for Learners with Developmental Disabilities.* Austin, Texas: Pro-ed.

Dunst, C. J., Trivette, C.M., and Deal, A. G. (1994). *Supporting and Strengthening Families: Methods, Strategies and Practices.* Cambridge, MA: Brookline Books.

Frea, W. (2000). 'Behavioral Interventions for Children with Autism.' In J. Austin and J.E. Carr (eds), *Handbook of Applied Behavior Analysis* (pp. 247–273). Reno, NV: Context Press.

Greenspan, S.I., and Wieder, S. (1999). 'A functional developmental approach to autistic spectrum disorders.' *Journal of the Association for Persons with Severe Handicaps, 24* (3), 147–161.

Hart, B., and Risley, T.R. (1995). *Meaningful Differences in the Everyday Experience of Young American Children.* Baltimore, MD: Paul H Brookes.

Hassall, R., Rose, J., and McDonald, J. (2005). 'Parenting stress in mothers of children with an intellectual disability: The effects of parental cognitions in relation to child characteristics and family support.' *Journal of Intellectual Disability Research, 49,* 405–418.

Hastings, R.P., and Johnson, E. (2001). 'Stress in UK families conducting intensive home-based behavioral intervention for their young child with autism.' *Journal of Autism and Developmental Disorders, 31,* 327–336.

Ingersoll, B.R. (2010). 'Teaching social communication: A comparison of naturalistic behavioral and development, social pragmatic approaches for children with autism spectrum disorders.' *Journal of Positive Behavior Interventions, 12*, 33–43.

Kaiser, A.P., Ostrosky, M.M., and Alpert, C.L. (1993). 'Training teachers to use environmental arrangement and milieu teaching with nonvocal preschool children.' *Journal of the Association for Persons with Severe Handicaps, 18*, 188–199.

Kanner, L. (1943). 'Autistic disturbances of affective contact.' *Nervous Child, 2*, 217–250.

Kasari, C., Gulsrud, A.C., Wong, C., Kwon, S., and Locke, J. (2010). 'Randomized controlled caregiver mediated joint engagement intervention for toddlers with autism.' *Journal of Autism and Developmental Disorders, 40*, 1045–1056.

Keen, D. (2007). 'Parents, families and partnerships: Issues and considerations.' *International Journal of Disability, Development, and Education, 54*, 339–349.

Keen, D., and Knox, M. (2004). 'Approach to challenging behaviour: A family affair.' *Journal of Intellectual and Developmental Disability, 29*, 52–64.

Keen, D., Rodger, S., Doussin, K., and Braithwaite, M. (2007). 'A pilot study of the effects of a social-pragmatic intervention on the communication and symbolic play of children with autism.' *Autism: The International Journal of Research and Practice, 11*, 7–15.

Keenan, M., Dillenburger, K., Doherty, A., Byrne, T., and Gallagher, S. (2010). 'The experiences of parents during diagnosis and forward planning for children with autism spectrum disorder.' *Journal of Applied Research in Intellectual Disabilities, 23*, 390–397.

Knox, M., Parmenter, T., Atkinson, N., and Yazbeck, M. (2000). 'Family control: The views of families who have a child with an intellectual disability.' *Journal of Applied Research in Intellectual Disabilities, 13*, 17–28.

Koegel, L.K., Koegel, R.L., Harrower, J.K., and Carter, C.M. (1999). 'Pivotal response intervention I: Overview of approach.' *Journal of the Association for Persons with Severe Handicaps, 24*, 174–185.

Koegel, L.K., Koegel, R.L., Shoshan, Y., and McNerney, E. (1999). 'Pivotal response intervention II: Preliminary long-term outcome data'. *Research and Practice for Persons with Severe Disabilities, 24* (3), 186–198.

Llewellyn, G., McConnell, D., Thompson, K., and Whybrow, S. (2005). 'Out-of-home placement of school age children with disabilities.' *Journal of Applied Research in Intellectual Disability, 18*, 1–16.

Lovaas, O.I. (1987). 'Behavioral treatment and normal educational and intellectual functioning in young autistic children.' *Journal of Consulting and Clinical Psychology, 55*, 3–9.

Lovaas, O.I. (1993). 'The development of a treatment-research project for developmentally disabled and autistic children.' *Journal of Applied Behavior Analysis, 26*, 617–630.

Lucyshyn, J., Dunlap, G., and Albin, R. (eds) (2002). *Families and Positive Behavior Support.* Baltimore, MD: Paul H Brookes.

Luyster, R.J., Kadlec, M.B., Carter, A.S., and Tager-Flusberg, H. (2008). 'Language assessment and development in toddlers with autism spectrum disorders.' *Journal of Autism and Developmental Disorders, 38*, 1426–1438.

MacDermott, S., Williams, K., Ridley, G., Glasson, E., and Wray, J. (2006). *The Prevalence of Autism in Australia: Can it be Established from Existing Data?* Australian Advisory Board on Autism Spectrum Disorders.

McGee, G.G., Morrier, M.J., and Daly, T. (1999). 'An incidental teaching approach to early intervention for toddlers with autism.' *Journal of the Association for Persons with Severe Handicaps, 24*, 133–146.

Mahoney, G., and Perales, F. (2003). 'Using relationship-focused intervention to enhance the social-emotional functioning of young children with autism spectrum disorders.' *Topics in Early Childhood Special Education, 23* (2), 77–89.

Manolson, H.A. (1985). *It takes two to talk: A Hanen early language parent guidebook.* Toronto, Ontario: The Hanen Centre.

Mundy, P., Gwaltney, M., and Henderson, H. (2010). 'Self–referenced processing, neurodevelopment and joint attention in autism.' *Autism, 14,* 408–429.

O'Connor, T.G. (2002). 'The "effects" of parenting reconsidered: Findings, challenges and applications.' *Journal of Child Psychology and Psychiatry, 43,* 555–572.

Prizant, B., Wetherby, A., and Rydell, P. (2000). 'Communication Intervention Issues for Young Children with Autism Spectrum Disorders.' In A.M. Wetherby and B.M. Prizant (eds), *Autism Spectrum Disorders: A Transactional Developmental Perspective* (Vol. 9, pp. 193–224). Baltimore, MD: Paul H Brookes.

Prizant, B., Wetherby, A., Rydell, P., Rubin, E., and Laurent, A. (2004). *Autism Spectrum Disorders and the SCERTS Model: A Comprehensive Educational Approach.* Port Chester, NY: National Professional Resources.

Rodger, S., Braithwaite, M., and Keen, D. (2004). 'Early intervention for children with autism: Parental priorities.' *Australian Journal of Early Childhood, 29,* 34–41.

Rodger, S., Keen, D., Braithwaite, M., and Cook, S. (2008). 'Mothers' satisfaction with a home-based early intervention program for children with ASD.' *Journal of Applied Research in Intellectual Disabilities, 21,* 174–182.

Rogers, S.J., Hall, T., Osaki, D., Reaven, J., and Herbison, J. (2000). 'The Denver Model: A Comprehensive, Integrated Educational Approach to Young Children with Autism and Their Families.' In J. Handleman and P. Harris (eds), *Preschool Education Programs for Children with Autism* (pp. 95–133). Austin, TX: Pro-ed.

Sallows, G., and Graupner, T. (2005). 'Intensive behavioral treatment for children with autism: Four-year outcome and predictors.' *American Journal on Mental Retardation, 110,* 417–438.

Sigafoos, J., O'Reilly, M., Ma, H.C., Edrisinha, C., Cannella, H., and Lancioni, G.E. (2006). 'Effects of embedded instruction versus discrete-trial training on self-injury, correct responding, and mood in a child with autism.' *Journal of Intellectual and Developmental Disability, 31,* 196–203.

Siller, M., and Sigman, M. (2002). 'The behaviors of parents of children with autism predict the subsequent development of their children's communication.' *Journal of Autism and Developmental Disorders, 32,* 77–89.

Sloper, P., and Turner, S. (1993). 'Determinants of parental satisfaction with disclosure of disability.' *Developmental Medicine and Child Neurology, 35,* 816–825.

Turnbull, A.P., and Turnbull, H.R. (1986). *Families, Professionals and Exceptionality: A Special Partnership.* Columbus, OH: Merrill Publishing.

Turnbull, A.P., and Turnbull, H.R. (2001). *Families, Professionals, and Exceptionality: Collaborating for Empowerment* (4th ed.). Upper Saddle River, NJ: Prentice-Hall.

Watson, L.R. (1998). 'Following the child's lead: Mothers' interactions with children with autism.' *Journal of Autism and Developmental Disorders, 28,* 51–59.

Wetherby, A., Watt, N., Morgan, L., and Shumway, S. (2007). 'Social communication profiles of children with autism spectrum disorders in the second year of life.' *Journal of Autism and Developmental Disorders, 37,* 960–975.

World Health Organisation (1992). *ICD-10 International Statistical Classification of Diseases and Related Health Problems* (10th ed.). Geneva: WHO.

Yoder, P., and Warren, S.F. (1999). 'Maternal responsivity mediates the relationship between prelinguistic communication intervention and later language.' *Journal of Early Intervention, 22,* 126–136.

Yoder, P., Warren, S.F., McCathren, R., and Leew, S. (1998). 'Does Adult Responsivity to Child Behavior Facilitate Communication Development?' In A. Wetherby, S.F. Warren and J. Reichle (eds), *Transitions in Prelinguistic Communication* (Vol. 7, pp. 39–58). Baltimore, MD: Paul H Brookes.

# CHAPTER 2

American Psychiatric Association (2000). *Diagnostic and Statistical Manual of Mental Disorders (DSM-IV-TR)* (4th ed.). Washington, DC: APA.

Arvidsson, T., Danielsson, B., Forsberg, P., Gillberg, C., Johansson, M., and Kjellgren, G. (1997). 'Autism in 3–6-year-old children in a suburb of Goteborg, Sweden.' *Autism: The International Journal of Research and Practice, 1,* 163–173.

Baranek, G.T. (2002). 'Efficacy of sensory and motor interventions for children with autism.' *Journal of Autism and Developmental Disorders, 32,* 397–422.

Baron-Cohen, S. (1991). 'Precursors to a Theory of Mind: Understanding Attention in Others.' In A. Whiten (ed.), *Natural Theories of Mind: Evolution, Development and Simulation of Everyday Mindreading* (pp. 233–251). Cambridge, MA: Basil Blackwell Inc.

Baron-Cohen, S., Leslie, A., and Frith, U. (1985). 'Does the autistic child have a "theory of mind"?' *Cognition, 21,* 37–46.

Bogdashina, O. (2003). *Sensory Perceptual Issues in Autism and Asperger Syndrome: Different Sensory Experiences, Different Perceptual Worlds.* London, UK: Jessica Kingsley Publishers.

Chakrabarti, S., and Fombonne, E. (2005). 'Pervasive developmental disorders in preschool children: Confirmation of high prevalence.' *American Journal of Psychiatry, 162* (6), Health Module.

Charman, T., and Baron-Cohen, S. (1992). 'Understanding drawings and beliefs: A further test of the meta-representation theory of autism.' *Journal of Child Psychology and Psychiatry, 33,* 1105–1112.

Charman, T., and Campbell, A. (1997). 'Reliability of theory of mind task performance by individuals with a learning disability.' *Journal of Child Psychology and Psychiatry, 38,* 725–730.

Courchesne, E., Karnes, C.M., Davis, H.R., Ziccardi, R., *et al.* (2001). 'Unusual brain growth in early life in patients with autistic disorder: An MRI study.' *Neurology, 57,* 245–254.

De Marchena, A., and Eigsti, I.M. (2010). 'Conversational gestures in autism spectrum disorders: Asynchrony but not decreased frequency.' *Autism Research, 3,* 311–322.

Dunn, W. (1999). *The Sensory Profile: A Contextual Measure of Children's Responses to Sensory Experiences in Daily Life.* San Antonio, TX: The Psychological Corporation.

Edelson, M.G. (2006). 'Are the majority of children with autism mentally retarded? A systematic evaluation of the data.' *Focus on Autism and other Developmental Disabilities, 21,* 66–83.

Filipek, P., Accardo, P., Baranek, G., and Cook, E. (1999). 'The screening and diagnosis of autistic spectrum disorders.' *Journal of Autism and Developmental Disorders, 29,* 439–474.

Frith, U (1989). *Autism: Explaining the enigma.* Oxford: Basil Blackwell Ltd.

Frith, U., and Happé, F. (1999). 'Theory of mind and self-consciousness: What it is like to be autistic?' *Mind and Language, 14,* 1–22.

Frith, U., Happé, F., and Siddons, F. (1994). 'Autism and theory of mind in everyday life.' *Social Development, 3* (2), 108–124.

Gal, E., Cermak, S.A., and Ben-Sasson, A. (2007). 'Sensory Processing Disorders in Children with Autism.' In R. Gabriels and D. Hill (eds). *Growing up with Autism: Working with School-Aged Children and Adolescents.* (pp. 95–123). New York, NY: Guilford Press.

Garnett, M.S., and Attwood, A.J. (1998). 'The Australian scale for Asperger's syndrome.' Retrieved 16 March, 2011, from http://www.aspennj.org/pdf/information/articles/australian-scale-for-asperger-syndrome.pdf

Gillberg, C., and Coleman, M. (2000). *The Biology of the Autistic Syndromes* (3rd ed.). London: MacKeith Press.

Gillberg, C., Gillberg, C., Rastam, M., and Wentz, E. (2001). 'The Asperger Syndrome (and high-functioning autism) diagnostic interview (ASDI): A preliminary study of a new structured clinical interview.' *Autism: The International Journal of Research and Practice, 5,* 57–66.

Gilliam, J. (1995). *Gilliam Autism Rating Scales*. Austin, TX: Pro-ed.

Hall, L.J. (2009). *Autism Spectrum Disorders: From Theory to Practice*. Upper Saddle River, NJ: Pearson Education Inc.

Happé, F. (1994). *Autism: An introduction to Psychological Theory*. London: UCL Press.

Happé, F. (1995). 'The role of age and verbal ability in the theory of mind task performance of subjects with autism.' *Child Development, 66,* 846–855.

Happé, F. (2000). 'Parts and Wholes, Meaning and Minds: Central Coherence and its Relation to Theory of Mind.' In S. Baron-Cohen, H. Tager-Flusberg and D. Cohen (eds), *Understanding Other Minds: Perspectives from Developmental Cognitive Neuroscience* (2nd ed., pp. 203–221). Oxford: Oxford University Press.

Happé, F., Briskman, J., and Frith, U. (2001). 'Exploring the cognitive phenotype of autism: Weak "central coherence" in parents and siblings of children with autism: I. Experimental tests.' *Journal of Child Psychology and Psychiatry, 42,* 299–307.

Heflin, L.J., and Alaimo, D.F. (2007). *Students with Autism Spectrum Disorders: Effective Instructional Practices*. Upper Saddle River, NJ: Pearson.

Holroyd, S., and Baron-Cohen, S. (1993). 'Brief report: How far can people with autism go in developing a theory of mind?' *Journal of Autism and Developmental Disorders, 23,* 379–385.

Howlin, P. (2003). 'Outcome in high-functioning adults with autism with and without early language delays: Implications for the differentiation between autism and Asperger syndrome.' *Journal of Autism and Developmental Disorders, 33,* 3–13.

Howlin, P. (2004). *Autism and Asperger Syndrome: Preparing for Adulthood* (2nd ed.). London: Routledge.

Jordan, R., and Jones, G. (1999). 'Review of research into educational interventions for children with autism in the UK.' *Autism: The International Journal of Research and Practice, 3,* 101–110.

Kanner, L. (1943). 'Autistic disturbances of affective contact.' *Nervous Child, 2,* 217–250.

Kientz, M.A., and Dunn, W. (1997). 'A comparison of the performance of children with and without autism on the Sensory Profile.' *American Journal of Occupational Therapy, 51,* 530–537.

Krug, D.A., Arick, J.R., and Almond, P.G. (1979). 'Autism Screening Instrument for Educational Planning, Background, and Development.' In J. Gilliam (ed.), *Autism: Diagnosis, instruction, management, and research*. Austin, TX: University of Austin Press.

Krug, D.A., Arick, J.R., and Almond, P.G. (1980). 'Behavior checklist for identifying severely handicapped individuals with high level of autistic behavior.' *Journal of Child Psychology and Psychiatry, 21,* 221–229.

Leekam, S.R., Libby, S.J., Wing, L., Gould, J., and Taylor, C. (2002). 'The diagnostic interview for social and communication disorders: Algorithms for ICD-10 childhood autism and Wing and Gould autistic spectrum disorder.' *Journal of Child Psychology and Psychiatry, 43,* 327–342.

Leekam, S.R., and Perner, J. (1991). 'Does the autistic child have a meta-representational deficit?' *Cognition, 40,* 203–218.

Leslie, A.M., and Frith, U. (1988). 'Autistic children's understanding of seeing, knowing and believing.' *British Journal of Developmental Psychology, 6,* 315–324.

Liu, K., King, M., and Bearman, P.S. (2010). 'Social influence and the autism epidemic.' *American Journal of Sociology, 15,* 1387–1434.

Lord, C., and Risi, S. (2000). 'Diagnosis of Autism Spectrum Disorders in Young Children.' In A.M. Wetherby and B.M. Prizant (eds), *Autism Spectrum Disorders: A Transactional Developmental Perspective* (Vol. 9, pp. 11–30). Baltimore, MD: Paul H Brookes.

Lord, C., Rutter, M., DiLavore, P., and Risi, S. (2001). *Autism Diagnostic Observation Schedule*. Los Angeles: Western Psychological Services.

Lotter, V. (1966). 'Epidemiology of autistic conditions in young children: I. Prevalence.' *Social Psychiatry, 1,* 124–137.

MacDermott, S., Williams, K., Ridley, G., Glasson, E., and Wray, J. (2006). *The Prevalence of Autism in Australia: Can it be Established from Existing Data?* Australian Advisory Board on Autism Spectrum Disorders.

Miller, L.J., Coll, J.R., and Schoen, S.A. (2007). 'A randomized controlled pilot study of the effectiveness of occupational therapy for children with sensory modulation disorder.' *American Journal of Occupational Therapy, 61*, 228–238.

Miller, L.J., and Lane, S.J. (2000). 'Toward a consensus in terminology in sensory integration theory and practice: Part 1: Taxonomy of neurophysiological processes.' *Sensory Integration Special Interest Section Quarterly, 23* (1), 1–4.

Miller, L.J., Lane, S.J., Cermak, S.A., Osten, E., and Anzalone, M. (2005). 'Regulatory-sensory Processing Disorders.' In S.I. Greenspan and S. Wieder (eds) *Diagnostic Manual for Infancy and Early Childhood: Mental Health, Developmental, Regulatory-Sensory Processing and Language Disorders and Learning Challenges* (pp. 73–112). Bethesda, MD: Interdisciplinary Council on Developmental and Learning Disorders.

Mundy, P., and Sigman, M. (1989). 'Specifying the Nature of the Social Impairment in Autism.' In G. Dawson (ed.), *Autism: Nature, Diagnosis and Treatment* (pp. 3–21). New York, NY: Guilford Press.

Muris, P., Steerneman, P., and Merckelbach, H. (1998). 'Difficulties in the understanding of false belief: Specific to autism and other pervasive developmental disorders?' *Psychological Reports, 82*, 51–57.

Ornitz, E.M., Guthrie, D., and Farley, A.H. (1977). 'The early development of autistic children.' *Journal of Autism and Developmental Disorders, 7*, 207–229.

Osterling, J., and Dawson, G. (1994). 'Early recognition of children with autism: A study of first birthday home videotapes.' *Journal of Autism and Development Disorders, 24*, 247–257.

Ozonoff, S., Rogers, S.J., and Pennington, B.F. (1991). 'Asperger Syndrome: Evidence of an empirical distinction from high-functioning autism.' *Journal of Child Psychology and Psychiatry, 32*, 1107–1122.

Ozonoff, S., South, M., and Provencal, S. (2005). 'Executive Functions.' In F. R. Volkmar, R. Paul, A. Klin, and D. Cohen (eds), *Handbook of Autism and Pervasive Developmental Disorders* (pp. 606–627). New York, NY: John Wiley and Sons.

Prior, M., and Ozonoff, S. (1998). 'Psychological Factors in Autism.' In F.R. Volkmar (ed.), *Autism and Pervasive Developmental Disorders* (pp. 64–108). Cambridge: Cambridge University Press.

Robins, D.L., Fein, D., Barton, M.L., and Green, J.A. (2001). 'The Modified Checklist for Autism in Toddlers: An initial study investigating the early detection of autism and pervasive developmental disorders.' *Journal of Autism and Developmental Disorders, 31*, 131–144.

Rogers, S. J., Hepburn, S., and Wehner, E. (2003). 'Parent reports of sensory symptoms in toddlers with autism and those with other developmental disabilities.' *Journal of Autism and Developmental Disorders, 33*, 631–642.

Rutter, M. (2000). 'Genetic studies of autism: From the 1970s into the millennium.' *Journal of Abnormal Child Psychology, 28*, 3–14.

Rutter, M. (2005). 'Aetiology of autism: Findings and questions.' *Journal of Intellectual Disability Research, 49*, 231–238.

Rutter, M., Bailey, A., and Lord, C. (2007). *Social Communication Questionnaire.* Torrance, CA: Western Psychological Services.

Rutter, M., Le Couteur, A., and Lord, C. (2003). *Autism Diagnostic Interview – Revised.* Torrance, CA: Western Psychological Services.

Schopler, E., Reichler, R.J., DeVellis, R.F., and Daly, K. (1980). 'Toward objective classification of childhood autism: Childhood Autism Rating Scale (CARS).' *Journal of Autism and Developmental Disorders, 10*, 91–103.

Smith-Myles, B., Tapscott-Cook, K., Miller, N.E., Rinner, L., and Robbins, L.A. (2000). *Asperger Syndrome and Sensory Issues: Practical Solutions for Making Sense of the World.* Shawnee Mission, KS: Autism Asperger Publishing Co.

Stone, W.L., and Hogan, K.L. (1993). 'A structured parent interview for identifying young children with autism.' *Journal of Autism and Developmental Disorders, 23,* 639–652.

Stone, W., Ousley, O., Yoder, P., Hogan, K., and Hepburn, S. (1997). 'Nonverbal communication in two- and three-year-old children with autism.' *Journal of Autism and Developmental Disorders, 27,* 677–696.

Swettenham, J. (1996). 'Can children with autism be taught to understand false belief using computers?' *Journal of Child Psychology and Psychiatry, 37,* 157–165.

Tager-Flusberg, H., and Sullivan, K. (1994). 'A second look at second-order belief attribution in autism.' *Journal of Autism and Developmental Disorders, 24,* 577–586.

Tomcheck, S.D., and Dunn, W. (2007). 'Sensory processing in children with and without autism: A comprehensive study using the Short Sensory Profile.' *American Journal of Occupational Therapy, 61,* 190–200.

Volkmar, F.R., Klin, A., and Cohen, D.J. (1997). 'Diagnosis and Classification of Autism and Related Conditions: Consensus and Issues.' In D.J. Cohen and F.R. Volkmar (eds), *Handbook of Autism and Pervasive Developmental Disorders* (2nd ed., pp. 5–40). New York, NY: Wiley.

Wetherby, A., and Prizant, B. (1993). *Communication and Symbolic Behavior Scales.* Chicago, IL: Applied Symbolix.

Wetherby, A., Watt, N., Morgan, L., and Shumway, S. (2007). 'Social communication profiles of children with autism spectrum disorders in the second year of life.' *Journal of Autism and Developmental Disorders, 37,* 960–975.

Wetherby, A., Woods, J., Allen, L., Cleary, J., Dickinson, H., and Lord, C. (2004). 'Early indicators of autism spectrum disorders in the second year of life.' *Journal of Autism and Developmental Disorders, 34,* 473–493.

Wimmer, H., and Perner, J. (1983). 'Beliefs about beliefs: Representation and the constraining function of wrong beliefs in young children's understanding of deception.' *Cognition, 13,* 103–128.

Wing, L. (1988). 'The Continuum of Autistic Characteristics.' In E. Schopler and G. Mesibov (eds), *Diagnosis and Assessment in Autism* (pp. 91–110). New York, NY: Plenum Press.

Wing, L. (1996). 'Autistic spectrum disorders.' *British Medical Journal, 312,* 327–328.

Wulff, S. (1985). 'The symbolic and object play of children with autism: A review.' *Journal of Autism and Developmental Disorders, 15,* 139–148.

Yirmiya, N., and Shulman, C. (1996). 'Seriation, conservation, and theory of mind abilities in individuals with autism, individuals with mental retardation, and normally developing children.' *Child Development, 67,* 2045–2059.

# CHAPTER 3

Allen, R., and Petr, C.G. (1996). 'Toward Developing Standards and Measurements for Family Centred Practice in Family Support Programs.' In G. Singer, L. Powers and A. Olson (eds), *Redefining Family Support: Innovations in Public Private Partnerships* (pp. 57–86). Baltimore, MD: Paul H Brookes.

Baker, B.L., McIntyre, L.L., Blacher, J., Crnic, K., Edelbrock, G., and Low, C. (2003). 'Preschool children with and without developmental delay: Behaviour problems and parenting stress over time.' *Journal of Intellectual Disability Research, 47,* 217–230.

Broggi, M.B., and Sabatelli, R. (2010). 'Parental perceptions of the parent–therapist relationship: Effects on early intervention outcomes.' *Physical and Occupational Therapy in Pediatrics, 30* (3), 234–247.

Brown, G. (2003). 'Family Centred Care, Mothers' Occupations of Care Giving and Home Therapy Programs.' In S.A. Esdaile and J.A. Olson (eds), *Mothering Occupations: Challenge, Agency and Participation* (pp. 346–371). Philadelphia, PA: FA Davis Company.

Carpenter, B. (2007). 'The impetus for family-centred early childhood intervention.' *Child: Care, Health and Development, 33* (6), 664–669.

Case-Smith, J. (1999). 'The Family Perspective.' In W. Dunn (ed.), *Pediatric Occupational Therapy: Facilitating Effective Service Provision* (pp. 319–331). Thorofare, NJ: SLACK Incorporated.

Corlett, J., and Twycross, A. (2006). 'Negotiation of parental roles within family-centred care: A review of the research.' *Journal of Clinical Nursing, 15* (10), 1308–1316.

Cuskelly, M., and Hayes, A. (2004). 'Characteristics, Contexts and Consequences.' In J.M. Bowes (ed.), *Children, Families and Communities: Contexts and Consequences* (2nd ed., pp. 29–51). South Melbourne, VIC: Oxford University Press.

Dabriwsja, A., and Pisula, E. (2010). 'Parenting stress and coping styles in mothers and fathers of preschool children with autism and Down syndrome.' *Journal of Intellectual Disability Research, 54* (3), 266–280.

Darlington, Y., and Rodger, S. (2006) 'Families' and Children's Occupational Performance.' In S. Rodger and J. Ziviani. (eds), *Occupational Therapy for Children: Understanding Children's Occupations and Enabling Participation* (pp. 22–40). Oxford: Blackwell Science.

Dempsey, I., Keen, D., Pennell, D., O'Reilly, J., and Neilands, J. (2009). 'Parent stress, parenting competence and family-centered support to young children with an intellectual or developmental disability.' *Research in Developmental Disabilities, 30* (3), 558–566.

Dillenburger, K., Keenan, M., Doherty, A., Byrne, T., and Gallagher, S. (2010). 'Living with children diagnosed with ASD: Parental and professional views.' *British Journal of Special Education, 37* (1), 13–23.

Dunlap, G., Fox, L., Vaughn, B., Bucy, M., and Clarke, S. (1997). 'In quest of meaningful perspectives and outcomes: A response to five commentaries.' *Journal of the Association for Persons with Severe Handicaps, 22* (4), 221–223.

Dunst, C., Johanson, C., Trivette, C., and Hamby, D. (1991). 'Family-oriented early intervention policies and practices: Family-centered or not?' *Exceptional Children, 58* (2), 115–126.

Dunst, C., Trivette, C., Davis, M., and Cornwell, J. (1994). 'Characteristics of Effective Helpgiving Practices.' In C.J. Dunst, C.M. Trivette and A.G. Deal (eds), *Supporting and Strengthening Families: Methods, Strategies and Practices* (Vol. 1, pp. 171–186). Cambridge, MA: Brookline Books.

Dunst, C., Trivette, C., and Hamby, D. (1996). 'Measuring the helpgiving practices of human service program practitioners.' *Human Relations, 49* (6), 815–835.

Dunst, C., Trivette, C., and Johanson, C. (1994). 'Parent–Professional Collaboration and Partnerships.' In C. Dunst, C.M. Trivette and A.G. Deal (eds), *Supporting and Strengthening Families: Methods, Strategies and Practices* (Vol. 1, pp 197–211). Cambridge, MA: Brookline Books.

Esdaile, S., and Olson, J. (2003). *Mothering Occupations: Challenge, Agency and Participation.* Philadelphia, PA: F.A. Davis.

Fox, L., Vaughn, B., Dunlap, G., and Bucy, M. (1997). 'Parent–professional partnership in behavioural support: A qualitative analysis of one family's experience.' *Journal of the Association for Persons with Severe Handicaps, 22* (4), 198–207.

Hannah, K., and Rodger, S. (2002). 'Towards family-centred practice in paediatric occupational therapy: A review of the literature on parent–therapist collaboration.' *Australian Occupational Therapy Journal, 49* (1), 14–24.

Harrison, C., Romer, T., Simon, M., and Schulze, C. (2007). 'Factors influencing mothers' learning from paediatric therapists: A qualitative study.' *Physical and Occupational Therapy in Pediatrics, 27* (2), 77–95.

Hassall, R., Rose, J., and McDonald, J. (2005). 'Parenting stress in mothers of children with an intellectual disability: The effects of parental cognitions in relation to child characteristics and family support.' *Journal of Intellectual Disability Research, 49* (6), 405–418.

Hastings, R., and Brown, T. (2002). 'Behavior problems of children with autism, parental self-efficacy, and mental health.' *American Journal on Mental Retardation, 107* (3), 222–232.

Hjorngaard, T., and Taylor, B.S. (2010). 'Parent perspectives: The family–therapist relationship and saying good bye.' *Physical and Occupational Therapy in Pediatrics, 30* (2), 79–82.

Humphry, R. (1995). 'Families who live in chronic poverty: Meeting the challenge of family-centered services.' *American Journal of Occupational Therapy, 49* (7), 687–693.

Kayfitz, A.D., Gragg, M.N., and Orr, R.R. (2010). 'Positive experiences of mothers and fathers of children with autism.' *Journal of Applied Research in Intellectual Disabilities, 23* (4), 337–343.

Keen, D. (2007). 'Parents, families and partnerships: Issues and considerations.' *International Journal of Disability, Development and Education, 54,* 330–349.

King, G., King, S., Rosenbaum, P., and Goffin, R. (1999). 'Family-centered caregiving and well-being of parents of children with disabilities: Lining process with outcome.' *Journal of Pediatric Psychology, 24* (1), 41–53.

King, S., Teplicky, R., King, G., and Rosenbaum, P. (2004). 'Family-centered service for children with cerebral palsy and their families: A review of the literature.' *Seminars in Pediatric Neurology, 11* (1), 78–86.

Law, M., Hanna, G., Hurley, P., King, S. (2003). 'Factors affecting family-centred service delivery for children with disabilities.' *Child: Care, Health and Development, 29* (5), 357–366.

Lawlor, M., and Mattingly, C. (1997). 'The complexities embedded in family-centred care.' *The American Journal of Occupational Therapy, 52* (4), 259–267.

Litchfield, R., and MacDougall, C. (2002). 'Professional issues for physiotherapists in family-centred and community-based settings.' *Australian Journal of Physiotherapy, 48* (2), 105–112.

MacKean, G.L., Thurston, W.E., and Scott, C.M. (2005). 'Bridging the divide between families and health professionals' perspectives on family-centred care.' *Health Expectations, 8* (1), 74–85.

Mirfin-Veitch, B., and Bray, A. (1997). 'Grandparents: Part of the Family.' In B. Carpenter (ed.), *Families in Context: Emerging Trends in Family Support and Early Intervention* (pp. 76–88). London: David Fulton Publishers.

Moes, D., and Frea, W. (2000). 'Using family context to inform intervention planning for the treatment of a child with autism.' *Journal of Positive Behavior Interventions, 2* (1), 40–46.

Novak, I. (2011). 'Parent experiences of implementing effective home programs.' *Physical and Occupational Therapy in Pediatrics, 31* (2), 198–213.

Novak, I., Cusick, A., and Lannin, N. (2009). 'Occupational therapy home programs for cerebral palsy: Double blind randomised controlled trial.' *Pediatrics, 124* (4), 606–614.

Osborne, L.A., McHugh, L., Saunders, J., and Reed. P. (2008). 'Parenting stress reduces the effectiveness of early teaching interventions for autistic spectrum disorders.' *Journal of Autism and Developmental Disorders, 38* (6), 1092–1103.

Pengelly, S., Rogers, P., and Evans, K. (2009). 'Space at home for families with a child with autistic spectrum disorder.' *British Journal of Occupational Therapy, 72* (9), 378–383.

Raina, P., O'Donnell, M., Rosenbaum, P., Brehaut, J., *et al.* (2005). 'The health and well-being of caregivers of children with Cerebral Palsy.' *Pediatrics, 115* (6), 626–636.

Rodger, S. (2006). 'Children and Families: Partners in Education.' In K.M. Kenna and L. Tooth (eds), *Client Education: A partnership Approach for Health Practitioners* (pp. 88–111). Sydney, NSW: University of NSW Press.

Rodger, S., Keen, D., Braithwaite, M., and Cook, S. (2008). 'Mothers' satisfaction with a home based early intervention program for children with ASD.' *Journal of Applied Research in Intellectual Disabilities, 21,* 174–182.

Rodger, S., and Keen, D. (2010). 'Child and Family-Centred Service Provision.' In S. Rodger (ed.), *Occupation Centred Practice for Children: A Practical Guide for Occupational Therapists* (pp. 45–74). Oxford, UK: Wiley Blackwell.

Rosenbaum, P., King, S., Law, M., King, G., and Evans, J. (1998). 'Family-centred service: A conceptual framework and research review.' *Physical and Occupational Therapy in Pediatrics, 18* (1), 1–20.

Seligman, M., and Darling, R.B. (2007). 'Professional–Family interaction.' In M. Seligman and R.B. Darling (eds), *Ordinary Families, Special Children* (pp. 279–314). New York, NY: Guilford Press.

Summers, J.A., Hoffman, L., Marquis, J., Turnbull, A., Poston, D., and Nelson, L.L. (2005). 'Measuring the quality of family–professional partnerships in special education services.' *Exceptional Children, 72* (1), 65–81.

Vaughn, B., Dunlap, G., Fox, L., Clarke, S., and Bucy, M. (1997). 'Parent–professional partnership in behavioral support: A case study of community-based intervention.' *Journal of the Association for Persons with Severe Handicaps, 22* (4), 186–197.

Washington, K., and Schwartz, I.S. (1996). 'Maternal perceptions of the effects of physical and occupational therapy services on caregiving competency.' *Physical and Occupational Therapy in Pediatrics, 16* (3), 33–54.

# CHAPTER 4

Bandura, A. (1997). *Self-efficacy: The Exercise of Control.* New York, NY: WH Freeman and Co.

Bondy, A.S. and Frost, L.A. (1994). 'The picture exchange communication system.' *Focus on Autism and Other Developmental Disabilities, 9* (3), 1–19.

Bourke-Taylor, H., Law, M., Howie, L., and Pallant, J.F. (2009). 'Development of the Child's Challenging Behaviour Scale (CCBS) for mothers of school-aged children with disabilities.' *Child: Care ,Health and Development, 36* (4), 491–498.

Broggi M., and Sabatelli R. (2010) 'Parent perceptions of the parent–therapist relationship: Effects on outcomes of early intervention.' *Physical and Occupational Therapy in Paediatrics 30* (3), 234–247.

Canadian Association of Occupational Therapists (2002). *Enabling Occupation: An Occupational Therapy Perspective* (Revised edition). Ottawa, ON: CAOT Publications.

Cardillo, J., and Smith, A. (1994). 'Psychometric Issues.' In T. Kiresuk, A. Smith and J. Cardillo (eds), *Goal Attainment Scaling: Applications, Theory, and Measurement* (pp. 173–212). Hillsdale: Lawrence Erlbaum Associates.

Carswell, A., McColl, A., Baptiste, S., Law, M., Polatajko, H., and Pollock, N. (2004). 'The Canadian occupational performance measure: A research and clinical literature review.' *The Canadian Journal of Occupational Therapy, 71* (4), 210–222.

Chan, C.C.H., and Lee, T.M.C. (1997). 'Validity of the Canadian Occupational Performance Measure.' *Occupational Therapy International, 4* (3), 229–247.

Clark, J., and Bell, B. (2000). 'Collaborate on Targeted Outcomes and Making Action Plans.' In V. Fearing and J. Clark (eds), *Individuals in Context: A Practical Guide to Client-Centred Practice* (pp. 79–90). Thorofare, NJ: SLACK Inc.

Deci, E. L., and Ryan, R.M. (2000). 'The "what" and "why" of goal pursuits: Human needs and the self-determination of behaviour.' *Psychological Inquiry, 11* (4), 227–268.

Dedding, C., Cardol, M., Eyssen, I.C.J., Dekker, J., and Beelen, A. (2004). 'Validity of the Canadian Occupational Performance Measure: A client-centred outcome measurement.' *Clinical Rehabilitation, 18* (6), 660–667.

Dyke, P., Buttigieg, P., Blackmore, A., and Ghose, A. (2006). 'Use of the Measure of Process of Care for families (MPOC-56) and service providers (MPOC-SP) to evaluate family-centred services in a paediatric disability setting *Child: Care, Health and Development, 32* (2), 167–176.

Evans, J., and Rodger, S. (2008). 'Mealtimes and Bedtimes: Windows to Family Routines and Rituals.' *Journal of Occupational Science, 15* (2), 98–104.

Green, B.L., McAllister, C.L. and Tarte, J.M. (2004). 'The strengths-based practices inventory: A tool for measuring strengths-based service delivery in early childhood and family support programs.' *Families in Society, 85* (3), 326–334.

King, G. (2009). 'A relational goal-oriented model for optimal service delivery of children and families.' *Physical and Occupational Therapy in Pediatrics, 29* (4), 384–408.

King, S., Rosenbaum, P., and King G. (1995). *The Measure of Processes of Care: A Means to Assess Family-Centred Behaviours of Health Care Providers.* Hamilton, Canada: McMaster University Neurodevelopment Clinical Research Unit.

Law, M., Baptiste, S., Carswell, A., McColl, M. (2005). *Canadian Occupational Performance Measure* (4th edition). Ontario: CAOT Publications ACE.

Law, M., Baptiste, S., McColl, M., Opzoomer, A., Polatajko, H., and Pollock, N. (1990). 'The Canadian Occupational Performance Measure: An outcome measure for occupational therapy.' *Canadian Journal of Occupational Therapy, 57* (2), 82–87.

Law, M., and Mills, J. (1998). 'Client-centred Occupational Therapy.' In M. Law (ed.), *Client-centred Occupational Therapy* (pp. 1–18). Thorofare, NJ: Slack Inc.

McCashen, W. (2005). *The Strengths Approach.* Bendigo, Australia: St Lukes Innovative Resources.

McWilliam, R.A., Tocci, L., and Harbin, G.L. (1998). 'Family centered services: Service providers' discourse and behaviour.' *Topics in Early Childhood Special Education, 18* (4), 206–221.

Majnemer, A. (2011). 'Importance of motivation to children's participation: A motivation to change.' *Physical and Occupational Therapy in Pediatrics, 31* (1), 1–3.

Marquenie, K., Rodger, S., Mangohig, K., and Cronin, A. (2011). 'Dinnertime and bedtime in families with a young child with autism spectrum disorder.' *Australian Occupational Therapy Journal.* doi: 10.1111/j.1440–1630.2010.00896.x

Mosey, A.C. (1973). *Activities Therapy.* New York, NY: Raven Press Publishers.

Nijhuis, B., Reinders-Messelink, H., Hitters, W., Groothoff, J., *et al.* (2007). 'Family-centred care in family-specific teams.' *Clinical Rehabilitation, 21,* 660–671.

Oien, I., Fallang, B., and Ostensjo, S. (2009). 'Goal-setting in paediatric rehabilitation: Perceptions of parents and professionals.' *Child: Care, Health and Development, 36* (4), 558–565.

Parker, D.M., and Sykes, C.H. (2006). 'A systematic review of the Canadian Occupational Performance Measure: A clinical practice perspective.' *British Journal of Occupational Therapy, 69* (4), 150–160.

Pizur-Barnekow, K., Patrick, T., Thyner, P.M., Folk, L., and Anderson, K. (2010). 'Readability levels of individualized family service plans.' *Physical and Occupational Therapy in Pediatrics, 30* (3), 248–258.

Poulsen, A., Rodger, S., and Ziviani, J. (2006). 'Understanding children's motivation from a self-determination theoretical perspective: Implications for practice.' *Australian Occupational Therapy Journal, 53* (2), 78–86.

Provost, B., Crowe, T.K., Osbourn, P.L., McClain, C., and Skipper, B.J. (2010). 'Mealtime behaviours of preschool children: Comparison of children with ASD and children with typical development.' *Physical and Occupational Therapy in Pediatrics, 30* (3), 220–233.

Raghavendra, P., Murchland, S., Bentley, M., Wake-Dyster W., and Lyons T. (2007). Parents' and service providers' perceptions of family-centred practice in a community-based, paediatric disability service in Australia.' *Child: Care, Health and Development, 33* (5), 586–592.

Rapp, C. (1998). *The Strengths Model.* New York, NY: Oxford University Press.

Rodger, S. (2010). 'Becoming More Occupation Centred when Working with Children.' In S. Rodger (ed.), *Occupation Centred Practice For Children: A Practical Guide for Occupational Therapists* (pp. 21–44). Oxford, UK: Wiley Blackwell.

Rodger, S., and Keen, D. (2010). 'Child- and Family-Centred Service Provision.' In S. Rodger (ed.), *Occupation Centred Practice for Children: A Practical Guide for Occupational Therapists* (pp. 45–74). Oxford, UK: Wiley Blackwell.

Rodger, S., Braithwaite, M., and Keen, D. (2004). 'Early intervention for children with autism: Parental priorities.' *Australian Journal of Early Childhood, 29,* 34–41.

Rodger, S., O'Keefe, A., Jones, J. and Cook, M. (in press). 'Parents' and professionals' perceptions of the Family Goal Setting Tool.'

Rosenbaum, P., King, S., Law, M., King, G., and Evans, J. (1998). 'Family-centred service: A conceptual framework and research review.' *Physical and Occupational Therapy in Pediatrics, 18* (1), 1–20.

Tam, C., Teachman, G., and Wright, V. (2008) 'Paediatric application of individualized client-centred outcome measures: A literature review.' *British Journal of Occupational Therapy, 71* (7), 286–296.

VanLeit, B., and Crowe, T.K. (2002). 'Outcomes of occupational therapy program for mothers of children with disabilities: Impact on satisfaction with time use and occupational performance.' *American Journal of Occupational Therapy, 56* (4), 402–410.

Wilkins, A., Leonard, H., Jacoby, P., MacKinnon, E., *et al.* (2010). 'Evaluation of the processes of family-centred care for young children with intellectual disability in Western Australia.' *Child: Care Health and Development, 36* (5), 709–718.

Wilkins, S., Pollock, N., Law, M., and Rochon, S. (2001). 'Implementing client-centred practice: Why is it so difficult to do?' *Canadian Journal of Occupational Therapy, 68* (2), 70–79.

# CHAPTER 5

Bailey, D.B., Bruder, M.B., Hebbeler, K., Carta, J., *et al.* (2006). 'Recommended outcomes for families of young children with disabilities.' *Journal of Early Intervention, 28* (4), 227–251.

Bailey, D.B., and Powell, T. (2005). 'Assessing the Information Needs of Families in Early Intervention.' In M.J. Guralnick (ed.), *A Developmental Systems Approach to Early Intervention: National and International Perspectives* (pp. 151–183). Baltimore, MD: Brookes.

Beach Center on Disability (2005). Beach Center Family Quality of Life Scale. www.beachcenter.org/resource_library/beach_resource_detail_page.aspx?intResourceID=2391&Type=Tool. Retrieved 17 September 2009.

Becker-Cottrill, B., McFarland, J., and Anderson, V. (2003). 'A model of positive behavioural support for individuals with autism and their families: The family focus process.' *Focus on Autism and Other Developmental Disabilities, 18* (2), 110–120.

Bell, M. (2007). 'Community-based parenting programmes: An exploration of the interplay between environmental and organizational factors in a Webster Stratton project.' *British Journal of Social Work, 37* (1), 55–72.

Bristol, M., Gallagher, J., and Holt, K. (1993). 'Maternal depressive symptoms in autism: Response to psychoeducational intervention.' *Rehabilitation Psychology, 38,* 3–10.

Bromley, J., Hare, D.J., Davison, K., and Emerson, E. (2004). 'Mothers supporting children with autistic spectrum disorders.' *Autism, 8* (4), 409–423.

Brookman-Frazee, L. (2004). 'Using parent/clinician partnerships in parent education programs for children with autism.' *Journal of Positive Behavior Interventions, 6* (4), 195–213.

Brookman-Frazee, L., Stahmer, A., Baker-Ericzen, M.J., and Tsai, K. (2006). 'Parenting interventions for children with autism spectrum and disruptive behavior disorders: Opportunities for cross-fertilization.' *Clinical Child and Family Psychology Review, 9* (3/4), 181–200.

Brown, G. (2004). 'Family-centred care, mothers' occupations of caregiving and home therapy programs.' In S.A. Esdaile and J.A. Olson (eds), *Mothering Occupations: Challenge, Agency and Participation*. Philadelphia, PA: F.A. Davis.

Crockett, J.L., Fleming, R.K., Doepke, K.J., and Stevens, J.S. (2005). 'Parent training: Acquisition and generalization of discrete trials teaching skills with parents of children with autism.' *Research in Developmental Disabilities, 28* (1), 23–36.

Drennan, A., Wagner, T., and Rosenbaum, P. (2005). *The Key Worker Model Of Service Delivery: Keeping Current Series*. Hamilton, ON: Child Centre for Childhood Disability Research, McMaster University.

Fingerhut, P.E. (2009). 'Measuring outcomes of family-centered intervention: Development of the life participation for parents (LPP).' *Physical and Occupational Therapy in Pediatrics, 29* (2), 113–128.

Francis, K. (2005). 'Autism interventions: A critical update.' *Developmental Medicine and Child Neurology, 47* (7), 493–499.

Graham, F., Rodger, S., and Ziviani, J. (2009). 'Coaching parents to enable children's participation: An approach to working with parents and their children.' *Australian Occupational Therapy Journal, 56* (1), 16–23.

Greber, C., Ziviani, J., and Rodger, S. (2007a). 'The four quadrant model of facilitated learning (part 1): Using teaching–learning approaches in occupational therapy.' *Australian Occupational Therapy Journal, 54* (s1), S31–S39.

Greber, C., Ziviani, J., and Rodger, S. (2007b). 'The four quadrant model of facilitated learning (part 2): Strategies and applications.' *Australian Occupational Therapy Journal, 54* (s1), S40–S48.

Hare, D.J., Pratt, C., Burton, M., Bromley, J., and Emerson, E. (2004). 'The health and social care needs of family carers supporting adults with autistic spectrum disorders.' *Autism, 8* (4), 425–444.

Ingersoll, B., and Dvortcsak, A. (2006). 'Including parent training in the early childhood special education curriculum for children with autism spectrum disorders.' *Topics in Early Childhood Special Education, 26* (3), 179–187.

Kaiser, A.P., and Fox, J.J. (1986). 'Behavioural Parent Training Research: Contributions to an Ecological Analysis of Families of Handicapped Children.' In J.J. Gallagher and P.M. Vietze (eds), *Families Of Handicapped Persons: Research, Programs, and Policy Issues* (pp. 219–235). Baltimore, MD: Brookes.

King, S., Rosenbaum, P., and King, G. (1995). *The Measure of Processes of Care: A Means to Assess Family Centred Behaviours of Health Care Professionals*. Hamilton, ON: Neurodevelopmental Clinical Research Unit, McMaster University.

Knowles, M.S., Holton, E.F., and Swanson, R.A. (1998). *The Adult Learner: The Definitive Classic in Adult Education and Human Resource Development* (5th edition). Houston, TX: Gulf Publishing Company.

Lanners, R., and Mombaerts, D. (2000). 'Evaluation of parents' satisfaction with early intervention services within and among European countries: Construction and application of a new parent satisfaction scale.' *Infants and Young Children, 12* (3), 61–70.

Law, M., Hanna, S., King, G., Hurley, P., *et al.* (2001). *Children with Disabilities in Ontario: A Profile of Children's Services. Part 3: Factors Affecting Family Centred Service Delivery for Children with Disabilities*. Hamilton, ON: Child Centre for Childhood Disability Research, McMaster University.

Lesar, S., Trivette, C.M., and Dunst, C.J. (1995). 'Families of children and adolescents with special needs across the lifespan.' *Exceptional Children, 62* (3), 197–199.

Mahoney, G., Kaiser, A., Girolametto, L., MacDonald, J., *et al.* (1999). 'Parent education in early intervention: A call for a renewed focus.' *Topics in Early Childhood Special Education, 19* (3), 131–140.

Mahoney, G., and Wiggers, B. (2007). 'The role of parents in early intervention: Implications for social work.' *Children and Schools, 29* (1), 7–15.

Mansell, W., and Morris, K. (2004). 'A survey of parents' reactions to the diagnosis of an autistic spectrum disorder by a local service.' *Autism, 8* (4), 387–407.

Neufeld, P. (2006). 'The Adult Learner in Client–Practitioner Partnerships.' In K. McKenna and L. Tooth (eds), *Client Education: A Partnership Approach for Health Practitioners* (pp. 57–87). Sydney: University of NSW Press.

Neufeld, P., and Kniepmann, K. (2001). 'Gateway to wellness: An occupational therapy collaboration with the National Multiple Sclerosis Society.' *Occupational Therapy in Health Care, 13* (3–4), 67–84.

Rankin, S.H., and Stallings, K.D. (2001). *Patient ducation: Principles and Practice.* New York, NY: Lippincott.

Rodger, S. (2006). 'Children and Families: Partners in Education.' In K. McKenna and L. Tooth (eds), *Client Education: A Partnership Approach for Health Practitioners* (pp. 88–111). Sydney: University of NSW Press.

Rodger, S., Braithwaite, M., and Keen, D. (2004). 'Early intervention for children with autism: Parental priorities.' *Australian Journal of Early Childhood, 29,* 34–41.

Rodger, S., and Keen, D. (2010). 'Child and Family Centred Service Provision.' In S. Rodger (ed.), *Occupation Centred Practice for Children: A Practical Guide For Occupational Therapists* (pp. 45–74). Oxford, UK: Wiley Blackwell.

Rosenbaum, P., King, S., Law, M., King, G., and Evans, J. (1998). 'Family-centred service: A conceptual framework and research review.' *Physical and Occupational Therapy in Pediatrics, 18* (1), 1–20.

Sanders, J.L., and Morgan, S.B. (1997). 'Family stress and adjustment as perceived by parents of children with Autism or Down Syndrome: Implications for intervention.' *Child and Family Behavior Therapy, 19* (4), 15–32.

Schuck, L., and Bucy, J. (1997). 'Family rituals: Implications for early intervention.' *Topics in Early Childhood Special Education, 17* (4), 477– 493.

Segal, R. (2004). 'Family routines and rituals: A context for occupational therapy interventions.' *The American Journal of Occupational Therapy, 58* (5), 499–509.

Seligman, M., and Darling, R.B. (1989). 'Models of Intervention.' In M. Seligman and R.B. Darling (eds), *Ordinary Families, Special Children* (pp. 152–182). New York NY: Guilford Press.

Simpson, R. (2005). 'Evidence-based practices and students with autism spectrum disorders.' *Focus on Autism and Other Developmental Disabilities, 20* (3), 140–149.

Smith, T., Donahoe, P.A., and Davis, B.J. (2000). 'The UCLA Young Autism Project.' In J. Handleman and S. Harris (eds), *Preschool Educational Programs for Children with Autism* (pp. 29–49). Austin, TX: Pro-ed.

Stewart, K.B. (2009). 'Natural environments or naturalistic learning opportunities: What is the evidence in early intervention?' *Journal of Occupational Therapy, Schools and Early Intervention, 2,* 2–5.

Thompson, L., Lobb, C., Elling, S., Herman, S., Jurkiewicz, T., and Hulleza, C. (1997). 'Pathways to family empowerment: Effects of family-centered delivery of early intervention services.' *Exceptional Children, 64,* 99–113.

Tonge, B., Brereton, A., Kiomall, M., Mackinnon, A., *et al.* (2006). 'Effects on parental mental health of an education and skills training program for parents of young children with autism: A randomized controlled trial.' *Journal American Academy of Child Adolescent Psychiatry, 45* (5), 561–569.

Turnbull, A.P., Summers, J.A., Turnbull, R., Brotherson, M.J., *et al.* (2007). 'Family supports and services in early intervention: A bold vision.' *Journal of Early Intervention, 29* (3), 187–206.

Wenger, E. (1998). *Communities of Practice: Learning, Meaning and Identity.* Cambridge: Cambridge University Press.

Wenger, E., McDermott, R., Snyder, W. (2002). *Cultivating Communities of Practice: A Guide To Managing Knowledge*. Cambridge, MA: Harvard Business School Press.

Wetherby, A.M., and Prizant, B.M. (2000). *Autism Spectrum Disorders: A Transactional Developmental Perspective*. Baltimore, MD: P.H. Brookes.

# CHAPTER 6

Aarons, M., and Gittens, T. (1992). *The Handbook of Autism: A Guide for Parents and Professionals*. New York, NY: Tavistock and Routledge.

Aldred, C., Green, J., and Adams, C. (2004). 'A new social communication intervention for children with autism: Pilot randomised controlled treatment study suggesting effectiveness.' *Journal of Child Psychology and Psychiatry, 45*, 1420–1430.

Boyce, W.T., Jensen, E.W., James, S.A., and Peacock, J.L. (1983). 'The family routines inventory: Theoretical origins.' *Social Science and Medicine, 17* (4), 193–200.

Dawson, G., and Adams, A. (1984). 'Imitation and social responsiveness in autistic children.' *Journal of Abnormal Child Psychology, 12*, 209–225.

Dawson, G., and Galpert, L. (1990). 'Mothers' use of imitative play for facilitating social responsiveness and toy play in young autistic children.' *Development and Psychopathology, 2*, 151–162.

Fiese, B.H., and Kline, C.A. (1993). 'Development of the family ritual questionnaire: Initial reliability and validation studies.' *Journal of Family Psychology, 6* (3), 290–299.

Hall, L.J. (2009). *Autism Spectrum Disorders: From Theory to Practice*. Upper Saddle River, NJ: Pearson Education Inc.

Hudry, K. (2009). 'Preschoolers with autism show greater impairment in receptive compared to expressive language.' Paper presented at the Asia Pacific Autism Conference in Sydney, Australia.

Ingersoll, B.R. (2010a). 'Brief report: Pilot randomized controlled trial of reciprocal imitation training for teaching elicited and spontaneous imitation to children with autism.' *Journal of Autism and Developmental Disorders, 40*, 1154–1160.

Ingersoll, B.R. (2010b). 'Teaching social communication: A comparison of naturalistic behavioral and development, social pragmatic approaches for children with autism spectrum disorders.' *Journal of Positive Behavior Interventions, 12*, 33–43.

Jensen, E.W., James, S.A., Boyce, W., and Hartnett, S.A. (1983). 'The family routines inventory: Development and validation.' *Social Science and Medicine, 17* (4), 201–211.

Kaiser, A.P., Ostrosky, M.M., and Alpert, C.L. (1993). 'Training teachers to use environmental arrangement and milieu teaching with nonvocal preschool children.' *Journal of the Association for Persons with Severe Handicaps, 18*, 188–199.

Keen, D. (2005). 'The use of non-verbal repair strategies by children with autism.' *Research in Developmental Disabilities, 26*, 243–254.

Keen, D., Couzens, D., Muspratt, S., and Rodger, S. (2010). 'The effects of a parent-focused intervention for children with a recent diagnosis of autism spectrum disorder on parenting stress and competence.' *Research in Autism Spectrum Disorders, 4*, 229–241.

Landa, R.J., Holman, K.C., O'Neill, A.H., and Stuart, E.A. (2011). 'Intervention targeting development of socially synchronous engagement in toddlers with autism spectrum disorder: A rondomized controlled trial.' *Journal of Child Psychology and Psychiatry, 52*, 13–21.

Lewy, A L., and Dawson, G. (1992). 'Social stimulation and joint attention in young autistic children.' *Journal of Abnormal Child Psychology, 20*, 555–566.

Llewellyn, G., Bundy, A., Mayes, R., McConnell, D., *et al.* (2010). 'Development and psychometric properties of the family life interview.' *Journal of Applied Research in Intellectual Disabilities, 23*, 52–62.

Lovaas, O.I., Koegel, R.L., Simmons, J.Q., and Long, J. (1973). 'Some generalization and follow-up measures on autistic children in behavior therapy.' *Journal of Applied Behavior Analysis, 6,* 131–166.

McWilliam, R.A. (2003a). *The RBI Report Form.* Nashville, TN: Center for Child Development, Vanderbilt University Medical Center.

McWilliam R.A. (2003b). 'Routines-based interview.' Nashville, TN: Vanderbilt Children's Hospital.

McWilliam, R.A., Casey, A.M., and Sims, J. (2009). 'The Routines-Based Interview: A method for gathering information and assessing needs.' *Infants and Young Children, 22* (3), 224–233.

Mahoney, G., and Perales, F. (2005). 'Relationship-focused early intervention with children with pervasive developmental disorders and other disabilities: A comparative study.' *Journal of Developmental and Behavioral Pediatrics, 26* (2), 77–85.

Nadel, J., and Pezé, A. (1993). 'What Makes Immediate Imitation Communicative in Toddlers and Autistic Children?' In J. Nadel and L. Camaioni (eds), *New Perspectives in Early Communicative Development* (pp.139–156). London: Routledge.

Peck, S., Wacker, D., Berg, W., Cooper, L., *et al.* (1996). 'Choice-making treatment of young children's severe behavior problems'. *Journal of Applied Behavior Analysis, 29,* 263–290.

Prizant, B., and Wetherby, A. (1985). 'Intentional communicative behaviour of children with autism: Theoretical and practical issues.' *Australian Journal of Human Communication Disorders, 13,* 21–59.

Reinhartsen, D., Garfinkle, A., and Wolery, M. (2002). 'Engagement with toys in two-year-old children with autism: Teacher selection versus child choice.' *Research and Practice for Persons with Severe Disabilities, 27,* 175–187.

Rogers, S.J., and Bennetto, L. (2000). 'Intersubjectivity in Autism.' In A.M. Wetherby and B.M. Prizant (eds), *Autism Spectrum Disorders: A Transactional Developmental Perspective* (Vol. 9, pp. 79–107). Baltimore, MD: Paul H Brookes.

Schlosser, R., and Lee, D. (2003). 'Evidence-based Strategies for Promoting Generalization and Maintenance.' In R. Schlosser (ed.), *The Efficacy of Augmentative and Alternative Communication: Toward Evidence-Based Practice* (pp. 533–552). London: Academic Press.

Scott, S., and McWilliam, R.A. (2000). 'A support approach to early intervention: A three-part framework.' *Infants and Young Children, 13* (4), 55–66.

Sigman, M., and Ungerer, J.A. (1984). 'Cognitive and language skills in autistic, mentally retarded, and normal children.' *Developmental Psychology, 20,* 293–302.

Siller, M., and Sigman, M. (2002). 'The behaviors of parents of children with autism predict the subsequent development of their children's communication.' *Journal of Autism and Developmental Disorders, 32,* 77–89.

Sytsma, S.E., Kelley, M.L., and Wymer, J.H. (2001). 'Development and initial validation of the Childhood Routines Inventory.' *Journal of Psychopathology and Behavioural Assessment, 23* (4), 241–251.

Warren, S.F., and Kaiser, A.P. (1986). 'Incidental teaching: A critical review.' *Journal of Speech and Hearing Disorders, 51,* 292–299.

Werner DeGrace, B. (2003). 'Occupation-based and family-centred care: A challenge for current practice.' *American Journal of Occupational Therapy, 57,* 347–350.

Wetherby, A., and Prutting, C. (1984). 'Profiles of communicative and cognitive-social abilities in autistic children.' *Journal of Speech and Hearing Research, 27,* 364–377.

Wimpory, D.C., Hobson, R.P., Williams, J.M.G., and Nash, S. (2000). 'Are infants with autism socially engaged? A study of recent retrospective parental reports.' *Journal of Autism and Developmental Disorders, 30,* 525–536.

Yoder, P., Warren, S.F., McCathren, R., and Leew, S. (1998). 'Does Adult Responsivity to Child Behavior Facilitate Communication Development?' In A. Wetherby, S.F. Warren and J. Reichle (eds), *Transitions in Prelinguistic Communication* (Vol. 7, pp. 39–58). Baltimore, MD: Paul H Brookes.

# CHAPTER 7

Alexander, D., Wetherby, A., and Prizant, B. (1997). 'The emergence of repair strategies in infants and toddlers.' *Seminars in Speech and Language, 18*, 197–212.

Bates, E., Camaioni, L., and Volterra, V. (1975). 'The acquisition of performatives prior to speech.' *Merrill-Palmer Quarterly, 21*, 205–226.

Beukelman, D.R., and Mirenda, P. (2005). *Augmentative and Alternative Communication: Management of Severe Communication Disorders in Children and Adults* (3rd edition). Baltimore, MD: Brookes.

Bondy, A., and Frost, L. (1994). 'The picture exchange communication system.' *Focus on Autistic Behavior, 9*, 1–19.

Carr, E., and Carlson, J. (1993). 'Reduction of severe behavior problems in the community using a multicomponent treatment approach.' *Journal of Applied Behavior Analysis, 26*, 157–172.

Donnellan, A., Mirenda, P., Mesaros, R., and Fassbender, L. (1984). 'Analyzing the communicative functions of aberrant behaviour.' *Journal of the Association for Persons with Severe Handicaps, 9*, 201–212.

Dunlap, G., Robbins, F., and Darrow, M. (1994). 'Parents' reports of their children's challenging behaviors: Results of a statewide survey.' *Mental Retardation, 32*, 206–212.

Durand, V.M., and Crimmins, D.B. (1988). 'Identifying the variables maintaining self-injurious behavior.' *Journal of Autism and Developmental Disorders, 18*, 99–117.

Flippin, M., Reska, S., and Watson, L.R. (2010). 'Effectiveness of the Picture Exchange Communication System (PECS) on communication and speech for children with autism spectrum disorders: A meta-analysis.' *American Journal of Speech-Language Pathology, 19*, 178–195.

Golinkoff, R.M. (1986). '"I beg your pardon?": The preverbal negotiation of failed messages.' *Journal of Child Language, 13*, 455–476.

Iacono, T., Carter, M., and Hook, J. (1998). 'Identification of intentional communication in students with severe and multiple disabilities.' *Augmentative and Alternative Communication, 14*, 102–114.

Keen, D. (2001). 'Analysis and enhancement of communication behaviour in children with autism.' Unpublished PhD thesis. University of Queensland, Brisbane.

Keen, D. (2003). 'Communicative repair strategies and problem behaviours of children with autism.' *International Journal of Disability, Development and Education, 50*, 53–64.

Keen, D. (2005). 'The use of non-verbal repair strategies by children with autism.' *Research in Developmental Disabilities, 26*, 243–254.

Keen, D., Sigafoos, J., and Woodyatt, G. (2000). 'Prelinguistic Behavior in Children with Autism.' In D. Fisher, C. Kennedy and B. Buswell (eds), *TASH 2000: Our Turn Now* (Vol. 1, pp. 35–38). Baltimore, MD: TASH.

Keen, D., Sigafoos, J., and Woodyatt, G. (2001). 'Replacing prelinguistic behaviors with functional communication.' *Journal of Autism and Developmental Disorders, 31*, 385–398.

Keen, D., Woodyatt, G., and Sigafoos, J. (2002). 'Verifying teacher perceptions of the potential communicative acts of children with autism.' *Communication Disorders Quarterly, 23*, 133–142.

Kublin, K., Wetherby, A., Crais, E., and Prizant, B. (1998). 'Prelinguistic Dynamic Assessment.' In A. Wetherby, S. Warren and J. Reichle (eds), *Transitions in Prelinguistic Communication* (Vol. 7, pp. 285–312). Baltimore, MD: Paul H Brookes.

Lucyshyn, J., Dunlap, G., and Albin, R. (eds) (2002). *Families and Positive Behavior Support.* Baltimore, MD: Paul H Brookes.

Matson, J., Benavidez, D., Compton, L., Paclawskyj, T., and Baglio, C. (1996). 'Behavioural treatment of autistic persons: A review of research from 1980 to the present.' *Research in Developmental Disabilities, 17*, 433–465.

Mayer-Johnson (1981). *Picture Communication Symbols.* Stillwater, MN: Mayer-Johnson.

Mesibov, G.B., Shea, V., and Schopler, E. (2005). *The TEACCH Approach to Autism Spectrum Disorders.* New York, NY: Kluwer Academic/Plenum.

Millar, D., Light, J., and Schlosser, R. (2006). 'The impact of augmentative and alternative communication intervention on the speech production of individuals with developmental disabilities: A research review.' *Journal of Speech Language and Hearing Research, 49,* 248–264.

Mirenda, P. (1997). 'Supporting individuals with challenging behavior through functional communication training and AAC: Research review.' *Augmentative and Alternative Communication, 13,* 207–225.

Mundy, P., Gwaltney, M., and Henderson, H. (2010). 'Self-referenced processing, neurodevelopment and joint attention in autism.' *Autism, 14,* 408–429.

O'Neill, R., Horner, R., Albin, R., Storey, K., and Sprague, J. (1990). *Functional Analysis of Problem Behavior: A Practical Assessment Guide.* Sycamore, IL: Sycamore Publishing.

Preston, D., and Carter, M. (2009). A review of the efficacy of the picture exchange communication system intervention. *Journal of Autism and Developmental Disorders, 39,* 1471–1486.

Prizant, B., and Wetherby, A. (1993). 'Communication in Preschool Autistic Children.' In E. Schopler, M. Bourgondien and M. Bristol (eds), *Preschool Issues in Autism* (pp. 95–128). New York, NY: Plenum Press.

Quill, K. (1997). 'Instructional considerations for young children with autism: The rationale for visually cued instruction.' *Journal of Autism and Developmental Disorders, 27,* 697–714.

Reichle, J., Halle, J.W., and Drasgow, E. (1998). 'Implementing Augmentative Communication Systems.' In A. Wetherby, S. Warren and J. Reichle (eds), *Transitions in Prelinguistic Communication* (Vol. 7, pp. 417–436). Baltimore, MD: Paul H Brookes.

Romski, M.A., Sevcik, R.S., Adamson, L.B., Cheslock, M., *et al.* (2010). 'Randomized comparison of augmented and nonaugmented language interventions for toddlers with developmental delays and their parents.' *Journal of Speech, Language, and Hearing Research, 53,* 350–364.

Sigafoos, J., Arthur-Kelly, M., and Butterfield, N. (2006). *Enhancing Everyday Communication for Children with Disabilities.* Baltimore, MD: Paul H Brookes.

Sigafoos, J., Woodyatt, G., Keen, D., Tait, K., *et al.* (2000). 'Identifying potential communicative acts in children with developmental and physical disabilities.' *Communication Disorders Quarterly, 21* (2), 77–86.

Wetherby, A., and Prizant, B. (1989). 'The expression of communicative intent: Assessment guidelines.' *Seminars in Speech and Language, 10,* 77–90.

Wetherby, A., Prizant, B., and Schuler, A. (2000). 'Understanding the Nature of Communication and Language Impairments.' In A.M. Wetherby and B.M. Prizant (eds), *Autism Spectrum Disorders: A Transactional Developmental Perspective* (Vol. 9, pp. 109–142). Baltimore, MD: Paul H Brookes.

Yoder, P., Warren, S.F., Kim, K., and Gazdag, G. (1994). 'Facilitating prelinguistic communication skills in young children with developmental delay II: Systematic replication and extension.' *Journal of Speech and Hearing Research, 37,* 841–851.

Zona, M., Christodulu, K., and Durand, V. (2005). 'Challenging Behavior.' In J. Neisworth and P. Wolfe (eds), *The Autism Encyclopedia* (p. 33). Baltimore, MD: Paul H Brookes.

# CHAPTER 8

American Psychiatric Association. (2000). *Diagnostic and Statistical Manual of Mental Disorders (DSM-IV-TR)* (4th ed.). Washington, DC: APA

Attfield, E. and Morgan, H. (2006). *Living with Autistic Spectrum Disorders – Guidance for Parents, Carers and Siblings.* London: Paul Chapman Publishing Ltd.

Audet, L.R. (2004). 'The pervasive developmental disorders: A holistic view.' In H. Miller-Kuhaneck, *Autism: A Comprehensive Occupational Therapy Approach* (2nd edition), (pp. 41–66). Baltimore MA: American Occupational Therapy Association.

Baer, D.M., Wolf, M.M., and Risley, T.R. (1968). 'Some current dimensions of applied behavior analysis.' *Journal of Applied Behavior Analysis, 1*, 91–97.

Beyer, J., and Gammeltoft, L. (2000). *Autism and Play.* London: Jessica Kingsley Publishers.

Bundy, A. (1997). 'Play and Playfulness: What to Look For.' In L.D. Parham and L.S. Fazio (eds), *Play in Occupational Therapy for Children* (pp. 52–66). St Louis, MO: Mosby.

Bundy, A.C. (2003). *Test of Playfulness Version 4.* Sydney: Department of Occupational Therapy, University of Sydney.

Case-Smith, J., and Kuhaneck, M. (2008). 'Play preferences of typically developing children and children with developmental delays between ages 3 and 7 years.' *Occupational Therapy Journal of Research: Occupation, Participation and Health, 28* (1), 19–29.

Craig, J., and Baron-Cohen, S. (1999). 'Creativity and imagination in autism and Asperger syndrome.' *Journal of Autism and Developmental Disorders, 29* (4), 319–326.

Desha, L., Ziviani, J., and Rodger, S. (2003). 'Play preferences and behavior of preschool children with Autistic Spectrum Disorder in a clinical environment.' *Physical and Occupational Therapy in Pediatrics, 23* (1), 21–42.

Dodd, S. (2005). *Understanding Autism.* Marrickville, Australia: Elsevier Australia.

Dominguez, A., Ziviani, J., and Rodger, S. (2006). 'Play behaviours and play object preferences of young children with Autistic Disorder in a clinical play environment.' *Autism, 10* (1), 53–69.

Dunn, W. (1997). 'The impact of sensory processing abilities on the daily lives of young children and their families: A conceptual model.' *Infants and Young Children, 9* (4), 23–35.

El'Konin, D.B. (1999). 'The development of play in preschoolers.' *Journal of Russian and East European Psychology, 37*, 31–70.

Gammeltoft, L., and Nordenhof, M.S. (2007). *Autism, Play and Social Interaction.* London: Jessica Kingsley Publishers.

Gorrod, L. (1997). *My Brother Is Different: A Book for Young Children Who Have a Brother or Sister with Autism.* London: National Autistic Society.

Gray, C. (2010). *The New Social Story Book.* Arlington, TX: Future Horizons.

Greenspan, S.I., and Wieder, S. (2009). *Engaging Autism: Using the Floortime Approach to Help Children Relate, Communicate and Think.* Philadelphia, PA: Da Capo Press.

Jones, E.A., and Carr, E.G. (2004). 'Joint attention in children with autism: Therapy and intervention.' *Focus on Autism and Other Developmental Disabilities, 19* (1), 13–26.

Kok, A.J., Kong, T.Y., and Bernard-Optiz, V. (2002). 'A comparison of the effects of structured play and facilitated play approaches on preschoolers with autism.' *Autism, 6* (2), 181–196.

Kuoch, H., and Mirenda, P. (2003). 'Social story interventions for young children with autism spectrum disorders.' *Focus on Autism and Other Developmental Disabilities, 18* (4), 219–227.

Libby, S., Powell, S., Messer, D., and Jordan, R. (1998). 'Spontaneous play in children with autism: A reappraisal.' *Journal of Autism and Developmental Disorders, 28* (6), 487–497.

Lim, S.M., and Chen, C. (2010). *It's Not Just Me: Enhancing The Development of Social-Emotional Learning in Children.* Singapore: KK Women's and Children's Hospital.

Lovaas, O.I. (1977). *The Autistic Child: Language Development through Behavior Modification.* New York, NY: Irvington Publishers.

Luthman, M.R. (2010). 'Parents'perspectives of their children with autism: On play, accomodations, home envrionments, and occupational therapy services.' *OT Practice, 15* (10), 11–16.

Marr, D., and Nackley, V. (2010). 'Using social stories and sensory stories in autism intervention.' *OT Practice, 15* (10), 17–20.

Meyer, D.J. (1997). *Views from our Shoes: Growing Up With A Brother or Sister with Special Needs.* US: Woodbine House.

Mostrangelo, S. (2009). 'Play and the child with autism spectrum disorder: From possibilities to practice.' *International Journal of Play Therapy, 18* (1), 13–30.

Morvay, B. (2010). *My Brother is Different: A Parents' Guide to Help Children Cope with an Autistic Sibling.* Perfect Paperbacks. Self published.

Moyes, R.A. (2001). *Incorporating Social Goals in the Classroom: A Guide for Teachers and Parents of Children with High-Functioning Autism and Asperger Syndrome.* London: Jessica Kingsley Publishers.

Muys, V., Rodger, S., and Bundy, A. (2006). 'Assessment of playfulness in children with Autistic Disorder: A comparison of the Children's Playfulness Scale and the Test of Playfulness.' *Occupational Therapy Journal of Research: Occupation, Participation and Health, 26* (4), 159–169.

Peralta, S. (2002). *All about My Brother.* Overland Park, KA: Autism Asperger Publishing Co.

Quirmbach, L.M., Lincoln, A.J., Feinberg-Gizzo, M.J., Ingersoll, B.R., and Andrews, S.M. (2009). 'Social Stories: Mechanisms of effectiveness in increasing game play skills in children diagnosed with Autism Spectrum Disorder using a pretest–posttest repeated measures randomized control group design.' *Journal of Autism and Developmental Disorders, 39* (2), 299–321.

Reed, C., Dunbar, S., and Bundy, A. (2000). 'The effects of an inclusive preschool experience on the playfulness of children with and without autism.' *Physical and Occupational Therapy in Pediatrics, 19* (3), 73–89.

Restall, G., and Magill-Evans, J. (1994). 'Play and preschool children with autism.' *American Journal of Occupational Therapy, 48* (2), 114–120.

Rigby, P., and Rodger, S. (2006). 'Developing as a Player.' In S. Rodger and J. Ziviani (eds), *Occupational Therapy with Children: Understanding Children's Occupations and Enabling Participation* (pp. 177–199). Oxford, UK: Blackwell Publishing.

Sherratt, D. (2002). 'Developing pretend play in children with autism.' *Autism, 6* (2), 169–179.

Sigman, M., and Ungerer, J. (1984). 'Cognitive and language skills in autistic, mentally retarded and normal children.' *Developmental Psychology, 20* (2), 293–302.

Skaines, N., Rodger, S., and Bundy, A. (2006). 'Playfulness in children with autistic disorder and their typically developing peers.' *British Journal of Occupational Therapy, 69* (11), 505–512.

Stone, W.L., Lemanek, K., Fishel, P., Fernandez, M., and Altemeier, W. (1990). 'Play and imitation skills in diagnosis of autism in young children.' *Pediatrics, 86* (2), 267–272.

Wieder, S., and Greenspan, S.I. (2003). 'Climbing the symbolic ladder in the DIR model through floortime/interactive play.' *Autism: The International Journal of Research and Practice, 7* (4), 425–435.

Wolfberg, P. J. (1999). *Play and Imagination in Children with Autism.* (pp. 13–22). New York, NY: Columbia University.

Young, R., Partington, C., and Goren, T. (2009). *Spectra: Structured program for Early Childhood Therapists Working with Autism.* Camberwell, Australia: Australian Council for Educational Research.

Ziviani, J., Boyle, M., and Rodger, S. (2001). 'An introduction to play and the preschool child with autism spectrum disorder.' *British Journal of Occupational Therapy, 64* (1), 17–22.

# CHAPTER 9

American Speech and Hearing Association (2004). *Auditory Integration Training: A Position Statement.* American Speech and Hearing Association Technical Report.

Baranek, G.T. (2002). 'Efficacy of sensory and motor interventions for children with autism.' *Journal of Autism and Developmental Disorders, 32,* 397–422.

Bennetto, L., Kuschner, E., and Hyman S. (2007). 'Olfaction and taste processing in autism.' *Biological Psychiatry, 62* (9), 1015–1021.

Blakemore, S.J., Tavassoli, T., Calo, S., Thomas, R., *et al.* (2006). 'Tactile sensitive in Asperger syndrome.' *Brain and Cognition, 61,* 5–13

Bogdashina, O. (2003). *Sensory Perceptual Issues in Autism and Asperger Syndrome: Different Sensory Experiences, Different Perceptual Worlds.* London: Jessica Kingsley Publishers.

Brown, N.B., and Dunn, W. (2010). 'Relationship between context and sensory processing in children with autism.' *American Journal of Occupational Therapy, 64* (3), 474–483.

Cohn, E., Miller, L.J., and Tickle-Degnen, L. (2000). 'Parental hopes for therapy outcomes: Children with sensory modulation disorders.' *American Journal of Occupational Therapy, 54* (1), 36–43.

Cornish, E. (1998). 'A balanced approach towards healthy eating in autism.' *Journal of Human Nutrition and Dietetics, 11,* 501–509.

Crane, L., Goddard, L., and Pring, L. (2009). 'Sensory processing in adults with autism spectrum disorders.' *Autism, 13* (3), 215–228.

Delfos, M. (2005). *A Strange World – Autism, Asperger's Syndrome and PDD-NOS: A Guide for Parents, Partners, Professional Carers, and People with ASDs.* London: Jessica Kingsley Publishers.

Dodd, S. (2005). *Understanding Autism.* Marrickville, Australia: Elsevier Australia.

Dunn, W. (1999). *The Sensory Profile: A Contextual Measure of Children's Responses to Sensory Experiences in Daily Life.* San Antonio, TX: The Psychological Corporation.

Dunn, W. (2001). 'The 2001 Eleanor Clarke Slagle Lecture. The sensations of everyday life: empirical, theoretical, and pragmatic considerations.' *American Journal of Occupational Therapy, 55* (6), 608–620.

Dunn, W. (2006). *Sensory Profile School Companion: User's Manual.* San Antonio, TX: The Psychological Corporation.

Dunstan, E., and Griffith, S. (2008). 'Sensory strategies: Practical support to empower families.' *New Zealand Journal of Occupational Therapy, 55* (1), 5–13.

Ellis, N.R. (1963). 'Toilet training the severely defective patient: An S-R reinforcement analysis.' *American Journal of Mental Deficiency, 68,* 98–103.

Gal, E., Cermak, S.A., and Ben-Sasson, A. (2007). 'Sensory Processing Disorders in Children with Autism.' In R. Gabriels and D. Hill (eds) *Growing up with Autism: Working with School-Aged Children and Adolescents* (pp. 95–123). New York, NY: Guilford Press.

Grandin, T. (1995). 'Thinking in pictures: My life with autism.' New York, NY: Doubleday Dell Publishing.

Gray, C. (2000). *The New Social Story Book.* Arlington, TX: Future Horizons.

Hall, L., and Case-Smith, J. (2007). 'The effect of sound-based intervention on children with sensory processing disorders and visual-motor delays.' *American Journal of Occupational Therapy, 61* (2), 209–215.

Herndon, A., DiGuiseppi, C., Johnson, S., Leiferman, J., and Reynolds, A. (2009). 'Does nutritional intake differ between children with Autism Spectrum Disorders and children with typical development?' *Journal of Autism and Developmental Disorder, 39* (2), 212–222.

Intellectual Disability Services Council, and Minda Incorporated (2001). *Are you ready: A toilet training package for people with intellectual disability.* Adelaide, SA: Catalyst Marketing and Communications.

Johnson, C., Handen, B., Mayer-Costa, M., Sacco, K. (2008). 'Eating habits and dietary status in young children with autism.' *Journal of Developmental and Physical Disabilities, 20* (5), 437–448.

Keen, D., Brannigan, K., and Cuskelly, M. (2007). 'Toilet training for children with autism: The effects of video modeling.' *Journal of Developmental and Physical Disabilities, 19* (4), 291–303.

Kienz, K., and Miller, H. (1999). 'Classroom evaluation of the child with autism.' *School System Special Interest Section Quarterly, 6* (1), 4.

Lim, S. M., and Chen, C. (2010). *It's Not Just Me: Enhancing The Development of Social-Emotional Learning in Children*. Singapore: KK Women's and Children's Hospital.

Mailloux, Z., and Roley, S.S. (2004). 'Sensory Integration.' In H. Miller-Kuhaneck (ed.), *Autism: A Comprehensive Occupational Therapy Approach* (2nd edition, pp. 215–244). Bethesda, MD: The American Occupational Therapy Association.

Marr, D., Gal, E., and Nackley, V. (2006). 'Sensory stories: Improving participation for children with sensory modulation dysfunction (SMD).' *Israeli Journal of Occupational Therapy, 15* (2), 41–53.

Marr, D., Mika, H., Miraglia, J., Roerig, M., and Sinnott, R. (2007). 'The effect of sensory stories on targeted behaviors in preschool children with autism.' *Physical and Occupational Therapy in Pediatrics, 27* (1), 63–79.

Marr, D., and Nackley, V. (2006). *Sensory Stories*. Framingham, MA: Theraproducts.

Marr, D., and Nackley, V. (2010). 'Using social stories and sensory stories in autism intervention.' *OT Practice, 15* (10), 17–20.

Martins, Y., and Young, R. (2008). 'Feeding and eating behaviors in children with autism and typically developing children.' *Journal of Autism and Developmental Disorder. 38* (10), 1878–1887.

National Autism Centre (2009). *National Standards Project – Addressing the Need for Evidenced-Based Practice Guidelines for Autism Spectrum Disorders*. Randolph, MA: National Autism Centre.

National Autistic Society (2010a). 'Sleep and autism: helping your child.' Retrieved 20 May 2010 from www.autism.org.uk/living-with-autism/understanding-behaviour/sleep-and-autism-helping-your-child.aspx.

National Autistic Society (2010b). 'Toilet training.' Retrieved on 20 May 2010 from www. autism.org.uk/living-with-autism/understanding-behaviour/toilet-training.aspx

Ozonoff, S., South, M., and Miller, J. (2000). 'DSM-IV defined Asperger Syndrome: Cognitive, behavioral and early history differentiation from high-functioning autism.' *Autism, 41* (1), 29–46.

Quill, K. (1997). 'Instructional considerations for young children with autism: The rationale for visually cued instruction.' *Journal of Autism and Developmental Disorders, 27* (6), 697–714.

Richdale, A.L., and Schreck, K.A. (2009). 'Sleep problems in autism spectrum disorders: Prevalence, nature and possible biopsychosocial aetiologies.' *Sleep Medicine Reviews, 13*, 403–411

Ritvo, E.R. (2006). *Understanding the Nature of Autism and Asperger's Disorder: Forty Years of Clinical Practice and Pioneering Research*. Philadephia, PA: Jessica Kingsley Publishers.

Rodger, S., Ashburner, J., Cartmill, L., and Bourke-Taylor, H. (2010). 'Helping children with autism spectrum disorders and their families: Are we losing our occupation-centred focus?' *Australian Occupational Therapy Journal, 57* (4), 276–280. doi: 10.1111/j.1440–1630.2010.00877.x

Rodger, S., Keen, D., and Braithwaite, M. (2004). 'Early intervention for children with autism: Parental priorities.' *Australian Journal of Early Childhood, 29* (3), 34–41.

Rodger, S., and Ziviani, J. (2011, in press). 'What is this "spectrum" I hear people talking about? A focus on Autism Spectrum Disorders.' In A. Bundy and S. Lane (eds). *Kids Can Be Kids: Supporting the Occupations and Activities of Childhood*. Philadelphia, PA: FA Davis.

Schlundt, D.G. (1995). 'Assessment of Specific Eating Behaviors and Eating Style.' In D. B. Allison (ed.) *Handbook of Assessment Methods for Eating Behaviors and Weight-Related Problems: Measures, Theory and Research* (pp. 241–302). Thousand Oaks, CA: Sage Publications.

Schmitt, L., Heiss, C., and Campbell, E. (2008). 'A comparison of nutrient intake and eating behaviors of boys with and without autism.' *Topics in Clinical Nutrition, 23* (1), 23–31.

Schreck, K., and Williams, K. (2006). 'Food preferences and factors influencing food selectivity for children with Autism Spectrum Disorders.' *Research in Developmental Disabilities, 27* (4), 353–363.

Shepard, C., Knoop, M., and Telarole, J. (2008). 'The effect of sensory stories on participation while getting a haircut for children with sensory processing disorders.' Unpublished master's thesis. Utica College, Utica, New York.

Sherick, J.R. (2004). 'The effects of sensory stories on behaviors in children with autism.' Unpublished master's thesis. The Ohio State University, Columbus, Ohio.

Segal, S., and Beyer, C. (2006). 'Integration and application of a home treatment program: a study of parents and occupational therapists.' *American Journal of Occupational Therapy, 60* (5), 500–510.

Smith-Myles, B., Tapscott-Cook, K., Miller, N.E., Rinner, L., and Robbins, L.A. (2000). *Asperger Syndrome and Sensory Issues: Practical Solutions for Making Sense of the World.* Shawnee Mission, KS: Autism Asperger Publishing Co.

Tomchek, S.D., and Case-Smith, J. (2009). *Occupational Therapy Practice Guidelines for Children and Adolescents with Autism.* Bethesda, MD: American Occupational Therapy Association.

Tonge, B., and Brereton, A. (2010). 'Dietary issues and autism – information for parents.' Retrieved 20 May 2010 from www.med.monash.edu.au/spppm/research/devpsych/actnow/factsheet17.html

Trecker, A., and Miller-Kuhaneck, H. (2004). 'Play and Praxis in Children with an Autism Spectrum Disorder.' In H. Miller-Kuhaneck (ed.) *Autism: A Comprehensive Occupational Therapy Approach* (2nd edition, pp. 193–213). Bethesda, MD: The American Occupational Therapy Association.

Wheeler, M. (2004). *Toilet Training for Individuals with Autism and Related Disorders.* Arlington, TX: Future Horizons.

Wilbarger, J., and Wilbarger, P. (2002). 'Wilbarger approach to treating sensory defensiveness and clinical application of the sensory diet. Sections in alternative and complementary programs for intervention.' In A.C. Bundy, E.A. Murray and S. Lane (eds) *Sensory Integration: Theory and Practice* (2nd ed.). Philadelphia, PA: F.A. Davis.

Williams, K., Dalrymple, N., and Neal, J. (2000). 'Eating habits of children with autism.' *Pediatric Nursing, 26* (3), 259–264.

Williams, K., Gibbons, B., and Schreck, K. (2005). 'Comparing selective eaters with and without developmental disabilities.' *Journal of Developmental and Physical Disabilities, 17* (3), 299–309.

# CHAPTER 10

Biklen, D. (1992). 'Typing to talk: Facilitated communication.' *American Journal of Speech-Language Pathology, 1,* 15–17.

Bondy, A., and Frost, L. (1994). 'The picture exchange communication system.' *Focus on Autistic Behavior, 9,* 1–19.

Bondy, A., and Frost, L. (2009). 'The Picture Exchange Communication System: Clinical and Research Applications.' In P. Mirenda and T. Iacono (eds), *Autism Spectrum Disorders and AAC* (pp. 279–302). Baltimore, MD: Paul H Brookes.

Green, V., Pituch, K., Itchon, J., Choi, A., O'Reilly, M., and Sigafoos, J. (2006). 'Internet survey of treatments used by parents of children with autism.' *Research in Developmental Disabilities, 27,* 70–84.

Greenspan, S.I., and Wieder, S. (2000). 'A Developmental Approach to Difficulties in Relating and Communicating in Autism Spectrum Disorders and Related Syndromes.' In A.M. Wetherby and B.M. Prizant (eds), *Autism Spectrum Disorders: A Transactional Developmental Perspective* (Vol. 9, pp. 279–306). Baltimore, MD: Paul H Brookes.

Gutstein, S.E., and Whitney, T. (2002). 'Asperger syndrome and the development of social competence.' *Focus on Autism and Other Developmental Disabilities, 17* (3), 161–171.

Hall, L.J. (2009). *Autism Spectrum Disorders: From Theory to Practice*. Upper Saddle River, NJ: Pearson Education Inc.

Heflin, L.J., and Alaimo, D.F. (2007). *Students with Autism Spectrum Disorders: Effective Instructional Practices*. Upper Saddle River, NJ: Pearson.

Keen, D., Couzens, D., Muspratt, S., and Rodger, S. (2010). 'The effects of a parent-focused intervention for children with a recent diagnosis of autism spectrum disorder on parenting stress and competence.' *Research in Autism Spectrum Disorders, 4*, 229–241.

Keen, D., Rodger, S., Doussin, K., and Braithwaite, M. (2007). 'A pilot study of the effects of a social-pragmatic intervention on the communication and symbolic play of children with autism.' *Autism: The International Journal of Research and Practice, 11*, 7–15.

Koegel, L.K., Koegel, R.L., Harrower, J.K., and Carter, C.M. (1999a). 'Pivotal response intervention I: Overview of approach.' *Journal of the Association for Persons with Severe Handicaps, 24*, 174–185.

Koegel, L.K., Koegel, R.L., Shoshan, Y., and McNerney, E. (1999b). 'Pivotal response intervention II: Preliminary long-term outcome data.' *Research and Practice for Persons with Severe Disabilities, 24* (3), 186–198.

Lovaas, O.I. (1987). 'Behavioral treatment and normal educational and intellectual functioning in young autistic children.' *Journal of Consulting and Clinical Psychology, 55*, 3–9.

Odom, S.L., Boyd, B.A., Hall, L.J., and Hume, K. (2010a). 'Evaluation of comprehensive treatment models for individuals with autism spectrum disorders.' *Journal of Autism and Developmental Disorders, 40*, 425–436.

Odom, S.L., Collet-Klingenberg, L., Rogers, S.J., and Hatton, D.D. (2010b). 'Evidence-based practices in interventions for children and youth with autism spectrum disorders.' *Preventing School Failure, 34*, 275–282.

Prizant, B., and Rubin, E. (1999). 'Contemporary issues in interventions for autism spectrum disorders: A commentary.' *Journal of the Association for Persons with Severe Handicaps, 24*, 199–208.

Prizant, B., Wetherby, A., Rydell, P., Rubin, E., and Laurent, A. (2004). 'Autism spectrum disorders and the SCERTS model: A comprehensive educational approach.' Port Chester, NY: National Professional Resources.

Raising Children Network (2011). Retrieved 4 January 2011 from http://raisingchildren.net.au/parents_guide_to_therapies/parents_guide_to_therapies.html

Roberts, J.M.A. and Prior, M. (2006). 'A review of the research to identify the most effective models of practice in early intervention of children with autism spectrum disorders.' Australia: Australian Government Department of Health and Ageing. Retrieved 23 January 2009 from: www.health.gov.au/internet/wcms/publishing.nsf/content/D9F44B55D76 98467CA257280007A98BD/$File/autbro.pdf.

Rodger, S., Ashburner, J., Cartmill, L., and Bourke-Taylor, H. (2010). 'Helping children with Autism Spectrum Disorders (ASD) and their families: Are we losing our occupation-centred focus?' *Australian Occupational Therapy Journal, 57*, 276–280.

Schopler, E., Mesibov, G., and Hearsey, K. (1995). 'Structured Teaching in the TEACCH System.' In E.S.E. Mesibov (ed.), *Learning and Cognition in Autism* (pp. 243–286). New York, NY: Plenum Press.

Simpson, K., and Keen, D. (2011). 'Music Interventions for Children with Autism: Narrative Review of the Literature.' *Journal of Autism and Developmental Disorders*, doi: 10.1007/s10803-010-1172-y.

Simpson, R. (2005). 'Evidence-based practices and students with autism spectrum disorders.' *Focus on Autism and Other Developmental Disabilities, 20* (3), 140–149.

# Subject Index

# Author Index